MW00762906

The Official

Party Host

HANDBOOK

By
DR. BONNIE

Text copyright © 2011 by Dr. Bonnie
All rights reserved. Published by Zakkem Publishing, a division of Zakkem
Productions.
Cover graphics and design by Jason Myer, Illustrations by Dr. Bonnie
No part of this publication may be reproduced, or stored in a retrieval system, or
transmitted in any form by any means, electronic, mechanical, photocopying,
recording or otherwise without written permission of the author(s). To contact
Dr. Bonnie, go to www.partyhost411.com

Life is one fabulous party at a time.

Table of Contents

I truly appreciate the support and dedication of my closest friends and family. Without you, I would not have as much experience hosting parties! Thank you for being such an inspiration – you know who you are!

We also thank the staff at My Mystery Party (www.MyMysteryParty.com) and Party Host 411 (www.PartyHost411.com) for their assistance and dedication to this project.

General Party 411

Chapter 1

Getting Started

Tag, you are it! It's your turn to host a party! *What do you do? Where do you start?* Well…you are in the right place, my friend! Let's get your party started! In this book, we'll discuss various types of events including all age groups, group sizes and themes. We'll cover etiquette, basic guidelines, suggested menus, party games, and more!

The ideal time to start planning most parties (i.e. for ~30 guests) is at least two months prior to your event date. With more guests on your invite list, you'll need more time to organize therefore the basic guideline is for every 20 guests beyond 30 guests, add a month of planning.

WHERE TO START:

Budget:

In order to plan, you'll need to start with a budget. How much money do you want to spend on the party? Whatever you decide, make sure you are comfortable with going 15% over that limit because that is typically what happens to hosts. Additional things arise beyond your control even with the most careful party planning. If you set your budget at $500.00, make sure it won't crash your finances when it rises to $575.00. If it's a potential finance crasher, back the budget up to $450.00! As you plan your party, you will make a virtual bank account and subtract from this budget - moving ideas around, changing items and deleting things as needed.

A basic guideline is ~ $20.00 to $35.00 per person for the average party. Home parties with snack food and board games are obviously a lot cheaper (i.e. ~$5.00 to $10.00 per person) and formal dinner parties at exclusive fine dining restaurants are more costly (i.e.~$50.00 to over $100.00 per person). Whatever you want to spend is available to you, that's the good news!

Invite List:

With your budget in mind, grab a pen and paper and write down your guest list. If you have a co-host, it is imperative that they are part of this process. This is the *most important* part of the party planning process as it dictates all other decisions that follow! The final invite list can increase or even decrease the original budget you set if you go over or under the amount of people you first intended to invite.

Here is the primary problem with guest lists: most people have more than one set of acquaintances. You might have family, friends from work, friends from school and friends from the neighborhood. Not all of these sets of acquaintances have met each other and the only thing in common is *you.*

You need to decide up front if you want to invite more than one set. *Do you invite people that do not know each other? Will they mesh and have fun or will it be awkward silence all night?* Chances are, if the groups are nothing alike, it will be difficult as the host to keep everybody happy for the night. This is a difficult decision so don't take it lightly! It will be more stressful and take more planning if you invite more than one set, as you'll be the *buffer* for the night. We all know it is hard to get to know people and the easy route is to stick close to the people that make you the most comfortable. The worst thing that can happen if you invite two or more different sets of acquaintances is to have two or more individual parties within your event. Then, you'll simply be torn the entire time while you try to tend to your hosting duties.

Here's an ideal strategy: everybody has email nowadays. Send a *Save the Date(s)* email to your preferred group and see how many will be able to attend your party on the given date(s). Keep your date a little flexible in the early planning stages and give your guests a couple of choices of event dates. When the preferred group responds, see who is available on what date. This is not an official invite – it's a simple survey to see when they will be available. Select the final date dependent upon the preferred guests you really want to attend. If all of the guests from your preferred group can attend on a given date and if this gives you enough guests for the party you want to host – you should stick with this invite list, finalize the date and go no further. However, if you don't have enough guests to make a party and / or you really feel compelled to invite another group - send a *Save the Date(s)* email to a second group and so on but send the *Save the Date(s)* in tiers with your most important group first, etc. Once you have enough on the guest list, you should stop the invites, as more is not necessarily better.

The exceptions to this dilemma of inviting people that don't know each other are mostly involved with graduations, wedding-related events and baby showers. These events are traditionally riddled with guests who are strangers but that's just something to deal with when hosting those types of events. These guests attend on behalf of the guest of honor and will expect to be uncomfortable at times so the strategies above do not apply. However, a personal party is a different scenario and you have to make the right decisions regarding your guest list. However, on the other side, we would never have known our best friends if we didn't meet them first, right?

SPECIAL ACCOMODATIONS:

Other considerations to make are with elderly guests, wide age range groups, smokers, guests with small children, guests with pet allergies, and guests that are known to drink over their limit and will need a place to stay for the night and / or a safe ride home. Let's discuss each special accommodation separately.

Elderly Guests:

Elderly guests typically have one or more special needs especially if they are not ambulatory or if they have dietary restrictions. Low sodium, sugar-free, lactose free, alcohol free, low fat are all common types of dietary restrictions.

As you invite elderly guests, add a line on the invitation asking for any dietary restrictions or special accommodations to be included with the RSVP. Then, it is up to the guests to let you know what their needs are. It's a great idea to have a few restricted dishes available anyway when you host an event with elderly guests.

In addition, elderly guests might need other accommodations with seating or with wheelchair access and / or walkers. Have all of your bases covered so they remain comfortable. Most will not want to impose on you and are not likely to make a fuss but it is your job to make sure they are taken care of at your party.

Wide Range Age Groups & Small Children:

Wide age range groups, such as with family reunions and wedding-related events, can be challenging. Most of the issues you will face as the host are about the food – second is the entertainment. If you are serving bacon wrapped filet mignons with asparagus and pureed cauliflower, don't expect your young guests to be excited about it. Have some chicken finger and French fry alternatives for the little tykes. Maybe mini grilled cheeses or pizzas will make them happy.

Party killers are discussed frequently throughout this book. A *party killer* is any event, item or person that brings a negative focus to the party and causes a mass hiatus from fun and / or an early-end cascade. One of the deadliest party killers is an unhappy child! Nobody wants to be around unhappy children for any length of time! Your little angels can turn into loud, demanding and very stressful characters when they have temper tantrums. People come to a party to escape and enjoy the company of others, not to become frazzled by angry toddlers! As a host, keep your young guests happy as clams!

Second to food, if you've only thought of adult entertainment such as maybe a pianist, you'll need to also occupy and entertain the youngsters. Youngsters would rather climb in the piano and play with the strings inside than listen to a pianist. Have something for them to do or you will pay for it! Depending upon the age group of the children will depend on what you provide to occupy their time. Maybe pay a teen to watch over them while they play party games? Alternatively, put on an awesome cartoon movie for them and have the adults take turns chaperoning the group. Whatever it is – make sure they are content and not getting into trouble! Bored kids are bad news!

Guests with small children need to be told whether small children are invited to your event. If you are going to have a wide age range group, you need to prepare for it well in advance. Make the decision up front when you create the guest list. If you decide to allow children, you'll need to make accommodations for these children (i.e. food, entertainment, safety) and do not leave it up to the parents! The guest will assume you have your bases covered and might show up without kid-friendly food or toys! *Disaster!* It will be *your fault* as the host – not theirs. You need to be proactive and take care of the little one's needs if you include them on the invite list.

In addition, if your home or party area is not safe for the kids, you might have an accident on your hands. If you know small ones are coming to the party, kid-proof the party area. No doubt, these mini people will explore your domicile while their parents mingle with other adults. It's not that parents don't pay attention to their kids but parents with kids tend to be more relaxed about their kids than others are. They're used to little Ella getting into the spice rack and dumping spices on the floor and won't be surprised when it happens at your home! Some parents think it is adorable when little Ella takes a crayon to the wall! You'll get endless apologies if this happens at your home but it won't take back the 10 minutes you had to spend cleaning it up and the hard feelings between the kids, parents and you for allowing the spice rack or the crayon to be within Ella's reach! You won't win as the host if you are not prepared for small children so cover your bases in advance if you invite them or forever be sorry you didn't!

Smokers:

Smokers, smokers, *smokers.* You can't live with them and you can't live with them...but if you invite smokers to your party, you'll need to assure they are comfortable. They are guests who deserve equal treatment even if they have a bad habit. You could probably pick more than one bad habit from every guest at your party so why should a smoker be singled out and inconvenienced. You can't expect a smoker to quit smoking for your party. That is just not going to happen. In fact, it is likely that the smoker will want to smoke even more when they are at a party! Smoking is associated with stress and parties can be stressful for shy and reserved individuals.

Smokers will need a place to smoke and extinguish their cigarettes, preferably outdoors many feet away from the entryway(s) to the party. Provide the smokers with adequate seating and multiple ashtrays. Check midway through the party to see if the ashtrays need to be emptied. Nothing is more disgusting and unkempt than a full ashtray!

The exception to accommodating smokers is your local laws on smoking. If the establishment in which you are hosting your party does not allow smoking on the premises, there is nothing you can do to accommodate the smokers. In addition, some places may not allow smoking next to commercial locations. Know the local laws and event location's rules regarding smoking before you set up your guests to get into trouble. If you know you are inviting smokers and smoking will not be permitted, let these guests know in advance.

Pet Allergies:

Pet allergies can be a difficult issue to deal with when considering your party location. According to the Asthma and Allergy Foundation of America, up to 30% of people that suffer from allergies include dog &/or cat allergies and about twice as many people are allergic to cats than dogs. Pet allergies can be rather severe for some with a complete swelling of the eyes, constriction of the airways and maybe even a case of the hives. You definitely don't want this to happen to any of your guests, as this will be a *party killer.*

If you have animals with fur and feathers and are inviting guests that you are not personally familiar with and they would not have knowledge of the pets in your home, it's worth it to include a small line about the types of animals present in the home on the invitation. If a number of people RSVP with *I'm sorry I can't come because I'm allergic to cats*…you might need to rethink your location.

If you are sending a *Save the Date(s)* email, include this information on this email if you're including a bunch of people who are not familiar with your pets. That way, you can make a decision about the location prior to having your invitations made.

Cocktails, Intoxicated Guests and Liability:

If you are serving cocktails, you should limit it to one or two per guest. You need to be a diligent host about taking away the keys of guests that might be intoxicated. If you have a guest that is intoxicated, do not allow them to drive or do anything dangerous where they may harm themselves or others.

Spending the night at your home is ideal to ensure that this guest doesn't drink and drive. As the host of a party, you may be liable if a guest that leaves your party gets into a drunken driving accident. Not only will you have possible legal issues from both the driver but the victim that they hit with their car, but also you'll feel eternally guilty for allowing them to drive away from your party in an illegal condition.

Breathalyzer devices are available for purchase at various locations on the internet and if you are going to serve alcohol, it might be worth it to do a quick breathalyzer check on your guests before they leave. It seems silly but you are protecting not only you, but also the guests and the potential victims on the road. Be sure to have the proper amenities for any guests who might need to spend the night. An extra toothbrush, shampoo, towel, etc. put into a guestroom (if you have it) with fresh linens is a good safety net.

This book does not serve as legal counsel – only as a swift kick of common sense. You should know the laws in your area regarding serving alcohol to guests prior to serving alcohol at any event.

LOCATION:

Indoor vs. Outdoor:

Decide if your party will be indoor or outdoor. When you *can* host a party outdoors, it is highly suggested. Everybody loves the fresh air and at night, the stars and the moon add an impeccable ambiance. Summer crickets chirping or crisp fall leaves falling onto the ground are perfect additions that you could never recreate inside! Guests tend to make less of a mess when outdoors, as there are fewer places to leave plates, napkins, etc. They seem to find the trash bins a little easier when outside and if spills happen, they are no biggie! However, if the weather is not perfect, it could be a night of misery for everybody so check the prior years for average temperatures and precipitation possibilities. *Too hot* or *too cold* is a *no-go!* From about 75-85°F is what you are looking for with a zero percent precipitation possibility. Outside of that temperature range is dicey! Check your 10-day forecast daily (i.e. go to www.weather.com) the 10 days prior to your event.

You should make the decision of *out versus in* depending upon your theme, the season and your local climate as well as the predictability of the weather. If you live somewhere such as Texas where weather is about as predictable as a toddler on the loose in a shopping mall...well, you need a backup plan and this will involve a lot more planning. Parties can be expensive and it would be a disaster to purchase food, décor and go through all the process and pain of planning just to cancel because of rain or plummeting temperatures!

All right, you've decided on indoor versus outdoor. *However, where do you have it?* Thirty people can have a memorable event in an apartment or you could rent a small hotel ballroom or hotel suite. It's up to you and the sky is the limit...well, maybe your budget is the limit, actually. Obviously, you can save a ton of cash by hosting it at your home. A living room is an ideal party area as long as it has a close restroom, of course. You will probably have to get additional seating, however, as the typical living room doesn't have 30 seats. You need to have a place for everybody to sit – even though everybody will not likely sit down at once. A backyard is great for an outdoor event – again, with a restroom that is close and a place to sit for every guest.

Most cities have nice parks and recreation center party rooms for you to reserve at no charge or at least at a minimal charge. If you go this route, check the park for the bathroom facilities, as you don't want to put your guests into a bad situation! There may be laws against alcoholic beverages in these locations so you'll need to check with the city first if you plan to serve cocktails.

Another alternative is a restaurant. From fast food chains to fine dining venues, most locations will have private dining rooms that you can use. You will typically pay per person and this amount normally doesn't equal to more than what the guests would pay for eating dinner there. Therefore, if you wanted to have a dinner party, this is an option for you.

Other locations for parties include bowling alleys, skating rinks, movie theaters, churches, schools, gymnasiums, museums, zoos and other establishments that have party packages available.

INVITATIONS:

Snail Mail vs. Evites:

You've created your budget, finalized your guest list and hammered down your location. Now it's time to send the invitation to your guests. This is the first impression that your guests will have of your event. The invitation is important if you are trying to impress!

The possibilities of invitations are endless. Select an easy evite (electronic invitation) from multiple vendors on the internet by simply searching the keyword *evite* in your search browser. These are relatively easy and simple to use for your guests. Guests can leave comments and see who else is on the invite list. If you have any updates to your party, you can post them at once for all to see or you can elect to send an email to your guests that have RSVP'd to notify of any changes.   Evites are acceptable nowadays due to the *go green* campaigns but it is much more fun to get a surprise invitation via snail mail! In addition, there isn't a whole lot of effort that goes into an evite so don't expect a lot of effort from your guests, either!

Remember that an invitation is the first impression of the event and evites scream *casual party!* Snail mail invitations are a step beyond the easy evite. It shows you had thoughtful planning of your party. Not that you didn't have thoughtful planning of an evite-invited party, but it does show extra effort. Guests will assume that if you didn't take the easy route on the invites, you won't cut any corners with the party. Purchase ready-made invitations at your local party store or specialty paper stores have more unique invitations and these stores can be found in most shopping malls across the country. They will also have more specialized pre-printed invitations. In addition, 24-Hour printing places will also print invitations for you and most have ready-made template choices. You wouldn't believe it, but you can get your wedding invites made at these places and they look quite spectacular! Last, if you are great at scrap booking, why not scrapbook an invite? It's always nice to receive a handmade invitation based upon your own creativity.

How will you get your guests' addresses for the snail mail? When you sent the *Save the Date(s)* email as discussed previously, that is the best time to ask for your guests' addresses. That way, you minimize the amount of times you need to send emails about your party to your guests. You don't want your guests thinking that being invited to your party is a big hassle! Ask everybody for his or her address, even if you already have it, so you can double check that you have the correct address.

FINAL PREPARATIONS:

Check List:
Make a master list of everything you will need to purchase for the big day (i.e. menu items, candles, decor, music, plates, utensils, etc.). Over the next couple of months, as you purchase these items, check them off your list. Chapter 2 has a master checklist for a universal party. Use it for all of your events by making copies of the pages.

One Week Prior:
Do an inventory of your plates, utensils, table coverings, tables, chairs, etc. depending on your confirmed guest count. These are important details that you do not want to overlook and by now, everybody should have RSVP'd. Contact any guests that have not RSVP'd to see if they plan to attend. You should have a finalized guest list by now. However, there might be a few last minute changes but nothing should fluctuate too terribly at this late in the game. Confirm rental equipment delivery, party staff including the entertainment, and in the case of an event away from home, confirm the location.

Organize party favors and party game equipment and prizes.

Two to Three Days Prior:
Send an email reminder of your party to your RSVP'd guests and ask them if they have any special requests for drinks, etc. This way, you'll be sure you are covered with each guests' drink of choice and food restrictions!

Add any additional items to your master checklist. Also, any guest who now has a situation preventing them from attending your party – even after they have RSVP'd – is likely to respond and tell you they will not be able to attend. It's unfortunate but it is human nature not to want to disappoint others so it is not as if your guests who cannot attend are going to be itching to let you know about their impending absence.

Start preparing any foods that can be frozen and keep for the big day. The more that's out of the way in advance of the 24 hour count down, the easier it will be on the big day. If you are having your party catered, you will need to submit a final head count either 72, 48 or 24 hours prior to your event – depending upon your contract.

If you are having your party in a location away from home, contact the representative to confirm how and when you will access the location on the day of the party.

24-Hour Countdown:

If you are having the party at your home, clean the house thoroughly. You'll have to keep it ultra-clean until the party! Go over your master list carefully and purchase any items you need. Arrange the decorations in each room of your home (or party area) that you will use for the following day. Check your master list one more time. You can never check it too much. Now is the time to develop obsessive-compulsive disorder – even if it is only a temporary case.

Get the serving trays and dishes ready, check wine glasses and polish silver if needed. Prepare any food that can be stored for 24 hours.

Day of the Party:

Finish the decorating in each room. Check the cleanliness of your home (or party area) and make adjustments as necessary. Prepare the last minute food items. For a formal dinner, dishes that bake in the oven or a crock-pot are preferred. This way, they are less maintenance and easy to figure out the exact time to serve dinner. Putting lasagna to bake in the oven for hour and 30 minutes is perfect if you stick it in the oven right before your guests arrive.

In the case of rainy or cold weather, check the coat rack (or clear the coat closet) and get the umbrella stand(s) ready on a rainy day.

Get the gift table, guest sign in table/podium and entryway decorated. Remember this is the first impression once your guests arrive and will set the tone of the event. Spend extra time on this location!

If you are serving cocktails, get your cocktail bar ready by cutting limes, lemons and putting cherries in a bowl. Get the ice buckets ready, blender in place, shakers, stir sticks and straws. Double check to be certain you have all of the mixers you will need. Don't hesitate to contact a close friend on their way to your event to pick up something that you might have overlooked!

Put on the ambiance music and if you are going to play a video or a picture slide show on your television without sound, put it on! If you have candles for ambiance, light them but in a safe, out of the way location. You don't want a guest tossing a jacket over a candle and kicking off your party with a house fire! That's a *party killer!* Get ready to have fun!

Chapter 2

Universal Master Checklist

Use the following universal master checklist for any event. Any item that doesn't apply to your event, simply check it off as complete or cross it out! Make copies of this list for your party so use this template repeatedly! Using a highlighter to signify a completed item is an effective method.

Getting Started:

2 months: _____Budget

2 months: _____Select party theme

2 months: _____Plan party games, make list of items needed
(*i.e. props, awards, etc.*)

2 months: _____Determine guest's attire

2 months: _____Select music playlist

1 month: _____Download songs or order CDs of music

Party Location:

2 months: _____Select location(s), get quotes

2 months: _____Put deposit on location

2 months: _____Tables for guests are adequate
(*add to rental list if not*)

2 months: _____Inclement weather accommodations
(*i.e. coat room/rack, umbrella stand*)

2 months: _____ Is the space adequate for party games

2 months: _____ Is there adequate parking

2 months: _____ Guestbook pedestal

2 months: _____ Gift table

2 months: _____ Adequate seating for your guests
(add to rental list if not)

2 months: _____ Restrooms are adequate

2 months: _____Linens – i.e. cloth, plastic, paper
(add to rental list if needed)

1 month: _____Plates, napkins, napkin rings, utensils
(add to rental list if needed)

1 month: _____Order rental equipment

1 week: _____Confirm rental equipment delivery

48 hours: _____Confirm time of access of location

24 hours: _____Home party - clean the house

24 hours: _____ Decorate and arrange furniture

Day of: _____Check bathrooms – soap, hand towels, toilet paper

Day of: _____Check coat rack or clear coat closet *(in inclement weather)* with open hangers for guest coats/raincoats

Day of: _____Check umbrella stand(s) availability
(in rainy weather)

Day of: _____ Light candles
(in a safe location)

Day of: _____ Start ambiance music

Day of: _____ Start movie / picture slide show without sound

Party Staff:

2 months: _____ Hire bartenders

2 months: _____ Valet service

2 months: _____ Hire servers

2 months: _____ Hire security

2 months: _____ Hire ticket takers

2 months: _____ Hire general staff

2 months: _____ Hire game attendants

2 months: _____ Hire entertainers

1 week: _____ Confirm all staff

Invitations and Guest Management:

2 months: _____ Invite list

2 months: _____ Extended guest list

2 months: _____ Send a *Save the Date(s)* email

2 months: _____ Consider special accommodations
    ___Smokers
    ___Elderly
    ___Small children
    ___Allergies
    ___Food restrictions

7 weeks: _____ Finalize party date

7 weeks: _____ Finalize guest list

7 weeks: _____Order custom invitations

6 weeks: _____Send party invitations
                (with/ without response cards and map)

5 weeks: _____Manage RSVPs

4weeks: _____ Out of town guests
                _____Hotel reservations
                _____Itinerary
                _____Maps
                _____Transportation during stay
                _____Transportation to/from the airport
                _____Tickets to locale events
                _____Dinner reservations

2 weeks: _____Call non-RSVP guests

2 weeks: _____ Out of town guests

2 weeks: _____ Table centerpieces

1 week: _____Confirm rental equipment delivery

Entertainment:

2 months: _____ Emcee

2 months: _____ Ambiance music

2 months: _____ DJ, band, musician

2 months: _____ Casino tables, dealers

2 months: _____ Fortuneteller booth

2 months: _____ Temporary tattoo booth

2 months: _____ Fun photo booth

2 months: _____ Balloon artist booth

2 months: _____ Clown, mime, magician

2 months: _____ Awards ceremony

2 months: _____ Toasts – written, scheduled, etc.

Day of: _____Organize games and party favors

Decorations:

6 weeks: _____Sketch room décor and make a list of what you need to purchase

6 weeks: _____Purchase online décor and party favors

2 weeks: _____Purchase votives / candles

2 weeks: _____ Purchase remaining party décor *(confetti, balloons, etc.)*

2 weeks: _____ Create table centerpieces

2 weeks: _____ Assemble party favors

Day of: _____Gift table décor

Day of: _____Gift table signage

Day of: _____Entryway décor

Day of: _____Table décor

Day of: _____Buffet table décor

Day of: _____Ceiling décor

Day of: _____ Set up guest sign in book and pedestal

Day of: _____ Welcome sign – i.e. easel type or banner

Day of: _____ Balloon bouquets

Day of: _____ Party favors

Day of: _____ Gift table décor

Day of: _____ Other theme-oriented décor

Day of: _____ Party favor display

Party Menu - Catered Event:

2 months: _____ Contact a caterer(s) and get quote(s)

2 months: _____ Sign contract with catering company

2 weeks: _____ Confirm caterer

48 hours: _____ Call caterer with a final count
        (Check the contract as it might be 24 or 72 hours)

Party Menu - Self-Catered Event:

2 months: _____ Find out if there are any guests food restrictions

2 months: _____ Plan party menu

6 weeks: _____ Make a non-perishable list

6 weeks: _____ Make a perishable list

2 weeks: _____ Inventory kitchen equipment

2 weeks: _____ Inventory serving trays, serving utensils, dishes, chafing dishes

1 week: _____Purchase liquor - if applicable

1 week: _____Purchase non-perishable items

48 hours: _____Purchase perishable items

48 hours: _____Purchase beverages

24 hours: _____Prepare food that can be stored

24 hours: _____Get serving trays and dishes ready

24 hours: _____Check wine glasses, polish if needed

24 hours: _____Arrange buffet table - if you have access

Day of: _____Prepare food

1 hour: _____Arrange food appetizers to be served first

< 1 hour: _____Light chafing dishes on buffet table

Party Favors, Games &/or Prizes:

2 months: _____Order custom t-shirts, giveaways

6 weeks: _____Order online party favors, theme-oriented prizes, party game props

6 weeks: _____Order trophies or award certificates for games or other events

1 week: _____Purchase gift cards for prizes

1 week: _____Organize items for party games

1 week: _____Purchase candy for tables and party favor bags

Documentation:

2 months: _____Hire photographer

2 months: _____Hire videographer

6 weeks: _____Purchase guest sign in book

2 weeks: _____Confirm photographer

2 weeks: _____Confirm videographer

2 weeks: _____Purchase table cameras
        (guests can take pictures of the event)

Chapter 3

Universal Party Etiquette

The following are the most popular general party etiquette questions. If you would like to have a question answered that is not addressed in this book, go to Party Host 411 at: www.PartyHost411.com and enter your party etiquette question on the contact form.

INVITES:

How long should you allow to receive an RSVP from a guest for an informal party?

RSVP literally means *respond please*. The host is asking the guests to let them know if they can come to the event so they can prepare for guests that will attend. The typical time range for an RSVP is 2 weeks for an informal party. If you are an invited guest, you know soon after receiving an invitation if you can make it so be kind and let your host know as soon as possible. A guest for an informal party should RSVP *at an absolute minimum* 72 hours prior to the party so the host can prepare for the number of guests s/he will have. If the event is catered, catering managers typically require a 48 or even a 24 finalized head count so a guest or numerous guests RSVP'ing within 24 hours or less to a party can mean disaster for the host. However, informal parties are usually not catered events.

Is an evite (electronic invitation service) considered lazy or is it just a sign of the times?

It's a sign of the times, actually. It's green, simple and convenient and shouldn't be looked down upon for an *informal* party. However, if you receive a wedding invitation via evite - that's *horrendous* and you should expect these two are hitchhiking it to Vegas because the bride's knocked up.

What is the latest time you can send out invitations?

If you don't send them two weeks in advance (*at least*), you cannot expect many on your invite list to attend. Typically, plans are made at least two weeks in advance so you are cutting it close.

What if you invite out of town guests to your party? Who is expected to pay for travel and lodging?

With any invite, guests know in advance of the costs they will incur if they decide to attend. It is up to the guests to pay for all travel and lodging expenses.   It's entirely acceptable to RSVP with a *no* if you, as the guest, cannot afford to or are unable to attend an out of town event for any reason. Of course, you are not required to divulge the reason for a negative RSVP but a host should never push the issue with out of town guests!

However, if the host has the room and especially if the invited guest is a family member, it is common courtesy to extend their guest room to the invited out of town guest. It is the host's responsibility to reserve the hotel rooms and make dinner reservations (outside of your party time) for all out of town guests. The out of town guests are not from the area and would be too difficult for them to know where to stay and where to dine. As an alternative, the host can simply provide the phone numbers and locations for the hotel and restaurants and slip it on an insert in the invitation.

How do I address my guests on the invitations?

If you are inviting a married couple, put Mr. & Mrs. John Doe. If one of them is a Dr., replace the title with Dr. If both are doctors, put Drs. John and Jane Doe.   When inviting a single male, put Mr. and to a single female, put Ms. For young teens and children, put Miss for females and Master for males. If you have a couple that are living together but not married, simply list them in any order such as Ms. Bunny Wilkens & Mr. Sammy White.   If you are inviting roommates that are not a couple, send them separate invitations.

Help with invitation etiquette! I have all of this stuff and don't know how to arrange it!

Put the folds of the invite (if there is one) towards the bottom of the invitation envelope. Some invites have envelopes inside of a larger envelope. The envelopes should be oriented the same direction and opened just like one of those Russian doll toys. Inside of the folded invitation is the reply card with an envelope that is self-addressed and stamped but not sealed!

DRESS

What is meant by a black-tie affair?

A black tie affair means there is a formal attire requirement. Men are expected to sport a tuxedo; hence, the black bow tie is attributed to the name of the event. Women are expected to wear full-length gowns. Think Hollywood glam!

What is meant by a semi-formal dress requirement?

Semi-formal has wide-ranging clothing options for both males and females. Modern fashion trends and the season will dictate the most appropriate attire for a semi-formal affair.

It's tricky for men as per tradition; men wear tuxedos for semi-formal affairs. Modern times have swayed this custom more towards a dark suit with matching jacket and trousers. Casual suits such as linens and cottons are not considered dressy enough for a semi-formal event.

For women, the dress length is not floor length – that's about the only requirement other than you shouldn't look like you just stepped out of the office! Traditionally, ankle length dresses are considered semi-formal. Cocktail dresses that are more on the formal side would be acceptable. No hemlines too far above the knees or massive cleavage up top as too much skin showing is not in the spirit of a semi-formal affair! The standard black dress is always a safe route.

What is the required or expected attire for a cocktail party?

Cocktail parties have absolutely the most variable attire that there is. If you are ever stressed about finding something to wear, this will be the event! The basic guideline is if the host doesn't specify the required attire on the invitation; try to match the location of the event. If it is a home party, ask yourself *how nice is the home?* If it is a 10 million dollar mansion, don't wear Bermuda shorts and a t-shirt! Choose an elegant cocktail dress on the verge of semi-formal attire in this case. If it's an apartment soirée, a nice business casual outfit will do just fine.

The second basic guideline is the invitation. An evite dictates casual attire. An invitation out of the package signifies attire that is middle of the road – not too casual and not too formal. A formal invitation shouts formal cocktail party attire is expected. Also, choose your fabrics according to the weather and the season.

For men, if it is after work during the week – keep your business attire on, as you're already dressed. Business attire is considered perfect for a cocktail party. Now it is time to wear your un-matching blazers and sports jackets if you desire. If you receive a formal invitation for a cocktail party at a mansion, dust off your suit with the matching jacket and trousers and put on a tie.

For women, your range is a mini skirt to ankle length with anything hovering around the knees preferred.   Save the floor length attire for formal events – don't wear these gowns to a cocktail party! Sequin appliqués and /or trim are all right but not a fully sequined garment as that would fall into a formal category. Moreover, please skip the feathers at a cocktail party…or any other time for that matter! After work hours, wear your office attire but drop the jacket if you are wearing a suit. If this party is on a weekend, wear a nice sundress if it's outdoors and a traditional little black dress that hits right above the knees if it is an indoor event.

What is meant by festive attire?

You can be the life of the party and take it literal if it is any time around a season such as Christmas or Valentine's Day. However, what your host *really* means is for you to wear something trendy, fun, and most likely in between business casual and cocktail party attire. Nevertheless, if you're feeling in the mood, why not dress up like Santa Claus or Cupid and say you misinterpreted the invitation? You'll definitely be the hit of the party!

GENERAL HOSTING

With a family reunion, anniversary celebration or other big event within a family or close circle of friends, what is the most appropriate way to ask the guests to help chip in for the cost of the party?

Easy enough! Put on the invitation that it is a potluck dinner and ask the guests to RSVP on what they will contribute to the meal. You will manage the menu as it comes in and you might need to ask the later guests to switch their dishes so the menu is balanced. This way, you are not collecting money from people and trying to keep it fair.

Once you ask for monetary donations, imaginary scandals arise and nothing ends up seeming fair. Don't go there unless you have a committee and appoint a treasurer and everybody contributes the exact same amount and anything leftover goes into a pot for the guest of honor. This is the only way to do it as far as collecting money from guests for a party goes.

You'd hate for gossip to start about Uncle Eddy not donating near as much as Aunt Myrtle or about the host pocketing the extra money because she couldn't have spent that much on the party. Obviously, parties are mini money pits and guests never realize how much money actually goes into hosting an event. If you've collected money, short of posting receipts on the wall, you're going to have a few conversations going on regarding what you did with the money if money was collected from guests. Again, don't go there if you can avoid it.

When is it appropriate to have a wishing well party or reception?

A wishing well event means the host collects money from the guests instead of gifts. These are traditionally held for weddings or baby showers but can be done for birthdays and graduations as well. As long as your guests *know up front* that they are being invited to a wishing well party, it is appropriate. With the exception that if you are hosting this party to make enough money for your rent – well, that's considered a loan! However, any guest that consents to attend your wishing well event to raise money for your rent will know in advance and all is fair!

Is it considered rude to throw your own birthday, anniversary party or other event?

Absolutely not! You are your biggest fan and are the most in tune to your needs, right? *Why can't you be your own party host?* Not everybody is lucky enough to have someone to host a party for him or her. Usually, within any given circle of friends, there's only one party planner who takes care of everybody's birthday celebrations and other events for the group. However, often enough, the party planner is forgotten or has a very unorganized last minute party thrown together for them. *Why should the party planner be shirked on their birthdays, promotions or anniversaries?* If you are the party planner or just find yourself without thoughtful friends, host your own event!

When are you expected to send thank you cards and is an email thanking them for the gift sufficient?

The basic guideline is when you receive a gift; the card should hit the mailbox within a week after the receipt of the gift. It should be a thoughtful note that you hand write and send in the mail or hand it to them next time you see them as long as it will be within a reasonable time. If you give it to them personally, let them know within a week that you have a card for them. Over a month is excessively long to wait for a thank you card so stick it in the mail! An email is too easy and is a lack of effort on your part. This person went to the store (or maybe online) and bought you a gift. You should have the same consideration for them and put effort in thanking them.

How do you set a table at an informal dinner party?

The plate is in the center with a napkin folded on top. To the left of the plate, the salad fork (smaller tongs) is on the outside and the dinner fork is next to the plate. All utensils are within 1 inch from the edge of the table. On the right side is the soupspoon on the far right, the teaspoon in the middle and the dinner knife next to the plate. To the top-right of the plate is the water glass with the wine glass slightly to the bottom right of the water glass.

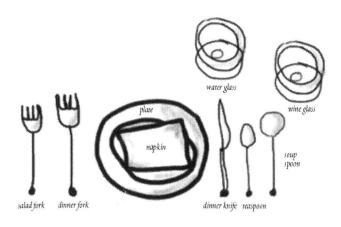

How do you set a table at a formal dinner party?

Regarding the figure above of the informal place setting, let's outline the differences. You place a charger underneath the salad plate and the napkin goes to the far left, on the other side of the salad fork.

Include a bread plate above the forks with a bread knife on top, handle pointing towards the salad plate. Immediately above the charger is the horizontal cake fork with the tongs pointing downward towards the table and to the right and a dessert spoon, also horizontal and pointing toward the left, again, the spoon edge is touching the table. Include a place card with the guest's name above the dessert spoon, slightly to the left. The water glass will move a tad upward and to the left and there will be both a red wineglass to the bottom right and then a white wineglass to the bottom right of the red wineglass. Below the white wineglass and to the right of the soupspoon will be a cup and saucer but you will not place this here until dessert.

Also, remember that glasses not in use are to be removed from the table and the charger is removed prior to the salad being served. If the diner doesn't want bread, soup, salad and /or dessert, you are to remove the tableware associated with these items immediately.

What is the rule on serving guests at a dinner party?

Service from the left side of the guests and clear from the right side of the guests.

Are you expected to tip the catering manager of the catering company that you hired?

Any gratuities are typically included in the contract. Nobody will turn down free money, but it is not expected. Most management positions are paid well enough they don't rely upon tips.

If you host a dinner party, shower, or other event at a restaurant, does the host have to pay for food?

Two ways to do this and either must be disclosed on the invitation. The first method is to have the guests order off the menu. If they do this, they typically pay for their own meal. As always, anytime your guests are obligated to pay for something, disclose it on the invitation! You could always decide to pick up the tab if you are feeling generous and you see that not everybody ordered the Australian lobster with truffle macaroni. Alternatively, buy rounds of drinks or desserts for everybody and have the wait staff put it on your tab.

If you have a private dining room and a set menu that you have chosen for your event, you (the host) pay for the food without debate! It's all about who chooses the food. You choose *you pay.*

Bachelorette parties! Who pays for everything? Is it acceptable to ask the attendees to pitch in for the night's events?

Being that bachelorette parties are typically given by young twenty-somethings that might not be financially set, it is acceptable to ask for donations or put a set amount on the invitation as an entertainment or transportation fee. As long as the guests know up front that they are expected to pay and you are not springing it on them after they arrive – it's fair and acceptable.

Elderly family members deserve big parties on monumental birthdays. However, most do not want a bunch of presents that they have no need for but rather might want cash for home projects or vacations. How do you tell the guests that this elder would prefer money in lieu of gifts?

The best way to do this is to put it on the invitation that there will be a money tree for *Aunt Myrtle's Vacation Nest Egg* at the event. Ask the guests to *Bring the Paper Presidents for Myrtle's Money Tree* or something else that is light-hearted.

How do you get guests to leave when the party is over? Do you play the song *Happy Trails?*

When the food and drinks are gone – the party is over. As long as you are feeding your guests, they'll be more likely to stick around. When they see everything packed up, they'll hit the road. You should stop serving food and drinks at least 45 minutes prior the party end and serve coffee. Remember to cautiously watch over your guests to ensure they didn't become intoxicated at your event. Even with a 1-2 drink limit, they might have found a way to get additional cocktails. If so, you'll have to ask for their keys. It's your responsibility not to allow your friends to drink and drive!

Which comes first – speeches or food? If you want to give a big toast or speech at your event, should you do it before or after dinner?

Do you want to listen to a speech when you are starved? Enough said! Speeches are after or during dinner, never before.

Plate chargers add festivity to a party table setting but when should they be removed?

A sign that you are about to be served is when the wait staff removes the chargers and un-used wine glasses. Remove them before any food items hit the table. They've done their job, which is a first impression of elegance.

GUEST ETIQUETTE:

If you are invited to an informal dinner party, should you B.Y.O.B. (i.e. bring your own booze) if the host doesn't mention it?

This one is tricky as it depends on how informal the party is. Here's the basic guideline: if you received an invitation through any means and it did not mention anything about B.Y.O.B., then bring the host a token gift (i.e. marble rye, bottle of wine, chocolates, etc.) but don't take it back when you leave - even if nobody eats or drinks it!

If you were invited via casual conversation or through a phone call then you B.Y.O.B. as this is not a planned event and you will just deplete another guests' beverage. That's very rude!

Am I expected to bring anything to the party for the host if I am not asked to do so?

Yes, a token gift is expected with any event unless it is a formal, staged event such as a wedding or graduation party, etc. More along the lines of personal, informal parties given at home, you should bring a small gift such as a bottle of wine or a tasty loaf of marble rye for everybody to share.

If I bring something for the guests to share at a party, do I take it with me when I leave if there is anything left?

Absolutely not! You brought it to share so you are to assume it was eaten and be done with it. Even if you see your Godiva chocolate tray was untouched, it is no longer yours and belongs to the host.

If you brought food or beverage in /on one of your own serving pieces, the host will return it to you and if s/he forgets, within a week it is appropriate to call the host and say that you're swinging by to pick up your serving piece and ask what the best time to come by will be.

Tipping service staff, waiters, valets, etc. How much is enough and how much is too much?

Wait staff of any kind should receive 15-20% of the bill. Over 25% is excessive.

Valets should receive a minimum of $2.00 per car and $3.00 to $5.00 is considered an average tip. Anything above $7.00 is excessive unless they kept a tight eye on your 100K Lambo at the front. In that scenario, you can fork over some extra dough as you probably have plenty to spare. Even if the valet service is free, you should tip! They are performing a valuable service to you and their salary depends upon your tips.

The tip meter goes down with any service if they are performing a bad or negligent service. Even with poor service, they are due the minimum tip, however. Maybe they were slammed with many guests at once to take care of and they don't mean to be slow in getting you what you need. It is not considered proper by any means to leave a written tip on the bill such as *if you provide good service, I'll leave a tip next time.* That is, of course, unless the server used foul language or crossed some other major etiquette line but in that case, you should either alert the manager and / or the party host so this server can be let go – at least for the evening. Everybody has a bad day but the server's boss will know if this is a repeating bad day! Some people are not cut out for the service industry.

For wait staff of a private party where there is no bill to calculate a tip from, look for a tip jar. If you are the host of the party, either tip the servers for the night or allow your guests to tip the servers by putting the tip jar on the bar. Anywhere from 0.50¢ to $1.00 is considered a fair enough tip for a cocktail. As a guest, if there is not a tip jar and it wasn't specified by the host, then you are not expected to tip but you can do it optionally. You might ask the host to be certain that you are not dissin' the servers all night, but if you tipped anyway, you'd be safe. To any party, it's wise to bring some change and some one-dollar bills. You never know.

If I'm invited to a party with friends, is it acceptable to bring my child along?

If the child wasn't extended an invite, it is not acceptable to bring your child unless you ask the host and the host agrees to accommodate the child(ren) for the night. Children need special accommodations and the host might not be prepared for your child(ren) if you do not notify them they are tagging along.

Chapter 4

Universal Tips for Décor

Depending on the theme and location of your party will depend on the exact décor you are to choose. First, choose a color scheme. Go for colors of the rainbow or select colors that go nicely together. Some themes mandate specific colors such as Halloween, Mexican Fiestas and Mardi gras. Don't use odd colors on these occasions, as your guests will be confused. Don't try to recreate the colors of Halloween – *it's too late.*

After you select the color, then you come up with a plan for the room according to props, centerpieces, balloon bouquets, lighting, and other ambiance such as smell, television slide shows, etc. all with your party theme in mind. Local party stores have most occasions covered as far as party décor is concerned.

Day After Sales:

Throughout the year, it is a good idea to hit the *day after* sales on the holiday party items. You can find unbelievable bargains the day after but might have to deal with the crowds as a trade off. Especially if you have a holiday party in mind for the upcoming year, you'll regret not grabbing the items at 75% off! Especially when you are checking out paying $15.00 for a package of balloons and confetti. You could have paid only $3.75 for both if you'd had just hit that sale last year!

Entryway:

First impressions cannot be undone! The most important décor is the entryway. This is where you need to pay the most attention and fork out the most money. Decorate the front walkway, the front door / entrance with fun streamers and balloons. If you have the budget, purchase a banner to put over the door/entryway. An easel sign is a nice touch at the entryway and if you throw a few helium balloons in the mix –

you've added some additional excitement and festivity. Balloon bouquets are party staples and can be weighted down with festive weights and placed anywhere throughout your party – including the entryway. Cardboard cutouts are always great if they are within the theme and in the case of a Hollywood or celebrity themed party, a red carpet with a camera click and flash soundtrack playing is a great effect.

When to Balloon and When not to Balloon:

Balloons are fundamental to party décor. There is not a party in the world that wouldn't be more festive with balloons. Balloons can range from a few primary colored balloons scattered about at a kid's party to an archway made out of elegant pearlized white balloons at a wedding.

Balloons should always be blown up with helium! They look so much better when they are floating aimlessly in the air in a bouquet or on the ceiling with hundreds of friends. A bouquet is a collection of about eight balloons with different lengths of ribbons tied together and weighted to the ground with a festively decorated weight. Make a festive weight by wrapping common household items such as cans of food in metallic wrapping paper and tying the top of the wrapping paper with some curled ribbon.

There are cheap helium tanks for sale at most party supply stores or have the balloons blown up for you by the party store on the day of the party. Most party stores need you to order helium balloons in advance to be sure they are ready on time. Don't forget you have to transport them to the party location so if you have a two-seater car, you'll only be able to transport a few at a time! Therefore, purchasing your own helium tank is probably smart if you are hosting a large event. The helium tanks from the local party store work fantastically and are easy to use! You shouldn't blow up helium balloons more than two - three hours prior to your party, however. This task should be one of the last on the list to do! Don't underestimate the amount of time it will take, either. Especially if you only have one tank, this can be time consuming so include enough time for balloon blowing in your schedule.

Elegant formal dinners can be the exception to the balloon rule, of course, but even a few metallic-colored &/or

pearlized helium balloon bouquets can add to the festivities of the most formal dinner parties and banquets, however.

Picture Walls and Arches:

Picture walls or arches are fantastic. Set up a display that your guests can stand in front of to have their picture made. Whether it is a simple wall of festive balloons or a wicker arch with flowers and vines for your guests to stand underneath - either way, your guests will appreciate the memories of having their picture made at your event.

Especially have either of these if you ask your guests to dress in costume! If they dress up like Fred Flintstone or Captain Jack Sparrow and don't have a picture of it later, they'll be pretty sore with you in the future! Taking a group shot is an added bonus. Everybody will want a copy and a great post-party *thanks for coming* email with a group picture as an attachment is an awesome hosting extra!

Centerpieces:

You will need to consider table centerpieces and if you have a buffet table, it needs to be highly decorated within the theme of your party. A *mutant party foul* is to leave a table undecorated! No table can be left plain! If you don't mind picking it up, table confetti is a great place to start. If hosting away from home, check with the representative of your venue (i.e. hotel, restaurant, etc.) to see if they have a confetti ban as some places don't allow it. Obviously, if you can find table confetti to match your theme – go with it. However, confetti won't do it alone and you need *something* in the center of each table. From a few flowers stuffed in a small western boot for a Wild West party to an elaborate mini ice sculpture for a holiday themed party – put something awesome in the center of each table.

Adding ribbons and flowers to unassuming objects in the theme of your party is all you really need. It should be interesting to look at, festive (that's where the balloons, ribbons and flowers come into play) and be within the theme of the party. There are premade centerpieces in nearly every kind of theme at your local party store. These are great but it will mean more to your guests if you come up with something unique and original. If you select shoes as the start of the centerpiece - maybe for a football or soccer team's end of the year banquet - they should be cleaned and sterilized! Remember, people are eating at these tables so a quick spray of a hose is not enough!

Decorating On Location:

Decorating your home is easy; decorating another venue can have its challenges. Speak to your representative well in advance of your party (i.e. hotel sales representative, restaurant manager, city recreation center manager, etc.) regarding the exact time you will have access to your party area *in advance* of your party. It's a rookie mistake not to get it in writing as part of your contract say on a hotel ballroom to have time to decorate in advance. It's an unfortunate happening if you are not allowed access to the ballroom until your party is scheduled to start, you know! It will take you at least two hours but more like four hours to decorate a party area. Obviously, the bigger the area, the more time it will take so maybe try to recruit some buddies for a big undertaking.

Prior to the event and in order to plan, ask for a schematic of the party room with the dimensions. This way, you can better plan for the décor and have a map of the room / area in advance for helpers to follow while decorating the day of the party.

Party's by Age Group

Chapter 5

Parties for Adults

There are five general categories of adult party styles. You want to ensure that at least most of your guests are in their comfort zone during your event. Before any event, perform a quick analysis of your guests to be sure you are in the correct zone when you are planning. It's easy to do. After creating your invite list, place each guest into one of the five categories discussed below – The Professionals, The Partiers, The Peter Pans, The Family Frenzy, and The Chillers. Most guests will be obvious as to what category they are in and any guest that seems to fit more than one category, place them in the one that fits them the most. Whatever stereotype is the majority on your invite list will dictate the general type of party you will host.

Here are a couple of examples: if you've invited 20 guests and 15 are Partiers and 5 are Peter Pans, the Partiers have the majority and the Peter Pans adapt for the night. Another example would be if you have 4 Chillers and 10 Peter Pans, the Chillers are adapting to a Peter Pan style party for your event and that's that! The Chillers might actually enjoy themselves and transform into a Peter Pan type of party guest!

Let's assume there are 5 main categories of adult party guests / party styles and discuss each individually.

The Professionals:

True professional party guests are conservative and tend to be more comfortable in a formal, structured environment. Often enough, party guests from the other categories discussed below, when attending a function for work, must become a professional party guest for a professional event. Therefore, the professional party group is often a blend of individuals from this and the other categories below in a variable mixture. Alternatively, the group can be a homogenous group of professionals that prefer a conservative, well thought-out environment. Whatever the reason, you'll need to follow the guidelines for hosting a professional event as outlined below.

The basic guideline hanging thickly in the air is that these folks remain professional at all times, at all costs. It doesn't mean that they cannot enjoy themselves but they are all on their best behavior. Some people might be straining to be someone they are not just for the event. For example, a Peter Pan invited to a Chiller party would still behave as a Peter Pan during the event but if a Peter Pan attends a Professional party, they will conform and behave as though they belong at the Professional party.

A professional party can be a personal party with guests that are strangers and / or are trying to impress one another. They might be colleagues, distant relatives, reunited school friends from a large school or reunited families with formal traditions – typically families with loads of cash. Formal wedding rehearsal dinners, charity galas, awards banquets, bridal showers, and baby showers where there are *mixed company* can also be professional groups. Whatever the reason for the professional constraint, this is how these events are so you must plan accordingly. Think *structured sophistication*.

Professional parties demand elegance and are more along the lines of cocktail parties on up to semi-formal or formal events. Not that you can't have a casual professional party but it is more difficult to pull off as the host. Professional party guests are not casual for these events by any means.

The invitations should be formal and include a self addressed, stamped RSVP card and envelope. On the invitation, outline the attire requirements (i.e. suit and tie required, etc). The invitation should not only disclose the date, time and location but also whom it is hosted by and what the entertainment will be. Disclose whether you will serve only light appetizers, heavy appetizers, or a formal dinner. A set agenda is necessary for a professional party. Slip a card matching the invitation that gives a mini version of your agenda so the guests know in advance what to expect. This will lend some comfort when they arrive to the event, as there won't be any unknowns.

The guests should have everything outlined for them upon entering the room. Your job as the host is to give your guests every possible chance to be comfortable upon their arrival. *Here is the food, here is where I can get a drink and this is what my focus is (i.e. entertainment).* Never host an open-ended professional party as you will stress out your guests and they will have a wretched time – these events are structured!

When in doubt, walk in your guests shoes and see what they will see, hear, smell when they arrive to your party. *Will they know what to do and will this be adequate for them to feel comfortable?* The first 15 minutes will set the tone for your event and if you fail here, you'll have a bunch of guests watching their timepieces for the remainder of the evening - judging when it is enough time spent at your event so they can bolt out of there!

With that said, let's focus on the different aspects of hosting a reception style party for this group of adults. Professional parties are often formal dinner parties or receptions so the basic guidelines outlined in other chapters will apply.

You have five senses and when you walk into any party area, you want to stimulate all five with your guests. Sight, smell, hearing, touch, and taste. Think about what your guests will see first, what will they smell when they walk in the room and what will they hear playing in the background? Hit the main three senses immediately as the guests enter the party area and then you'll knock their taste & touch senses later on and *seal the deal.*

Lighting should be low as low lighting leads to elegance and sets the mood. People are more comfortable in low lighting. Candles are necessary but shouldn't be the only source of light and should be placed in safe locations. Refrain from Christmas light strands for a professional environment as these lead to a more informal or festive elegance and are great for certain parties (i.e. masquerade balls), but not for the professional events.

Party décor should be classy, not gauche . Refrain from using party store cardboard cutout displays with these events as those are cliché and not for these style of events. If you want large displays or banners, have them made or get a professional to paint them for you on wood or other sturdy substrate. Cardboard is taboo with professional events so save it for the categories of parties discussed below. Think simple.

Balloons are universal for all parties. Always strive for elegant color choices with professional parties. Metallic or pearlized balloons are chic so use these for professional events. Using PVC pipes, create an archway and cover it with the balloons using twine. It should be large enough to span your entryway so your guests can walk through this piece to the party area. Remember, first impressions are lasting! When made correctly, it will look fabulous but not one inch of pipe can show through the balloons so arrange the balloons correctly on the arch and fill any spaces with elegant flowers that are in season. If you use confetti for the tables and buffet line décor, it should be small, gold or silver and plain shapes. Do not use cutesy cutout confetti with professional events. Lightly sprinkle the confetti on the white table clothes around the centerpieces but don't overdo it.

The table centerpieces should be simple yet well designed and graceful. A crystal vase holding a simple flower arrangement with the bottom covered in tulle and tied with a satin bow around the center of the vase is a perfect choice. Surround this vase with votives as candles lend to sophistication and set the mood of the room. For long tables, a beautiful table runner on top of a white tablecloth with multiple votives and rose petals sprinkled about in the center is also a great choice.

The ambiance music should be timeless and classy. Classical is a number one choice for professional parties. If you can find a classical soundtrack in the theme of your party, that's ideal. If you think classical music is too formal for your party, a light top 40 mix would be appropriate but nothing too hard or controversial. Stay clear of top 40 music and unless you want to give 80-year old Aunt Myrtle a heart attack, avoid rap music and heavy metal like the plague! She might not make it through the balloon archway!

Entertainment at a professional party might be directed by the type of event you are having, for example, in the case of an awards banquet. Maybe consider a pianist or maybe a guitarist for the first segment of the event. Then, the sky is the limit for the main event such as a DJ (again, directed to play soft hits and traditional wedding style music). Possibly host a murder mystery party, as these are perfect for guests who don't know each other but be sure to select one for your professional crowd. Murder Mystery Parties by nature are not made for this group but you can pull it off by getting your guests out of their shell for a bit. The boxed sets in the stores tend to be risqué so refrain from selecting these. Also, don't select a comical or silly theme for this group as your guests will likely not be comfortable enough to play their roles in this setting. Read the available character lists and sample game materials to determine if it fits the group. This will give you enough direction to see if it is right for your guests. The suggested parties from My Mystery Party for a professional group are Anonville Manor, The Murder at Franklin Vinatra's Birthday Celebration and the Fine Wine, Good Friends and a Wicked Murder. There are also corporate quality games such as Widgets, Inc. or Corporate Chaos, which has its own mock corporate website for the guests to view in advance.

Other forms of entertainment for a professional party would be to hire a local Jazz or Blues band or maybe actors to put on a tasteful show of any kind for your group. A Casino Night might be yet another option for this group but you are veering towards playfulness and this group might not be comfortable interacting in this manner.

Last, let's discuss the final additions. The party area should smell clean but not overwhelming. Do not select heavily scented candles or flowers for your tables. Smell is about 75% of taste so the food will *taste like roses or fresh cotton* and that just isn't appealing. If this is a holiday party, have some apple cider candles burning in the opposite corner of the room from the food and not on the individual guest tables. If you are seating your guests during your party, you are to make nametags (or have them made by a printer) and direct your guests to their table upon their arrival. The nametags (place setting placards) should be elegant on decorative formal stock or hand written in formal calligraphy if possible.

The Partiers:

Partiers appreciate a more relaxed environment and typically, these parties are focused on cocktails. Partiers' gatherings can be hosted for a variety of reasons. Maybe these are friends, family or close-knitted colleagues but whatever the reason, these groups of people love to have fun. A party for this group can be elegant as described above with the professional events but it's not necessary so there is no need for the additional effort and costs. After a couple of cocktails, this group of guests will not pay much attention to the sights, sounds and smells but more on having laughs with the other guests.

Invitations can also vary for these events. If you desire to have a formal invitation, do it. However, this group won't expect it and you don't need to go the extra mile. These folks are likely to know each other and /or are more relaxed of a crowd so you do not have to outline the attire for your group. They'll simply wear what they want to wear and / or the girls might contact each other to see what they're wearing. Typically, they'll go by the basic guideline of the event location. Evites are acceptable with this crowd and actually easy to manage RSVPs. This crowd are the most likely to leave messages on the evite message board for the other guests to see and this builds pre-party excitement. If it is an informal event, sending an email to these types of guests won't be the end of the world. This a laid-back group of people so you have a lot of leniency as a host. Remember that the invitation dictates the formality of the event. Don't host a formal dinner by sending an email as the invitation.

A formal dinner remains formal, even with the partier crowd. The only exception will be the décor and entertainment in this case. Let's focus on a cocktail / reception style party for this group of adults. Just because these folks are laid back doesn't mean that you have to ignore the basic rules of hosting. Again, sight, smell and sound all come into play. Put your mind as a partier guest and ask yourself what should they see first? Ultra-festive décor and of course, easy access to the bar for cocktails but remember the limits of hosting – one to two cocktails per guest.

You can have lighting that is more festive with these types of parties. Low lighting leads to comfort so don't stray from this rule, but kick it up a notch with neon lights, black lights and maybe some fun Christmas light strands placed in fun places like around the bar, etc. If you have a dance floor, the more lights the better! A light show is perfect and this group of all groups will appreciate it! A cocktail and a dance floor with a lively DJ or fun house music is the ultimate party for this group!

Party décor should be fun. Your statement is *wooo hooo!* This is the group where you can get away with the party store cardboard cutout displays. Cliché is accepted and appreciated and lends to fun. Balloons are universal for all parties and depending upon your theme, always strive for bold color choices with this group. Still select metallic or pearlized balloons but the opaque, flat color primary colored balloons will be more laid back and add to the fun. No need to spend time and money on a balloon archway as you're wasting your efforts on this group. Instead, purchase an inexpensive helium tank from the party store and blow up helium balloons (within two to three hours prior to the party), tie long ribbons of varied lengths and secure to a festively decorated weight (again, available at party stores in the balloon aisle). Strategically place these balloon bouquets around the room.

Purchase large, cutesy cutout confetti in bold colors within the theme of your event and sprinkle on all serving tables and guests' tables. It's all right to go to the extreme with the confetti with these parties.

Centerpieces should bring a smile to the guests' faces. Throw formal elegance out the window and do something funny yet pleasing to the eye. Maybe for a Mardi gras party, make paper mache painted jester heads and make them appear as though they are bursting out of the table with a feather boa and confetti surrounding them. The possibilities are endless but if the centerpieces do not bring a smile to your face, keep brainstorming and find something that does.

The ambiance music should be slightly louder than the professional party should but you want your guests to be able to talk to each other. This isn't a teen party! The music should be top 40 as that is pleasing to most and is typically lively and familiar since it gets the most radio play. However, if you are a group of country & western music lovers or head bangers – by all means, play a heavy mix of what the majority of the guests like to hear. However, don't exclude someone who enjoys a different genre of music – throw in a song or two for him or her so they can enjoy the audio sensory as well.

Entertainment for a group of partiers is endless. This group would enjoy absolutely anything. Interactive murder mystery parties are ideal for this group; however, the easier games should be selected. You want the mystery to be slightly easy so the guests don't lose themselves in the story and lose interest. A big mistake is to choose a moderate sleuther that says *not for novices* as cocktails can kill this type of mystery party. My Mystery Party's games are listed by age as far as difficulty goes so a game listed as 13 years to maybe even 14 years and up is suggested for this event.

Other forms of great entertainment for partiers would be a DJ and dance floor or a Casino Night is great! Any type of band - especially a retro band of any kind – is another perfect choice. Party games are ideal for this group as well as a simple board game night. *Why not choose a costume party / ball for this group?* This is one of the groups that you could get away with requiring them to come in costume! Whether it is for a murder mystery where you assign their character and costume or if it is for Halloween or maybe even Mardi gras, this group will enjoy dressing up for a change. Even the ones who are hesitant to do so will enjoy themselves in the end.

The most important part about these parties is to make sure that your guests do not drink too much to harm themselves *and* that they have safe transportation. Not only is it your responsibility to ensure everybody that is served a cocktail is of legal age, but it is also the hosts' responsibility to ensure that nobody is harmed by the amount of cocktails they consume and that they do not drive while intoxicated. It's a good idea to limit the amount of cocktails for your guests to one or two and cut off all alcohol consumption at least an hour before the end of the party. Instruct the bartender to watch for problems with your guests' consumption of alcohol.

Occupy your guests with dessert and coffee for an hour before you officially end your party. You're responsible if anything happens to your guest via alcohol poisoning both at your party and once the intoxicated guest leaves your event. You never thought you could end up in jail by hosting a party, right. Well, it could be a possibility. You should know the laws in your location / region regarding hosting events with alcohol prior to your event.

At a hotel or other establishment, one way to minimize your liability is to give your guests tickets for only one - two cocktails. Then, if the guest decides to drink more than that limit, they are to purchase it from the bar directly. Bartenders are trained to look for guests that have had too much and will cut them off when it is necessary. This still doesn't get you off the hook; it only shows you minimized your negligence. It is your duty to take the keys and call a cab or provide a place to sleep for the guests that have had too much to drink and are unable to drive their cars. Purchase an inexpensive breathalyzer from multiple places on the web and give your guests a quick test on their way out. However, these are not 100% reliable as you are not trained to use them so don't allow a guest to drive if they are anywhere close to the legal limit.

As further insurance, have a taped line on the floor and ask your guests to walk the line a few times. Just make it light-hearted and say that you are asking it of everybody. There's nothing wrong with requiring a guest to pass a test or two before leaving with their keys if you have served them alcohol. It just shows you are a responsible host and that you care about their safety and the safety of others on the road. If you have any doubt, keep them around and do not let them behind the wheel. It's probably best if you take keys when the guests arrive and check them back out as they leave, by the way, as you don't want any *end of the night stubbornness*.

You could, if budget wasn't an issue, rent a limo service for the night. Have the guests chip in and split the cost of the service but disclose this on the invitation, of course. Who wouldn't rather pay $70 for a limo service for a night instead of a $5000 to $10,000 or more DUI? Have the limo pick up the guests and then take them back home as the party is winding down. You'll have some guests who are ready to leave before others and some guests that want to stick it out until the end so the order of the limo taking them home will work its way out. If you rented a large limousine such as a Hummer limo or maybe even a party bus, they can take up to 15 – 20+ guests at once. If you rented it for ~ 7 hours, you could consider it would take them ~1.5 hours to get everybody to the party (taking multiple trips) and about ~1.5 hours to take most of the guests back home (again, with multiple trips). Then, you are looking at four solid hours of party time in this scenario.

Some of the partiers might not be big social drinkers so they will elect to skip the limo service and drive themselves. It's still your responsibility to ensure they keep the deal and remain sober. If this party is at a hotel, encourage your guests to book a room so they don't have to worry about transportation. Maybe even rent a few of the big suites and assign your guests to rooms within the suites. If this party is at your home, get your guest beds, cots and sleeping bags ready because it might turn into a slumber party.

In summary, the host is responsible for the safety of the guests and it is *your duty* to ensure that you don't allow an intoxicated individual behind the wheel! Check the laws in your area and contact your local PD for advice on ensuring you are the proper host when serving alcohol to guests. This book doesn't serve as legal counsel by any means - just as a literary kick to the head of common sense and ethical values.

The Peter Pans:

The next category is filled with adults who are kids at heart and are thereby named the Peter Pans. This group is the most creative and self-entertaining group that you will ever have the pleasure to host. This group enjoys life at the fullest and can be happy in any environment. They love to play games and are thrilled at the chance to dress in costume. Some members of this group might enjoy a cocktail or two but cocktails are not really the focus with the group. They are all about having a blast with friends and playing out a childhood fantasy.

These types of parties can be as elaborate as renting an amusement park for a few hours, renting bowling lanes or hosting a board game night in your living room. If a teen or maybe even a child would enjoy it…this group will love the chance to escape to their childhood for the night. The bottom line is that these events are casual events but you should have structure, an itinerary of what you will be doing throughout the event. Peter Pans don't want to dress up in formal attire unless they're going to have an Oscar Night, Masquerade Ball or a Murder Mystery that goes in line with the formal attire. Costume parties are perfect for this group. Children love to play dress up and so do the adults in this group! Just give them any excuse to dress as Fred Flintstone, the Queen of England or Richard Simmons and *they're in!*

The party décor should be nearly child-like and very fantasy oriented. Go over the top with your theme and include your party food with the décor by giving it fun names within the theme. Think Willy Wonka and the Chocolate Factory or Alice in Wonderland when you are decorating the party area. The larger than life fantasy themed decorations will add to the fun and festive mood of the party. Think child décor but with an adult persuasion. Brightly colored balloons maybe in odd color combinations. Loads of Christmas light strands in multiple colors and shapes and hang dramatic banners and cutouts within your theme of the party.

This group will appreciate party games. They are all about interaction and having fun. Ask that they create their own disco ball upon arrival if you host a Groovy Seventies bash. Arts and crafts are not off limits for this group! Remember that these folks are not afraid of being childlike! If you are not fortunate enough to be a member of this category of adult party guests, put your mind in the frame of mind of a 10 year old when you are planning this event. Would a 10 year old have fun doing this activity? If it is yes, then put a slight adult twist to it. In the case of the disco ball, give them all real scissors, hot glue guns and Gorilla glue –they are adults, you know! If it is Halloween, a pumpkin-carving contest is necessary! However, you must manage safety if you give them knives and cocktails at the same time. It's suggested to do these activities *pre-cocktail.*

Murder mystery parties were made for this group. They'll enjoy them no matter what theme you throw at them. They'll be able to get into the more moderate sleuthers as their focus will be on entertainment and not cocktails.

DJ and dancing are great, bands are all right but not quite interactive enough for this group so unless you had a 50-50 split with Partiers and Peter Pans – you should stay clear of bands. This group wants to have control of the entertainment as they are focused on interacting with the other guests and less on paying attention to a show of any kind.

Family Frenzy:

There is no doubt that the Family Frenzy category is one of the most difficult parties to host – even more so than the professionals are. At least the professionals are predictable. This group is demanding, needy and has special accommodations out the wazoo! Typically, the age range as well as the variable personality types is what make this tricky to host. You'll likely have an even split between each type of group discussed in this chapter with an additional realm of children and teens. For this reason, you just do the best with the decisions you make as the host.

It's highly suggested to make a party planning committee out of some close family members to discuss the party plans in advance. Don't put it all on yourself - split the hosting responsibilities. If it is for Granny's 80th birthday, all of Granny's children should split the cost and hosting responsibilities equally – unless, of course, one child is a plastic surgeon and the other is a short order cook at a fast food restaurant. Then, the surgeon should foot the bill and the burger flipper should do most of the actual legwork. Sweat and tears don't cost money. There always has to be a lead host, however, as families will always navigate towards debating about the small details. Someone up front needs to volunteer as the main host and all parties must agree that this individual has the final say in all situations.

Graduations, wedding parties, big birthdays, reunions, and holidays are all primary reasons for these events. The designated host is always tasked with the most grueling decisions regarding the travel plans, lodging and entertainment for all family members.

Invitations should be *more than* specific and detailed when dealing with family. You will hear about it and it will become a topic of conversation during the event behind your back if you leave out any minor detail. Over-think the invitation. Is there any possible detail that you could disclose that you haven't thought of? Request special accommodations with the RSVP. You thereby place the responsibility on the guest to tell you what they'll need and what they cannot have as far as food and other allergies go. That way, when they arrive and they don't have a humidifier in their hotel room, it won't be your fault and you won't feel guilty and have to rush around the day of your event and fill their individual needs. Be ready to run *some* errands once the out of town guests arrive and slap a smile on your face when you do it. Look at it from his or her perspective as it is difficult to travel and everybody knows it can be stressful and it's never as comfortable as being safe at home.

Family Frenzies can range from formal affairs to casual events hosted at home. Bridal showers and baby showers are in a later chapter and weddings are not fully discussed in this book, as that is yet another dimension of party hosting. In any case, this is where you will deal with the biggest range of accommodations from travel to allergies to food restrictions and you have to be a tentative host.

Because the events are so variable, it is difficult to put your finger on the way to decorate for a general family party. It is best to go by the guidelines in the specific sections (i.e. Halloween, Holiday parties, etc). You'll get the most complaints from this group but you'll also have the most leeway and praise from loved ones. Get ready to get a hard time from the elders of the group no matter how well you plan. It's their job and a rite of passage to be able to grumble about not having walnuts in their pancakes for breakfast because one of the grandkids has a tree nut allergy or because you don't have lactose-free milk for their cereal.

Make sure that you follow the list of special accommodations and travel / lodging for out of town guests on the master party checklist (see Chapter 2). Other than that, follow all of the guidelines for the type of party that you are hosting because with this age range, you will never please everybody's tastes on food, environment or entertainment. You can only do your best to hit the middle of the road to please everybody.

The Chillers:

The guests in the Chiller category are beyond relaxed and extremely laid back. This group just wants to chill and do absolutely nothing but be with friends. Pajama parties with a few cocktails and snacks are all that is necessary for this group.

Invitations are always informal, as this group doesn't even know what an RSVP is besides: *Can you come to my party? Yeah, I'll be there sometime between seven and nine.* A phone call or an email stating the party is at your home or local pub, etc. is all that is needed for this group. They will rarely go to the effort of responding to an RSVP or go online to view an evite. As far as attire goes, don't expect anything beyond casual and if you requested pajamas as the required attire, they'd thank you for it.

Party décor is a waste of time. This group would think it was unnecessary, as they are an informal group of people. If you feel compelled to do something maybe because it's someone's birthday, a few balloons at the party table with a birthday cake is as extreme as you should go.

Entertainment is being with each other and doing nothing. A laid-back game of poker, a movie with popcorn or a subdued board game is the maximum amount of entertainment you should plan, this group despises schedules and structure. These are free flowing minds that don't like to be restrained and told what to do. Music will be the focus in this party and there is no need for a DJ /dance floor. This group of guests is not going to dance or appreciate what you paid the DJ. Put the radio on the majority of your guests' favorite local station and be done with it.

Everything about this party is informal so *fly by the seat of your pants* with this one as long as you have enough party snacks / food and beverages. That's all you need to worry about with this event. Easy! Well, besides getting the guests to leave at a reasonable hour. This can be challenging as these guests are in *chill mode* and aren't in a hurry to do anything...including go home. The best way to clear out your guests is to stop serving food and if that doesn't give this group the hint, make a joke out of it and play the song "Happy Trails" by Van Halen. That's a sure sign the party is over.

So there you have the five categories of adult parties. When you formulate your guest list, it is wise to categorize each guest into the category they fit the best: Professional, Partier, Peter Pan, Family or Chiller. With the exception of a professional party that is dictated by the event itself, the category represented by the majority of the guests will rule. If you end up with more family than partiers, you must follow the guidelines for a family frenzy party or if you have more Peter Pans than chillers, it's going to be an interactive fantasy-filled event and so on! If you stick with this method, you'll have most of your guests in their comfort zone and you're party will be a success!

Chapter 6

Parties for Teens

Teen parties come with the main responsibility of ensuring the teens have a safe yet fun time. They are still minors so it is the host's responsibility as the parent / adult to ensure the safety of the guests *at all costs.* Never trade fun for safety just to be a cool parent or to gain popularity points for your teen. In the end, it is never worth it.

Security:

If you plan to have over 30 teens in any given location, you should hire a security guard. Most police departments allow their officers to pick up part-time jobs as security guards for various events around the city. Contact your local police department to find out how to hire an officer or two for your teen's event. Different cities will have various hourly rates that you are to pay the officer(s) but the police department should tell you the average rate for hiring them. Expect anywhere from 15$ - 20$ per hour in a small town to maybe 100$ per hour or more in a big city. With more than 100 guests, hire multiple security guards and so on. This is to show the kids that there is law and order at the party and it's not the time to allow their hormones and immaturity to take control and drive them to act like wild animals. If you've ever seen a teen movie where the kid hosts a party without the parent's knowledge, well…that's what you will get the morning after if there are not adequate chaperones and security guards with a large group. Hollywood didn't make up this scenario out of thin air, it really happens! Even if raised properly, most teens do not possess the consequence-driven higher thinking capabilities like adults. The frontal cortex of the brain develops last and sometimes not completely until their twenties! They might not realize the obvious consequences of playing football inside the house until they break your expensive vase. It doesn't mean they are malicious, it might mean they didn't have the conscious thought of *consequence*.   Understand where their brains are coming from and deal with these folks at your party but allow them to have a good time. If one teen starts to climb the wall, others are certain to follow so nip the first one in the bud by putting a stop to the behavior and then it's done and forgotten. Be proactive in all instances and your bases are covered.

Entertainment is the Focus:

Teen parties can range from elaborate Sweet Sixteen Balls held at an elegant ballroom to casual home parties in the family living room. Teens don't fit into the same stereotypical groups as adults do. They are genuinely uniform as far as their interests go in general (with exceptions, of course) and most will appreciate any type of party as they are just getting to experience life and enjoy different styles of events. You really can't go wrong with a teen party and the possibilities are endless. The main issues with teen parties that go bad are with making them too childish. Teens want to grow up and show that they are not kids anymore. The worst thing you could do is force your teen to have a fairy tea party and expect their friends not to make fun of them on Monday at school. Teens can be verbally vicious to each other so don't give their friends any ammunition! Peer pressure is one of the worst things that teens are going through in this stage of their life so keep their party positive at all costs.

Other than being too childish, you could go wrong if you didn't have a focus, as *entertainment* is the #1 priority of a teen party. Food will be the least amount of focus for this group! You obviously need to serve food but 9 times out of 10, you will have over bought food for your teen's event. If you have 100 bored kids in a room, expect trouble to break out at any given moment. *Keep them busy at all costs!*

We established that party themes are *endless*, but let's outline some of the top scenarios for teens. Let's look at some of the proven teen themes that have stood the test of time. These are all quality parties that are age-appropriate and lend to an exceptionally great time by all.

Lock Ins:

A Lock In is an overnight party where the guests are *locked in* and unable to leave for the night. With the exception if a parent needed to pick up their child, obviously.

A traditional Lock In is held in a gymnastic center on the gym floor. This is a perfect environment to put sleeping bags and to host the night's events. What is more fun than a bouncy floor and trampolines for energetic teens? The gym staff will typically cover the chaperoning for the night and will supervise the kids during trampoline time. Feel free to stay all night and help chaperone. The gym will likely require consent forms to be signed from the parent(s) of each child. A Lock In can also be held at a recreation center, a church, or maybe even a roller-skating rink.

Overnight Lock Ins are fun for teens but can be difficult to chaperone. The best chaperones for these parties, if not the staff of the establishment or yourself and your adult friends, are young twenties that have proven to be dependable and reliable. Young twenties pride themselves on finally being adults and shouldn't try to stoop down to the teen level to gain acceptance from them. If this happens, however, you are in big trouble, as the chaperones can become enablers for the teens. If you are hiring twenty-somethings as chaperones and do not know them, do a thorough background check. Ask for reputable references and anyone who provides shaky references is to be in the discard pile! Local colleges are great places to hire young adults. Professors, ex or current bosses as well as parents are great references to call. You'd hate to hire someone that just got out of prison for a conviction of contributing to a minor! Also, have a criminal background check done as these don't cost as much as a lawsuit will when all of the parents sue you for negligence when your chaperones break out the alcohol or take the kids egging houses! As the parent host, you are liable for every child's safety! If minors become intoxicated, damage property or break the law in any other manner – the primary blame will lie with the adult host. However, remember that this book doesn't serve as legal counsel - only as a literary kick to the head of common sense and ethics.

Masquerade Balls and Costume Balls:

Teens love to dress up! Especially in adult-style costumes. Either a Masquerade or Costume Ball would likely be the first experience of such a party for most of the guests – given that this is hosted in a hotel ballroom, that is. You can rent a hotel ballroom from approximately $2000 to over $20,000 for about a four to 5 hour span. This will usually cover the food and beverages. Also, expect a 20-24% service fee and a sales tax on top of that. Therefore, if you are quoted $2000, expect your total bill at the end of the night to be ~ $2685. Get everything in writing in a contract prior to your event so you know your total costs. Monetary surprises are never good. The price is highest on Saturday nights and tends to be higher in May to July as during these months, you are competing with weddings. Make an appointment with the sales representative for the hotel and look at the room you are thinking about renting. Look where the electrical outlets are and see what they will do for you regarding a stage and dance floor. Talk to your DJ in detail about the audio-video needs and make certain the hotel can accommodate their needs. Give the DJ the sales rep's number and have him/her talk to them to see what you will need to provide, if anything. Before putting down a deposit, make sure there will be enough seating and food for your guests, ask about the availability of any décor, and by all means – ask for a complementary guest suite or two so you can spend the night and not worry about driving home after the long night. Most of the time the sales representative will throw in a room or two as a bonus.

Local Country Clubs will also lease their ballrooms to members and most will lease the ballrooms to non-members as well. The prices vary by the club and the type of ballroom but are typically comparable to the hotel ballrooms. However, you will not have as many amenities as a hotel does and the ability to get a free suite for the night.

The teens have probably attended home costume parties since they were five years old but having it at a ballroom is a definite step up and very memorable! There will be excitement in the air of anticipation of what will come next. The teens might not appreciate classical music associated with the traditional masquerade ball but there's nothing set in stone when it comes to teens (or kids) so choose whatever music the teens want to listen to – it's their party and you want them to have fun. Make sure the DJ is lively and plans to host dance floor games with the group. The more the atmosphere changes, the less likely your teens will become bored and veer towards trouble. Contests for the best costume and dance contests are always big crowd favorites.

Kidnap Breakfast:

A kidnap breakfast is a reverse surprise party for your guests. You pick them up or *kidnap them* and take them to breakfast either at a restaurant or at your home. Then, you have their parents pick them up or bring them all home after breakfast.

In advance of your party, you must call every parent and ask permission to *kidnap* (i.e. pick them up without advance warning) their teen the morning of your kidnap breakfast. Make the parents *pinky swear* that they will not leak a bit of news out about your surprise breakfast. Recruit enough drivers to carry all of your kidnapped teens in advance of your party. Select a morning, preferably a Saturday morning, when you know that most of your friends will be at home in their beds. Make reservations at your local breakfast diner or have someone prepare a big delicious breakfast at your home while you are out kidnapping your friends.

One by one, you are to arrive at your friends' homes and wake them up and take them with you. They are not allowed to brush their hair, put on makeup or change clothes *unless they are wearing something inappropriate, that is.* Do not allow this person to text or call and wake up the guests you haven't picked up to warn that you are on your way as they will, no doubt, get ready for your breakfast party!

As you pick up the next guest, every guest that has previously been picked up is to help wake up the next guest…and so on. Be ready for some morning grumpies!

Enjoy breakfast and then either arrange for the parents to pick the guests up at the breakfast location or bring them home! Take plenty of pictures!

Casino Night:

A Casino Night for your teen is an exciting change of pace for teens. Teens are not old enough to gamble so they'll be thrilled to pretend doing so for a night. Again, teens want to be grown ups and this gives them a chance to pretend for the night. All the same rules will apply for a Casino Night discussed in a prior chapter, minus the cocktails, of course.

Murder Mystery Party:

Murder Mystery Parties are a blast for teens. Without cocktails to muddle the brain, these folks will be able to harness their extra energy to figure out whodunit.

My Mystery Party has a large selection of teen appropriate games that are both murder and non-murder games. Some parents will have an issue with their teen attending a *murder* mystery party so the non-murder options are there. However, about 10% to 15% of the murder mystery parties held are with church groups. Overall, it's socially acceptable to play a game of crime sleuthing for a night.

Murder mystery parties are discussed in a previous chapter and all rules for these parties will apply for teens with the exception that there will not be a murder in the non-murder variations of the mystery party games and therefore, one of the guests will not become a victim during the game. However, another type of crime will occur such a thievery, kidnapping, etc.

Scavenger Hunt Party or Amazing Race Party:

Scavenger Hunt Parties originated as teen parties but even adults enjoy the challenge. These are high energy, fast-paced hunts for items either about town, within the neighborhood or within a given building such as a church, school, etc. The best method for a scavenger hunt is to acquire fun photographs of the hunted items with the team members in the picture. That way, there are elaborate items to find and not just bottle caps, strings and leaves and you have a memorable photo of the task. Make a scrapbook of all of the teams' photos after the party for a great book of memories! There are hunts where the guests travel about town and look for items in the task list or others that ask you to stroll about on-foot in a neighborhood and hunt for items.

My Mystery Party also has a large selection of teen appropriate scavenger hunts available by instant download or as boxed sets so the host never has to see the task list and can play along with the rest of the group. These parties will typically take 30-40 minutes for the guests to arrive, divide into groups and listen to the rules. The actual hunts are typically two hours and then the judging period takes about 30-45 minutes.

Amazing Race parties are an upscale variation of a scavenger hunt party. You will need to recruit help for your various stations around your location that you choose to host your hunt (i.e. neighborhood, city, etc). You will set up stations with challenges for the guests to complete before receiving the envelope to go to the next location. The challenges can be anything from a simple hula-hoop challenge to a complex riddle or puzzle. Be creative and change up the challenges from physical to mental to a combination of both so you even it out for the guests. Not everybody is an athlete and not everybody is a mathematician either! The winner will be the team that completes all challenges at all locations and crossing the finish line first.

An alternative is to eliminate the last team that makes it to each station to reduce the amount of teams as the race proceeds. If you do this, allow the disqualified players to follow along to the next station to watch the teams still in the race compete on the challenges. You wouldn't want to just kick the disqualified players out of the game altogether! This way, the more delicate and / or longer challenges are at the final stations as there won't be as many teams participating. Therefore, it won't take as long and the race can be completed within a manageable time.

Luau:

A backyard luau is a teen staple. You don't have to have a swimming pool to host a luau, as a traditional Hawaiian luau isn't always around a swimming pool. However, it's always by the ocean so try your best to recreate the beach with sounds (play a tidal wave soundtrack in the background), smells (light a few candles that are beach or ocean-spray scented), and sights (get beach party décor and some tiki torches (with citronella inside if there are insects in your area). Put colorful beach towels on lawn chairs and add some fun hula-hoop contests. Host a limbo challenge while playing fun Hawaiian music.

Make your own limbo pole by purchasing two ~2" diameter by ~5-6' length wooden dowels at your local home and garden store. Also, purchase ~ 3-4" length pegs to insert into each dowel to hold the crossbar. You'll also need to purchase a ~ ½" diameter, ~ 4-5" length crossbar.

If you don't have a drill or other tool to put the pegs inside of your wooden dowels, use wood glue but be sure to get the pegs in the exact location as the corresponding peg on the other dowel. You don't want a crooked crossbar! Bury the wooden dowels in the yard about four to five feet apart and check to see that the pegs are even prior to playing. Play fun music while you host this contest!

Luaus are discussed further in Chapter 8 and all rules will apply to teen parties.

Sole Survivor Party:

Divide your guests into two teams (i.e. tribes) by giving each team a different colored bandana (i.e. red and blue). Elect two captains and allow them to choose their own teams but this leads to the last person picked getting their feelings hurt and therefore, is not suggested. Either pre-select the teams, have every other person that arrives go on an opposing team or pull the teams at random from a hat.

Once the teams are set, have them go through various challenges such as obstacle courses or puzzles, etc. Maybe have a video game challenge (i.e. Rock Band or Super Mario on the Xbox) or a quick game of Go Fish with a deck of cards. The challenge can be essentially anything you choose. As each team loses a challenge, they have to vote someone off their team. As you don't want any guests being bored for the rest of the game, allow them to make a third team of cast offs (i.e. purple team). This cast off purple team will compete with the original two teams (red and blue) and if they win a challenge, both of the original teams must vote someone off their team. The cast offs never have to vote anyone off their team but you can elect to have them sit team members out of a challenge so you can have equal number of players – depending upon the challenge. They cannot sit the same player out in two challenges, however, until everybody has sat out a challenge.

Once the original teams get to 50% of what they once were, you will combine the red and blue teams. For example, if you started off with 20 people with 10 players on each team (red and blue) and once 10 people have been voted off and are on the cast off team (purple), combine the original two teams (red and blue) into one team (choose either red or blue for this merged team) who will now go against challenges with the cast off team. Now when the cast off team wins a challenge, only one player from the opposing team needs to be voted off. If the cast off team loses a challenge, no players are voted off and the next challenge is played.

When you get down to three players on the original team, the cast off team can cast a vote for the winner of sole survivor.

Vampire Party:

With the vampire movies and television shows being the rave, why not throw a vampire party any time of the year? Invite your friends to the party with an invitation in the shape of a coffin. Instruct them to choose their favorite vampire from any movie, book, and television show and dress accordingly.

Decorate your home in gothic, Transylvanian castle décor and play eerie pipe music in the background as a fun yet spooky vampire ambiance. As an alternative, a thunderstorm track will set an ultra-eerie mood.

Serving blood fondue – with both cheese and chocolate – is awesome! Turn white cheese and white chocolate into *blood* by adding red food coloring and maybe a drop or two of blue to deepen the color. Add one drop of blue first and then add red until you see the color of blood. If you overshoot it, add another drop of blue and keep going back and forth until it is perfect. Don't overdo it on the food coloring though!

Play games such as pin the fangs on the vampire bat (or your favorite celebrity's face). A vampire party would not be complete without watching the crowd's favorite vampire movie!

One Color Party:

Spice up a normal party game night with a One Color Party! Choose a color and go with it! Invitations, décor, guests' attire, party food, etc. Absolutely everything must be that color! An alternative to a one-color party is to have a black & white party where everything is black and white.

Shopping Mall Extravaganza:

If you have a shopping mall in your city with an attached hotel or a hotel nearby – why not shop all day and stay in the hotel for fun party games and room service? The guests can take a break from shopping and go swimming, have lunch at the hotel, go to the arcade or whatever other attractions the hotel has to offer. Then back to shopping! If you have the budget, give each guest a certain amount of money to spend at the mall and / or on the invitation, instruct the guests to bring some spending cash for shopping! End the shopping affair with a movie and then back to the hotel room for some fun party games. My Mystery Party has a shopping mall scavenger hunt available for download or as a boxed set. However, check with the mall manager to see if scavenger hunts are allowed first! Some malls don't want the hassle and distraction of a scavenger hunt and could ask you to leave! That's a party killer for sure!

Chapter 7

Parties for Kids

Think back on your childhood and recall your best birthday celebrations. Childhood parties are *memorable* and make a lasting impression kids! Kids look forward to their birthday all year and some might start planning what they want to do for next year the day after their birthday.

Birthday parties are extremely important to most children and as a parent; it is your duty to give them unique experiences. It's important that they are captivating and fun and a little learning is never a bad thing too!

Let's discuss kid's parties in detail starting with the available party themes, parent issues and general tips with décor and then we'll get into the various types of parties available to host for your child.

Party Themes:

Kid's parties are no different from the rest - you have two layers – the theme and the type of party and the combinations are nearly infinite. The first thing you need to do is ask your child what theme they want their party to be (i.e. princess, sports, pirate, etc). Then, ask them to select the three most important things they want to do at their party (i.e. roller skate, ice skate, bowling, etc).

Outline the various combinations to them such as a princess roller-skating party, a princess ice skating party or a princess bowling party. Go back and forth with them until they are truly excited about the theme and focus! If they seem indecisive about it…pick another night to discuss it, as kids can be fickle. You want to be certain you are within their perfect idea of a birthday party or you won't have a truly happy child on their birthday. Not that it is all right to spoil a child and give them whatever they want but on their special day, they should *feel* special!

Things to Consider Regarding Parents:

Before you have a rock climbing party or a murder mystery party – think about your children's friends. Do you know their parents well enough to take their children rock climbing at the mall? If the answer is no, then don't do it. Will the parents be irritated if their son comes home and says he was the murder victim at your child's murder mystery party? If you don't know the answer, don't do it! However, both a rock climbing party and a murder mystery party can be a blast for a kid's party but don't put yourself in a situation where you are explaining yourself and talking your way out of a corner when the guests' parents are frustrated with you.

Disclose everything on the invitation and you'll be just fine. In addition, My Mystery Party offers non-murder mystery parties available for instant download and as boxed sets. As far as the rock-climbing goes, you'll need a parental consent form signed by most places by each parent before they will allow children to climb the rock wall. Check with the establishment for their rules before hauling a bunch of kids up there!

Party Décor:

Party décor for kid's parties should be within the birthday child's favorite color and the theme they have chosen. If they wanted a frog theme but their favorite color is pink – then you have pink frogs and *that's that.* The décor should be bright and fun and you can't have too many balloons and streamers with a kid's party. Now is the time to pull out the streamers and make a wild party area. Bright colored balloons tied to anything in the party room are the way to go. Kids aren't much for elegance, they're about fun!

Now, let's discuss the traditional, easy to host types of kid's parties, starting with the away from home parties and moving to the home hosted events.

ON LOCATION PARTIES:

Roller Skating:

It seems that roller skating rinks have been around forever. Today, many adults have fond memories of going to the skating rink as kids and why should your child be any different? Skating rinks are known for birthday party packages and are usually offered as a set price per invited guest. The typical range for a roller-skating party is anywhere from $8.00 to $12.00 per child. Some rinks might have set prices for a party up to a maximum amount of skaters. For example, a basic package might run you $99.00 plus tax for up to 12 skaters. This will vary depending upon the location of the rink, of course.

You will receive, with most basic packages, admission and skate rental, a set amount of soft drinks, invitations, cups, napkins and plates. Expect the party table to be reserved for a designated 1-2 hour period for your guests to have cake and the birthday child to open presents. Some rinks might provide a birthday t-shirt for the birthday child. If there is an arcade in the rink, you might receive tokens for the birthday child and their guests. There may be additional upgrades such as pizza, goodie bags for the guests, etc. that are available as upgrades with birthday packages and most of these are outlined on their web pages.

Your guests can either bring roller-skates / rollerblades or the rink has skates available for rent (this charge is typically included in the party package). For children who have never skated before, ask the staff members to give a lesson or two and look out for them on the skating floor. It's a good idea to ask a few adults to chaperone the guests on the skating floor – especially if they are young guests.

The DJ in the skating rink will most likely dedicate a song or two to the birthday kids of the day over the P.A. system.

Overall, this is a no-hassle party as everything is taken care of for you besides the birthday cake. Nowadays, you might even find a skating rink that does offer a birthday cake in their package, however!

Most rinks offer a private party where you can rent the rink exclusively for your party for a set amount of time – typically two hours. This will run ~ $400 but will vary depending upon location and package and is done outside of their normal session times.

It is not suggested to take your child and their guests to the rink without purchasing a birthday package. Your child will feel snubbed if there is a board at the front that says Happy Birthday Sally, Dave and LeAnn and her name isn't listed! In addition, the DJ of the roller rink will tell Sally, Dave and LeAnn Happy Birthday on the PA system but not to your child. In addition, your child will notice the fact that other birthday parties are going on and she isn't one of them. You don't want your child to feel slighted on her birthday just to save a few bucks! In the end, that is not worth it. If you can't afford an away from home party this year, host an economical yet fabulous home party and wait until next year to have a skating party.

Ice Skating:

Ice skating rinks have been around for ages but their popularity is increasing over time. Ice skating rinks, like roller-skating rinks, have birthday party packages and are arranged as a set amount you will pay per invited guest. The typical range for an ice-skating party is anywhere from $8.00 to $12.00 per child and this will vary depending upon the location of the rink.

Some children will not have their own ice skates but they are available for rent at the rink and this fee is typically included in your birthday party package. With ice-skating not being quite as widespread as roller-skating (especially in the southern states), it might be a wise idea to ask a few of the staff of the ice rink to help your guests skate and give them a lesson or two. There's always a staff member on the ice to ensure everybody is safe, but it doesn't hurt to ask for a couple more for assistance. There might be a charge for formal private lessons along with your party and you should expect about $50.00 for a 30-minute session for one instructor per 10 students.

There is always a party room that will be reserved for your party with a set time for you to have pizza (or other food), and birthday cake. At this time, the birthday child will open presents. The rink will usually decorate the room for you but you should ask up front. If they do not decorate, ask when you will have access to the room and throw a few balloons and streamers in there for a festive party effect.

Overall, this is a no-hassle party as everything is taken care of for you besides the birthday cake. Nowadays, you might even find a skating rink that does offer a birthday cake in their package.

If you have the cash, why not rent the rink? After the public skating session times, most rinks will rent their rink to you for exclusive ice skating or even for a game of broomball. This will run you about $300.00 per hour depending upon the location of the rink.

Bowling / Laser Tag:

Bowling or Laser Tag parties can be a lot of fun! If you plan to host a large party (~ more than eight guests), don't choose to go bowling as guests will have to separate into groups per lane and some guests will never get to have fun with the birthday child! If you are having a small party, bowling is a great idea, however. As long as your party doesn't take up more than two lanes then all of the guests can interact as a big group. As far as laser tag goes, don't invite more guests than can go into the laser tag arena at once. You wouldn't want a portion of your guests waiting outside of the arena while the others are inside having fun. That isn't a good experience for your guests!

Host a bowling party or laser tag party one of two ways. One way is to rent the lanes (or purchase admission for laser tag sessions) for a set amount of time and host your own event at the table next to your bowling lanes. Purchase food at the counter for your guests and ask the manager in advance if they wouldn't mind you bringing in a birthday cake (ask ahead to prevent any snags in your plans to host it without the assistance of the establishment). You might find that this is slightly cheaper than officially booking a birthday party but it's not always the case!

Bowling alleys and laser tag arenas, like skating rinks, offer birthday packages as well. This should include a dedicated host, décor, lane rental, shoe rental for bowling, food & drink as well as a private party room for you to have cake and open presents. Usually, you'll need to provide your own cake but not always so ask in advance.

If this is a bowling alley that is associated with an arcade, laser tag, etc., they will have an upgrade at an additional fee to allow your guests to have arcade tokens, a laser tag pass, etc. Why not do both bowling and laser tag? Play with the numbers and see what your best option is financially as sometimes, things you don't need are included in the birthday packages such as the tablecloth, décor, party hats that your guests might not want to wear, etc.

Check with the manager of the bowling alley &/or laser tag arena to see if they make birthday announcements on the P.A. system or have a sign at the front that lists the birthday kids of the day. If so, you should purchase the birthday party package as this may not seem like a big deal to you, but it will be to your child if everybody else's birthday in the place is acknowledged but theirs!

Skateboarding:

Skateboarding is a popular pastime for kids and skateboarding parks and parties are growing increasingly popular as more professional skateboarders become famous for their talents.

Some outdoor skate parks are owned by the city and are free to the public so if you host a party at a public outdoor skate park, be prepared with everything you will need (i.e. birthday cake, napkins, forks, cups, beverages, etc). It might be a great idea to bring along a first aid kit with you as bumps, bruises and scrapes are synonymous with skateboarding. Keep that in mind as far as host-liability is concerned as well. You'll need many chaperones for these parties, especially with kids that are new to skateboarding.

Make safety equipment mandatory and do not allow kids to skateboard without parental consent and the proper attire. Injuries are *party killers* and you don't want a broken arm on (you and) your child's conscious! Your child will forever remember his best friend Jason broke his arm on his 10th birthday – not that you hosted an awesome skateboarding party for him. Not a great memory!

Many skate parks are privately owned and offer birthday packages. The packages will typically run between $14.00 to over $20.00 per person and will include admission, a loot bag, a drink, free rental of gear or at least 50% off the rental gear (i.e. board, helmet, pads). Some parks will give a coupon for a free future session to the guests in the loot bags.

There is staff on site that can supervise your guests and help those that might not know what they are doing! At most private parks, for an additional fee (~ $8.00 per guest), have a group lesson as part of your party package. There will most likely be upgrades for your packages such as pizza (or other food items). You will probably need to bring your own birthday décor, table wear and birthday cake.

Check with the manager in advance to see what type of parental consent forms/ waivers, if any, will need to be signed by each child's parent. If they will need these forms, have them available for the parents to sign as they drop off their kids for the party or give a copy in advance with the party invitation with a line instructing to bring the signed for with you to the party. You'd hate a child not to be able to participate due to a consent form oversight!

Fast Food Restaurant:

There are plenty of fast food restaurant chains that cater to small children on their birthday. There are packages available anywhere from $8.00 to $13.00 per child (depending on the location and restaurant).

With these packages, you'll receive a meal for each guest, a dedicated host, loot bags for the guests, complimentary invitations (sometimes these are available via download from their webpage), gift for the birthday child, and organized fun games and activities. If you select a restaurant that has a play yard, your guests will love you for it!

Kid's Restaurants:

Kid's restaurants (i.e. Chuck E. Cheese) were created with kid's parties in mind! This is the ideal place for a birthday party and a guaranteed no-hitch event.

Depending upon the restaurant, you are looking at spending about $12.00 up to over $20.00 per child. Again, this depends upon the location and the birthday package you select. What typically comes with a basic package is one - two hours of a reserved party table, a small present for the birthday child (i.e.

medallion, inflatable birthday crown, etc.), and recognition for the birthday child (on a blackboard at the front entrance, during the show, on the PA system, etc). Also included are soft drinks, tokens for each guest, slices of pizza, tableware, party décor, a dedicated party host, and invitations. Typically, you'll be able to upgrade to include bonus tokens, Mylar balloons, and additional presents for the birthday child, etc.

These are highly energetic parties and the kids are guaranteed to have non-stop fun. Every child should have an experience with a kid themed restaurant party at least once.

Arcade:

Many of the locations discussed above have an arcade in some manner associated within them. However, there are establishments that have rooms full of video games with possibly multiple floors of fun! These establishments usually also offer birthday packages.

Depending upon the arcade will depend upon the available package but these typically range from $15.00 to over $30.00 per person. An arcade party is one of the more expensive parties per person but if you think about what you spend at the arcade when you take your child, you know it adds up quickly!

What you will typically receive with their birthday packages are menu items (i.e. pizza or other food items), soft drinks, and a set amount of game tokens loaded on a card for each guest. The birthday child typically receives a bonus amount of tokens for the games. Some packages will allow upgrades of unlimited game play per person for a set amount of time (i.e. one hour) and this is the way to go! Kids won't spend their tokens at the same rate and it is difficult to look at a kid that runs out of tokens and tell them they'll have to wait for everybody else to finish using their tokens. That's not fun for a child! Therefore, the unlimited amount of tokens is great – especially at the final hour.

Rent a Gymnasium:

Some gyms focus on small kids and others are primarily focused on gymnastics training for all ages. Either way, you can host a birthday party at most locations.

The gyms that focus on youngsters (i.e. ages one -5) have the more elaborate party packages with various themes to select from. Party packages will vary by gym and location but expect exclusive use of the facility for a one - two hour period, a dedicated party host, party supplies (napkins, plates, candles, and balloons), invitations, a special gift for the birthday child and loot bags for the guests. These parties have a wide range of cost per child but expect anywhere from $12.00 to $25.00 per child.

If you don't have a small child gym in your area, contact your local gymnastics center. They likely have party packages available or will have pricing and availability to rent the gym for a period. They should provide adequate staff to supervise your guests on their equipment (i.e. trampolines, gym floor, etc.) but you will most likely be responsible for all of the party décor, tableware, food, etc. with these locations.

Zoo Party:

It's probably best to take your group to the local zoo for an adventure instead of trying to find a birthday party package and being constrained to a schedule. Animals are unpredictable and if the Baboons are being amusing and your guests are having a blast watching them, you don't want to make the kids leave the exhibit because you've got the party room scheduled for the next hour. Have the cake and present opening ceremony when you get back home before the parents pick up the kids – that's the best way to handle it.

Zoo parties can be an awesome experience but you should have plenty of chaperones for the children you are taking with you. Establish a buddy system and a plan for a lost child (i.e. if you get lost, go straight to a police stand and show them what a police stand looks like). Speak to the group in advance on how important it is to stay together. Put a wristband on each guest with your name and phone number on it as well.

Most zoos have after hour events for private parties or group discounts so check the zoo's website and contact the event sales representative to see what they can do to accommodate your party in advance.

Amusement Park Adventure:

It's probably best to take your group to the local amusement park for an adventure instead of trying to purchase a party package. Amusement parks are conducive to free will and less for schedules.

Most amusement parks have after hour events for private parties or group discounts so check their website and contact the event sales representative to see what they can do to accommodate your party in advance. Most will give a discount for a large group.

Amusement Parks can be a blast but you should have plenty of chaperones for the children you are taking with you. Establish a buddy system and a plan for a lost child (i.e. if you get lost, go straight to a police stand and show them what a police stand looks like). Speak to the group in advance on how important it is to stay together. Put a wristband on each guest with your name and phone number on it as well.

Nature Hike & Picnic:

If your child is one with nature and would like a hiking experience with friends, host a nature hike and picnic party! *Safety first!* Plan your route carefully and ensure that the weather is going to be perfect. Don't go into unknown territory, stay on the beaten path and have a definite plan. Now is not the time to go charting territories like Magellan! Bring along a first aid kit and plenty of chaperones for a nature hike.

For the picnic, remember the food safety rules. Perishable food is only safe to eat for up to two hours once it hits the temperature danger zone (40°F-140°F) and remains at room temperature (~ 72°F). On warm days (~ 85°F), this period can be reduced to only one hour! Therefore, if you have tuna salad sandwiches (or any other perishable food items) and it is ~ 80-85F outside, you have one hour to start eating so no more than an hour hike before the picnic!

Stuff a Bear Party:

Many shopping malls have locations themed to build your own stuffed animals. These locations usually offer birthday party packages and the basic packages are priced quite reasonably but you'll probably end up spending more. The basic packages start around $10.00 per person and depending upon the location and package, will go up from there. Realize the guests will create their own stuffed bear but it will be *naked* at this basic cost so you're probably looking at forking over some dough for each guest to purchase a dress or other accessories for their bear and this can add up quickly.

For the basic package, expect a dedicated party host, a stuffed toy bear to build for each guest (with accessories optional and an extra charge), a photo of the party, a party favor for each guest, free printable invitations, and some may offer a coupon for free access to a virtual website that the guests can access after the party.

Look into the offered virtual websites by the various party establishments, as some children's websites will peddle upgrades that the kids will certainly want to have. The kids might gain free access from your birthday party coupon into the main virtual room of the site where a few fun activities are available for them to do but in order to get through the *other five doors to more exciting things*, they'll need their parent's credit card. You don't want to irritate the parents of your guests in the end.

Science Party:

If you have a science museum in your area, check to see if they offer birthday party packages. Some will allow you to rent the facility after hours and others will give you a great group discount. Especially if your museum has a children's museum section, this might be an awesome place to host your next event!

Some cities might even have companies that host personal science parties at your home. Make sure that you see references and valid testimonials before ever allowing anyone into your home to interact with children, however.

Rent a Limousine:

Every child should have the experience of riding in a limousine at least once! They see the celebrities riding in them and have an intense curiosity of what it must be like to do the same.

For a limousine, depending upon the company, the type of limo you desire and how long you wish to rent it will determine what you are charged.

The range for an 8-10 person limo for four hours will run you about $450.00 plus a tip for the driver. Renting a Hummer Limousine will obviously be closer to $1100.00 for this time period but will carry more guests. A party bus is a cheaper alternative to carry more guests as well but it is not as trendy or suave as a limousine.

Typically, the limo is rented on an *as directed* basis where you instruct the driver where to take you and your guests. You will receive a business card from the driver with their phone number and each time the driver drops you off, they will park the limo in the nearest location and await your call. Be sure to give the limo driver at least 5-10 minutes to pick you up as some locations you may go to will not allow the limo to park! Don't wait until your guests are waiting in the heat, rain, sleet or snow to call for the limo.

Take the guests essentially anywhere once you rent the limousine. Take them to eat, bowling or even to a Medieval Dining Establishment. You have a set amount of time so make sure to use every minute!

HOME PARTIES:

Beauty Pageant Party:

If your little one has been following the pageants each year and can't wait to be in one of her own…a beauty pageant party might be the answer!

Invite your guests and disclose exactly what your party will entail. Instruct the guests to come up with a two-minute talent routine of their choice, bring eveningwear and active wear and be ready to answer some fun interview questions. Swimsuits are optional and frowned upon by some parents so tread cautiously with the swimsuit competition. It's probably better to switch it to an active wear competition where the girls can come up with their cutest outfit!

Design a runway in your home for the guests to model their outfits.   Outline the runway with crepe paper, tape on the floor, and / or balloon bouquets but not tall balloon bouquets or you won't be able to see the fabulous modeling!

Start with the evening gown competition with the host parent asking a fun interview question at the end of the runway to each contestant. The interview question can be absolutely anything such as "do you ever think you will live on Mars and why" or "do you think chocolate cake should be served before or after dinner and why?" The girls will certainly giggle at each other's answers and have loads of fun. Have a video camera during this event, for sure!

Follow it up with the talent routine portion of the pageant. Tell the audience members to be ultra-supportive of everyone and there will be deductions of points for anyone saying anything negative about someone else! Encourage sportsmanship!

Last is the active wear competition. Allow the guest to show their modeling skills while flaunting their favorite outfit. This is the best time to do cake and presents. You'll need someone to manage this while you (or someone else) get the awards ready. The awards can be simple certificates, ribbons or purchase trophies such as inexpensive ones from a local party store or more costly varieties from a local sporting goods store. The trophies from a sporting goods store will need to be ordered in advance of your party and will cost about $8.00 for the cheapest trophy on up. Be sure to give them plenty of time (i.e. 4 weeks) to get your trophies made. Another alternative is to purchase tiaras from the local party goods store. They usually have these in packages of four to eight as party favors and these would be excellent for an awards ceremony.

When the pageant is over, tally up the votes but no matter what; do not select only one winner. Make *everybody* the winner of the pageant and exclaim it is a tie! Or give a different award to each child for something such as: the most photogenic (take their individual pictures during the pageant and show everybody the best picture of the day), the best model of evening wear, the best interview, the best talent routine, the best model of active wear, the most personality, the best sportsmanship, the best smile, etc.

It's not a positive experience for most if you only select one winner, as this is not truly a competition but rather a party where all guests should leave feeling good as if they've had a blast. You don't want someone to feel as though they lost but should have won or to be embarrassed because they did so poorly as compared to the other girls as that's how feelings get hurt!

Rent a Blow Up Bounce House:

If you plan to have a home party, you have to have a focus on entertainment. With kids (and teens), that is the most important part of the party planning – how are you going to keep them entertained?

Nothing says *drain of energy* like a bounce house! There are tons of companies out there that will deliver, set up and monitor the bounce house next to your home (or other location) for a set amount of time. They can tell you exactly what they offer and how much they charge per hour. Some companies have popcorn machines, fictional characters that will come with the rental (i.e. someone dressed as Barney, Mickey Mouse, etc.), and other items to rent along with the bounce house. Have plenty of adult supervision on hand for these active parties.

Rent a Karaoke Machine and have a Super Star Party:

Every kid has a musical idol. Now it's time for them to be a star for a day. Rent a karaoke machine and instruct the invited kids to dress as their favorite musical idol. On the RSVP, ask them for their five favorite songs to have some of them available in the karaoke selection. When the kids arrive, take turns putting on a show for each other! Get your video cameras ready!

Rent a Petting Zoo:

Some local farms or zoos may provide a service for you to rent a petting zoo. These will typically run between $1000 to over $2000 for about four hours. Expect to have 10-12 animals at your home during this time and the types of animals will vary. Most of the time, these animals are well trained and can be counted on to behave but please remember – these are animals and can never be trusted 100%.

Some companies might have pony rentals where your guests can take turns riding a pony! Again, even though these are highly trained animals, they are still *animals*. You will share in the liability if anyone gets hurt, as it is your party so do not be negligent and make sure there are tons of chaperones available when there are animals involved.

Scavenger Hunt Party:

My Mystery Party has tons of themes of scavenger hunt parties available for download instantly upon purchase as well as boxed sets with the task list sealed so the host can play along. Scavenger hunts are highly energetic parties and are extremely memorable events. They are contagious as once your child attends a scavenger hunt party, they'll want their next party to be a scavenger hunt!

There are *about town* photo hunts where the guests divide into teams and travel around town looking for items on their task list. The tasks are written as such to provide memorable pictures – not just pictures of a statue or a random book in the library but of the team members posed in a specific and hilarious way with the item they found. These scavenger hunt pictures make for great memory books for the birthday child. There are also *on foot* neighborhood hunts and building hunts available and cars will not be necessary with these types of hunts.

With kid's parties, you'll need plenty of chaperones to supervise the hunts, as the kids will be super energetic as it is a competition. Scavenger hunts are one of the most fun and memorable parties and are relatively inexpensive as compared to the other parties. Download some of the kits for under $20.00 and this provides entertainment for an unlimited amount of guests!

Non-Murder Mystery Party:

My Mystery Party has tons of themes of non-murder mystery parties available for download instantly upon purchase as well as boxed sets with the clues sealed and ready to go. These downloadable kits start at under $30.00 and again, it is inexpensive as compared to the other parties as it is providing entertainment for ~ $2.50 per child as most kits will accommodate about 12 children. There is some associated assembly with the downloaded kit such as paper and ink that will increase this cost slightly but still nowhere near what it will cost for most of the parties outlined above. The boxed sets are more as the staff will prepare the kit, etc. but these are a hosting dream as everything is ready to go for the day of the party.

My Mystery Party's mystery party games are played in a series of rounds. With kid's parties (~ ages 5-9), they are less focused on characters and character building but more upon solving multiple mysteries as a group. When you get to the ages 10+ mysteries, more focus is put on the characters and their involvement with the crime. Younger kids, however, might feel bad if they were the *bad person* so the authors are very sensitive to not singling out a child and making them the *intentional* perpetrator.

Mystery parties are a unique option for a kid's party but will take some dedication by the host parent to read the instructions prior to the game. Having a few adult/teen chaperones to facilitate the party is suggested, as the younger guests might need a little help if they are playing a game where they are the minimum age in the range. These parties, however, are unique, very fun and the guests will talk about them for a long time!

Sports Party:

If your child is an athlete or has an interest in sports, you might consider hosting a sports party for them. Host a soccer or football tournament or a party with various sports-related challenges as the focus of entertainment. Instruct your guests on the invite to wear athletic clothing so they will come prepared for the fun! Continue the sports theme with the food and party décor and be sure to have many sports drinks for the exhausted athletes.

Tea Party:

For the younger ladies, a tea party is a wonderful change of pace for a birthday party. Little girls love playing dress up and pretending to be adults! Have an elegant table setting with grown up tableware. Ask the girls to wear their favorite outfit of their mommy's (with their permission, of course). Hats and over-sized high-heeled shoes are a timeless tradition and feather boas are a plus!   Pick up feather boas from your local craft store for ~ $5.00 to $10.00 a piece and this is an awesome party favor!

Serve hot tea with tons of sugar and honey (use decaf, please).   Cookies should be served and the girls should be instructed to speak to each other about how their (pretend) careers have been going. Ask each of them to pretend they are an adult during the tea party and to imagine that they are in the career of their choice. If they want to be a doctor or a duck feeder - they are to pretend as though that is what they are!

Of course, after the tea, they can participate in fun party games!

Hire a Professional Entertainer:

Nothing says tradition like a clown, mime, magician and puppeteer for a kid's party. If you want to have a home party but want someone else to be in charge of the entertainment, do an internet search for a clown, mime, magician and / or puppeteer for hire.

These folks will keep your guests entertained for a couple of hours. Break up the shows with food and birthday cake, and of course the presents.

The prices of hiring these individuals will vary with the individual or agency that represents them but you are looking at an average of $50.00 per hour *and up.* You will be required to pay a deposit upon booking the entertainer and most of the time it is non-refundable. You will pay more for hiring an entertainer from an agency but they are likely to be more reputable and the agency will probably have done background checks on these entertainers. It's all right to ask them if they have done a background check including a criminal history check. After all, it's your home they are coming to and your child in which they will interact!

Other types of entertainers are jugglers, balloon artists, face painters, caricature artists, holiday characters, stilt walkers, fortunetellers.

Fashion Show:

Invite your guests to participate in your child's birthday fashion show. Not too far of a spin off from the beauty pageant party but this one is not a competition. You'll assign your guests to the various themes of outfits and then compose a final show at the conclusion of your party. On the invitation, assign each guest to a different theme of outfit such as a ballerina, soccer player, party girl, eveningwear, etc.

When the guests arrive, they are immediately to go to their modeling lesson where they will learn (from you as the host parent or other assistant) how to model like a high fashion model. Do a YouTube.com search for 'how to model' and show the video to your group. Also, show the guests a quick clip of a fashion show to get the party started. If you have a television in the room, have some prerecorded episodes of *Top Model* or other fashion-related shows playing without sound.

After the guests learn to model correctly, they are to go to hair and makeup. Here, they will have their hair done in the style of their assigned outfit. Hire a hairstylist and makeup artist or get some adult/teen volunteers to help with this.

Once the hair and makeup is done, the guests are to get their outfits ready for the runway. Play fun spirited music in the background while the guests model their outfit to the audience. The audience is the guests who are not currently modeling as well as the chaperones.

After the fashion show, it is time for birthday cake and presents! If you videotaped the fashion show, play it on the screen for them to watch as they enjoy their cake!

Makeover / Spa Party:

Little girls love to be pampered! Hire a few stylists and nail technicians or recruit some adult/teen volunteers and transform your living room into a day spa! Have stations for manicures, pedicures, hair and facials. Skip massages for a kid's party – it's not necessary at this age.

Serve tons of chocolate covered strawberries and chocolate truffles!

Dance Party:

If you have a big enough party area for a dance floor, turn on the music and have a dance party! Kids love to *cut a rug* and especially if you have a play list of their favorite songs, they'll be entertained for a long time!

Break up the dance party with party games that can be played in the dance floor area. Have a dance contest, of course!

The kids need a constant change of direction and any form of entertainment will become boring if done at the same pace for too long. It's important to have an interactive DJ and plenty of dance-related party games ready to keep changing the pace.

Actors, Directors Party:

If your child is into acting, allow them to shine at their own birthday party. When all of your guests have arrived, select the leaders to act as the team captains. Hand the team captains a clapboard (pick up toy clapboards at your local party store or on the internet).

The team captains are to draw a scenario from a hat. The scenario will have as much information as you would like them to have for a two-minute skit that they will perform in front of the group. Offer a complete script for them to follow and allow the captain to act as the Director and cast the roles and run the rehearsals. For older kids, give them only a premise (i.e. you are in the school lunchroom and are trying to prevent a food fight) for the skit and allow them to make up their own skit as a group.

At the conclusion of the party, the groups are to perform their skits in front of the group. Have plenty of adult / teen volunteers to help the groups. Be sure to video tape these performances!

Arts & Crafts Party:

Arts and Crafts are a universal activity for all to enjoy. Most kids love to create something wonderful. Schedule random craft project times during the party such as jewelry making, decorating picture frames, making houses out of Popsicle sticks, etc.

Things that need to dry will need to be made first. The guests will take home all of their projects when they leave or deliver things that need additional drying time such as painted projects or paper mache art.

Lego Parties:

If your child is into legos and s/he has enough legos for a ton of kids to enjoy making things...why not make a party of it?

To get the lego party started, announce for the kids to make certain items such as an airplane and give them a time limit and a prize for whoever makes the best one. Allow them to make a city or other structure together as a team by having them draw individual components from a hat such as Cars on the streets, the Police Station, Homes, etc.

Don't forget to take breaks to eat birthday cake and open presents!

Luau / Swimming Pool Party:

Tread ultra-cautiously when having a party involving a body of water and small children. The adult to child ratio should be one adult to two - three kids and the adults need to be attentive while the kids are not only in the water, but also anywhere near the water. Weak swimmers are always provided with life vests and not allowed to go near the deep end of the pool.

The adults, of course, should be excellent swimmers as well. Hiring professional lifeguards is necessary. These parties are almost not worth having for small kids but if you are set on doing it – do not skimp on lifeguards. Hire as many as you can and recruit additional adult chaperones to watch the kids diligently. Again, having a swimming party for kids is not suggested but if done right and with proper supervision, can be a lot of fun.

If you do decide to host a swimming pool party, do not allow jumping into the water, diving or running around the pool. Have a time-out penalty assessed for each violation and remain strict to it. Schedule games to play in the pool to keep the kids focused and do not allow them to become wild while in the water.

Kids should not eat immediately prior to swimming so only give light snacks until swim time is over. When you eat lunch/dinner and serve cake, the kids should not be allowed to swim for an hour so you should do this at the conclusion of the party.

Even if you rented a recreation center pool, a Country Club pool or other public pool, it is still your responsibility for the safety of the children. Ask for additional lifeguards (you will probably have to pay for it but it's worth it) and invite plenty of adult chaperones.

Home with Party Games:

A traditional home party with random party games is always an easy and economical choice. Allow your child to choose a theme and then change the party game names and props to fit the theme. There are tons of party games in this book for all ages. To make them fit your theme, put a key word in the title and slightly change the props.

Be sure to read the required game gear and gather up the required props for each game so you are not scrambling the day of the party. With home parties, have food as part of the fun! Allow the guests to make their own pizza (assemble the toppings) and design their own cupcake!

Party Theme 411

Chapter 8

Distinctive Party Themes

You have your guest list, location set and party date finalized and now it is time to decide upon the theme. You might have already had an idea for a theme when you first conceptualized hosting the party but now that you know whom you will invite, the location and the date, it's time to put your theme in concrete.

Consider Guests' Attire:

Regarding your invite list, think about what you want your guests to wear. With adult parties, you should take time to categorize your party guests and see which group the majority of your guests fit into (see Chapter 5). Think about if they will enjoy dressing in costumes, dressing in semi-formal attire or going all out with formal attire. Maybe they would prefer casual attire or even pajamas. Kids and teens are easy to please as far as attire goes and will go along with any plan you create. Adults take more thought as far as attire is concerned.

Costumes can be simple props such as animal-ear headbands or masquerade masks all the way to elaborate medieval knights and maidens. You know your guests the best and will know if they'll be on board with having to purchase and / or create a costume ensemble. If your group fits the partier or Peter Pan category, go for a wild costume event, as these parties are the most memorable. Even the most conservative and shy person will have fun if they are dressed up like a nerd, elephant or maybe even a pumpkin. Who wouldn't have fun dressed up like a pumpkin? Don't stray from a costume party because of age because even nursing home residents wouldn't mind getting dress up in silly attire for a night!

Nevertheless, if your guests are types that are more professional or family with wide age ranges they'll most likely be more comfortable in normal attire – whether it be casual, semi-formal or formal. The adults from the Chiller category won't want to be told what to wear unless it is pajamas.

Consider Themes:

With the guests' attire being considered, decide what you want to do at your party. Do you want to do a murder mystery party game, scavenger hunt challenge, formal dinner, informal dinner, board game night, party game night, etc.

Next thing to do is to assign a theme to your main activity. Do you want to host a Mexican fiesta, a backyard barbeque or maybe a decade-themed event? Mix it up and host a Nifty Fifties murder mystery party, a pirate themed backyard barbecue, or maybe a Mardi gras party game night? The combinations are nearly endless!

Now let's discuss the most popular party themes for most ages and groups.

Casino Night:

Casino parties are always a scream and the cost and set up will vary greatly depending upon your budget. From a deck of cards and poker chips to an elaborate room of Vegas quality gaming tables and professional dealers – these parties run the spectrum.

The typical casino party is a semi-formal affair. Think about what you would wear nowadays to a Las Vegas casino. Of course, there are some casinos where you'd be fine in shorts and flip flops and other gaming rooms that approach formal attire requirements like the old days. If you choose to make it a formal affair, call it a VIP or Celebrity Casino party.

What about games? A moderate budget would support purchasing a felt game table toppers (i.e. blackjack, craps, poker, etc). Some of the felt table toppers are cheaply made but will do the trick for a casual party whereas others come close to Vegas quality but of course, you will pay more for them. There are companies in most big cities to hire both the dealers and lease the full-sized gaming tables. For about three - four tables along with the dealers for each table, expect to pay $1,000.00 to $2,000.00 for a five to six-hour party. Most companies will also provide a bartender for your event at an hourly fee as well.

Who deals? Again, this depends upon your budget. If it fits in the budget, hire a few folks as the dealers. This will free up your valuable time to host properly. In addition, you couldn't do it all anyway and would need to recruit some friends and these friends would have been party guests!

What do you gamble for? The big question is – do you use real money? Well, in most states it's considered illegal to gamble for real money so we will only discuss using fake money. This generates another question – *how much fun is it to gamble for fake money?* This is a great question, by the way!

You solve this issue by having an end of the night auction for prizes. The guests' incentive for winning the most money is to be able to purchase the most prizes at the auction! It is suggested to place a limit on the amount of prizes each guest can win (i.e. two - three prizes) as this will keep one person from walking away with all the prizes - which can happen! The auction prizes can be as simple as a $5.00 gift certificate to a fast food restaurant to an expensive video game system or even more elaborate prizes depending upon your budget.

An alternative is to ask your guests to each bring a prize with a minimum monetary value. Set a minimum and not a maximum for obvious reasons – allow the high rollers to spend as much as they want as that only adds excitement to the auction! However, without a minimum value, your frugal friends might just bring a stick of gum wrapped up in a box! It's also preferred if you have the prizes wrapped in gift paper or gift bags. This adds mystery to the auction as the guests are then bidding on unknown prizes.

Any guest who doesn't contribute to the prize pool is not eligible to participate in the auction! This will cause sore feelings among guests if Jason wins the best prizes but didn't bring a prize of his own!

As an alternative to prizes, have an award ceremony for the big winner(s) and the biggest loser of the night. Pick up a trophy from your local sporting goods store (good quality for around $8.00) or even at a local party store (cheap quality but gets the point across). Alternatively, use ribbons or awards certificates. Create a template in Microsoft Word, make a pdf of the file and add text box fields. On your party night, add your guests' names into the text box fields and print!

What kind of money do I use? This is again, up to your budget. Pick up fake money at your local party store in the party favor section. Alternatively, if you are an expert with Adobe Photoshop software, why not Photoshop your face, the guests' faces or other common icon into some money that you create on the computer? Make different denominations or make them all 100-dollar bills. Have a certain amount of money available to each guest upon arrival. Then, have the option for them to buy poker chips to gamble or they can simply hold on to their cash for the auction. Unbelievably, some guests will take the option of not buying poker chips as not everybody enjoys gambling.

Burning question: what if a guest runs out of cash - won't they get bored? You have a few options here. First, you should make a timed penalty in any scenario to prevent the guests from doing unrealistic bets on the tables and soaking the fun and energy out of the group. When a guest runs out of cash and they want to continue to gamble, set a 15 minute or 30 minute penalty on them before they can get more money from the host. They'll be all right with having to watch others at the tables for some time. They can use this time to freshen up, enjoy some appetizers, etc.

Document how much money these guests get from the bank throughout the night and they are to pay the entire debt back before the auction – with a 10 percent interest fee. Split this 10 percent interest fee among the guests who never had to re-draw from the host bank.

An alternative is if you did not hire professional dealers and you have volunteers running your tables, allow these broke players to earn their money back by dealing at the tables for a set amount of time.

Yet another alternative to this is if you set up a karaoke stage or other type of stage in your party area, allow these broke players to work as a lounge performer for a set amount of time to earn their cash back! This can add some hysterical memories to your party. Maybe add a tip jar and allow the other players to give him/her tips while they perform.

Run your casino for a set amount of time. At the end of this time, ask the guests to cash their chips in and give the guests back the bills according to the amount of chips they turned in. Start the auction with any random prize. Allow the guests to bid on the prizes until there is a winner. Ask the winner to open the gift in front of everybody if it's gift-wrapped. Allow the next player who wins a present either to switch with the last person who opened one or to select the one for auction and so on.

Red Carpet Oscars Party:

There's nothing more glamorous than an Oscars party is! Send an invite in a tin can movie reel box (these can be purchased from the internet) or glue your invitation to clapboards for a fun effect. It would be acceptable to do a simple evite as you can choose from ready-made invitations and track your RSVPs easily. This is not a formal party but rather a quirky themed party where your guests are dressing in *costume* formal attire so the evite is all right in this situation. We've established thus far that any party requiring formal attire requires a formal invitation. This is the one exception as this is not a *serious* formal attire party.

Ask that your guests dress as though they are attending the Oscars and have a red carpet in your front walkway. Glitter and feather boas are expected!   Purchase a red carpet piece from a local carpet dealer or possibly from a local party store. As an alternative, paint some craft paper red and allow drying thoroughly before your party! Hire some local teens or local actors if you have the budget to dress as paparazzi and take pictures of your guests as they stroll down the red carpet. Have a videographer film fake interviews by one of the paparazzi members and keep this as a memorable video! Give everybody a copy after your event!

Announce each guest over a PA system as they arrive to your event and greet them with appetizers and a cocktail (for adults). Pass out pens and ballot sheets that have the nominees already listed so the guests can vote prior to the awards show. Nominees are typically listed at least a month prior to the award show so check the official website at www.oscars.org when you are ready to make your ballot sheets.

Make sure to have adequate seating where everybody has a clear view of the television set or projector screen if you have a media room. If you don't have enough room in one area, it is acceptable to make two party areas. The television or movie screen is the focus and the guests need to be comfortable! If you don't have adequate seating around a television for everybody, find another home to host the party – no exceptions!

During the awards show, serve appetizers and cocktails with a non-alcoholic option for adults and yummy beverages such as milkshakes and smoothies for teens.

Food for an Oscar party should be elegant. Champagne or non-alcoholic champagne, lobster stuffed mushrooms, shrimp cocktails and Godiva chocolates are great choices. Definitely skip the hamburgers and hotdogs! You want to mock what the celebrities will be dining on for the night!

Make a separate ballot for the best/ worst dress or suit on the red carpet, the best/worst interview on the red carpet and the best / worst hairstyle of the red carpet. At the end, tally the votes to see which celebrity wins each category.

Purchase a plastic Oscar and present it to the guest who got the most Oscar winners correct after the awards show! Demand an acceptance speech from the winner!

Masquerade Ball / Costume Ball:

You don't have to host either type of Ball during the Halloween season. Balls can be hosted for all ages at any time throughout the year.

First thing to do is to decide on a solid theme for your Ball. *Do you want your guests to bring a simple masquerade mask or go all out and wear elaborate costumes? Maybe you want everybody to dress as a character from the Lion King or you want to host a Mardi gras themed Ball?* The sky is the limit on the type of Ball you want to have and there are no wrong types of Balls. Be unique!

The invitation will vary by theme but for a typical masquerade ball, you'd likely include a paper mask in the invitation design. If you are doing a Victorian style masquerade ball, print your invites on parchment paper and scroll them. These will require a hand-delivery or mail the scroll invites to your guests in a small box.

For a Mardi Gras Ball, decorate with green, purple and gold and include tons of confetti, beads, sequins and feathers to create a fun Carnival atmosphere. (Mardi gras celebrations are discussed further in Chapter 15).

For other types of Masquerade Balls and Costume Balls, use soft lighting as these are elegant events. Light candles and maybe candelabras but put both in safe areas of the party room away from flammable items. Nowadays, there are fake plastic candles available that look like real lit candles. These are worth it for safety during your event.

Colors for a traditional masquerade ball are bold such as deep reds, purples and metallic colors such as gold or silver. Drape velvet on the walls and don't be afraid to use over-sized feather plumes in metallic vases with metallic-gold or even black spray-painted tree branches for a gothic yet elegant feel.   Soft white Christmas lights around the room also add to elegance. Drape the chairs in tulle fabric and tie with elegant bows that hang to the floor.

When available, use sterling silver serving dishes and goblets and fine china for serving your guests.

Most Balls are upscale formal attire events but you don't have to have a crazy-huge budget to host one. Balls can be hosted at home but you'll need space to designate as the dance floor (or a ballroom with a dance floor installed). If you are doing this at home, clear out the furniture from the center of the room and have seating along the walls.

Hire a DJ (or make a long mix CD) to play classical ballroom music. Obviously, hiring an orchestra is the best scenario but most people are on a budget. Classical music is the tradition but not a must. The Phantom of the Opera sound track is great for masquerade parties. Play modern music at your Ball if you so choose. Hiring an emcee for your party is preferred.

The dance floor is ready; the music is playing so now what? That's what your emcee is for, actually. You want this person to keep the party moving and exciting. Have them stage costume contests where the contestants parade about and the guests will vote via handclap for their favorite. Have a dance contest and designate a panel of judges to tap out couples as they lose with the last two remaining couples going head to head in the next song. The audience clap vote is necessary to determine the winning couple.

For children's masquerade parties, hire a face painter to paint the masks onto the kids as they arrive to your party. That way, the parents will not have to purchase their child a mask for your party! Also, have a spirited piñata designed in your theme and have the kids take turns beating it with a plastic bat while blindfolded until the candy spills out. The kids scamper all over the dance floor and pick it up! For party favors, give beads and a cute mask along with some candy.

Wine Tasting:

Create a wine-tasting party ambiance with classical music playing softly, and low level lighting in the party room. Light plenty of candles (and place in safe areas) or purchase the fake plastic candles and assemble around the party area.

Choose about three to eight different varietals of wines from a specific region. Do any combination of reds and whites but half-and-half is common. In most stores, the wines are separated by region. Go on a scouting mission to any wine store or local grocery store and view the selection and select different varietals to assign to each guest to bring to the party and include a price point range for each.

Between you and the bottles your guests bring, there will be approximately 1.5 ounces per sample for each tasting. Each bottle equals about 10 tasting samples. Keep a few extra bottles for drinking after the official tasting, as your guests might want to enjoy their favorite wines they tasted.

You should have some backup bottles just in case a guest forgets to bring their assigned wine! It happens and you don't want to be left with not enough wine at your wine tasting. Ask each guest to bring a cheese pairing with his or her respective wines or supply these. A quick internet search on your chosen wines with their best pairing is all you need to do.

Either set up mini-tables with 'wine stations' around the room and each wine has its own table - or have one long buffet style table with each wine and its cheese pairing close together.

There are two ways to deal with glasses.   Supply the wine glasses as one per person. Be sure to assign wine charms in case a guest puts their glass down and forgets where they put it.

As the guests taste the wines, they will dump the remaining wine from their glass in the wine dump bucket (have a few available). Have a rinse bucket as well, but realize that this can dilute the next glass of wine if any water is left in the glass. A wine rinse is best, yet wasteful.

Pair the correct type of wine glass with each wine. Red wine is paired with a round shaped glass and white wine is to be served in a smaller, more fluted glass (but not as narrow like a champagne flute). It is best to assign one white and one red glass to each guest or just offer enough of each type of glass for each guest for each wine so the guests can be sure to have the right glass at all times. Have plenty of little plates for your samples of cheese with each wine.

Tasting Cards: on each table by each bottle of wine (or on the large buffet table by each wine station), write as much information down on a note card regarding the wine as possible. Do research on the types of wines that your guests will bring so add to the fun and increase everybody's knowledge of the wines they taste! However, if you don't have the time - then no worries - they'll still taste and enjoy the wines!

Scoring Sheets: make scoring sheets and place next to each wine station so the guests can score each wine based upon appearance, aroma, body, taste, and finish. Ask the guests to tally their score sheet and place into a large wine goblet, ice bucket, or any other container next to the wine. At the end of the tasting, tally up the scores to determine the best tasting wine of the night. There are plenty of free wine tasting scorecards available for download on the internet.

Get these items ready before your event: pens, wine dump buckets, wine as well as water glasses, paper napkins, the cheese pairings with crackers and some plain French bread or water crackers to cleanse the palate in between each tasting.

For each wine station, use simple white tablecloths with white unscented candles. Add bunches of grapes and grape leaves or possibly decorate with seasonal or holiday items such as autumn leaves if the party is in the fall or holly, evergreen twigs, etc.

In addition to the cheese pairings, on a separate table, offer grapes and other fruit such as strawberries, cherries, apples, apricots, etc. If you choose one large buffet table - instead of actual wine 'stations', you will need a nice focal piece so use wine buckets filled with ice and bottles of wine centered around a large tiered platter with any type of Hors d' oeuvres on it.

You will need foods that pair nicely with the wines that you will offer. When you decide on the type of wine to assign each guest, do some research on the ideal type of food pairing and have this ready for the party. You can always interview or hire a sommelier from your local fine dining restaurant if money is not an option.

If you are having the one long, buffet table - then make sure to keep the paired items close together and make note cards for the wine as well as the types of cheeses. These labels should state the name and general flavor of the cheese and the origin. If you have time, do research on the history of the cheese for added fun. Each cheese should have its own cutting board and cheese knife or you should cut the cheese in advance of the party and serve it on a cheese-serving tray. You'll also want to provide many interesting breads (i.e. French breads, sourdoughs, etc.) and different styles of party crackers. If money is not a problem, add some caviar.

Keeping within the theme of the party, a fruit topped cheesecake is perfect for dessert! Maybe serve dessert wine with the cheesecake or brew up some coffee to have with dessert...especially if your guests will be driving. You should encourage guests to take taxis if possible and never allow an intoxicated guest to get behind the wheel.

Pirate Party:

Create a pirate tavern ambiance with pirate music playing softly, pirate decor and any pirate movie playing without the audio (i.e. Pirates of the Caribbean, etc.) if there is a television in the party
room.

Decorate with a nautical theme. You are at port, but the sea is near. Play an ocean ambiance track (or the music as above) very low in the background. Use ropes and netting with starfish and barnacles as décor. Make plenty of Jolly Roger Flags, place them on poles and stands, and line them around the walls as if they are docked pirate ships.

Insist that everybody speak as a pirate. On the web, there are plenty of pirate dictionaries available (such as on www.PartyHost411.com).

For food, you should serve pirate-worthy delicacies such as smoked meat dishes and potatoes. For adults, pirates love rum so you should serve tropical rum drinks such as pina coladas and daiquiris.   Also, don't forget the lemonade-inspired drinks and lime sherbet punch, as you don't want your pirates to get scurvy!

The guests should dress as pirates or at a minimum, hand them a bandana, fake earring loop and eye patch as they arrive and they can take these home as party favors.

Pirates love to hunt for treasure so a scavenger hunt such as the Out of This World Hunt from My Mystery Party found at the address: (www.mymysteryparty.com/aroutofthwop1.html) is an excellent choice for pirate party entertainment. However, this party would require you to go 'about town' and search for land-lubbing pirate items. As an alternative, hide *Pieces of eight (pirate coins)* around your house, yard or neighborhood and send the pirates on a treasure hunt.

Luau:

The meaning of the word Luau is *feast.* Hawaiian natives gather with family and friends to enjoy life with great food, friends and entertainment! Flower leis, ukuleles and hula-hoops always seem to make their way into the festivities!

Luaus are traditionally held for special events but can be held any time throughout the year! A luau should invite relaxation. Choosing to host a luau for first time friends is a great idea as they'll be in a relaxed and fun environment from the start!

First, design the perfect invitation! Think of flower leis, pineapples and ukulele shapes as the starting point. Along with your invitation, sprinkle some tropical metallic confetti and include a lei bracelet for the women. Purchase fun Hawaiian-inspired Luau decor for your home from your local party store and start in the front walk way!

Remember that first impressions set the tone for your party! Fresh pineapples and coconuts make for great starts with table centerpieces and buffet lines! Grab some fresh tropical flowers and add them anywhere to add the décor.

When the guests walk in, present them with a flower lei and snap their picture in front of a flower and balloon wall. Hand them a cocktail (non-alcoholic fruit juice for minors) in a carved out pineapple! No luau would be complete without hibiscus flower straws, colorful paper umbrellas and loads of fresh fruit garnish (i.e. pineapple wedges, etc.) on all beverages.

The party should be hosted in the backyard, preferably by a poolside but having a pool for a luau is not mandatory. Play a cool Island music CD and light tiki torches. Add citronella in them if you live in an area endemic for annoying mosquitoes! Keep the bugs away as they are not invited!

Set up an appetizer table with a raffia table skirt with a coconut and pineapple centerpiece laden with silk Hawaiian flowers. Again, adding festive flowers and confetti everywhere will complete your look. Use beachcomber hats upside down with festive-colored napkins inside to hold munchin' items such as crackers, chips and nut mixes and don't forget the macadamia nuts! Throw metallic palm tree confetti around the table for a fun, festive effect.

Play a fun game of limbo! Hire performers (or recruit friends) to play the ukulele and to perform a hula dance for your guests while they dine on roasted pork, ham and pineapple kabobs, tropical fruit salad, macadamia nut crusted chicken fingers (follow our almond crusted recipe but switch for macadamia nuts), and banana bread. For an informal party for teens, order a Canadian bacon (or ham) and pineapple pizza – often called the Hawaii Special.

Limousine Party:

You can't go wrong with renting a limousine and having a night out on the town – especially if there are adults that might want to enjoy cocktails! This will give them a safe night out without having to worry about driving.

For a limousine, depending upon the company, the type of limo you desire and how long you wish to rent it will determine what you are charged.

The range for an eight to ten person limo for four hours will run you about $450.00 plus tip for the driver. Renting a Hummer Limousine will obviously be closer to $1100.00 for this time period but will carry more guests. A party bus is a cheaper alternative to carry more guests as well.

Typically, the limo is rented on an as directed basis where you instruct the driver where to take you and your guests. You will receive a business card from the driver with their phone number and each time the driver drops you off, they will park the limo in the nearest location and await your call. Be sure to give the limo driver at least 5-10 minutes to pick you up as some locations you may go to will not allow the limo to park! Don't wait until your guests are waiting in the heat, rain, sleet or snow to call for the limo.

Go absolutely anywhere as long as you stay within your time limit. Make it a big night and go for fine dining and dancing or maybe since you spent so much for transportation; make it an inexpensive night of a few drinks at the local pub and then a game of bowling? If you live in a big city, make it worth the time and finally go to those out of the way places you've wanted to go since you won't have to worry about finding a place to park.

There is nothing wrong with asking your guests to pitch in for the limo if this is a casual party without a strict designated host. You can simply get together as a big group of friends and decide to make a night of it and split the costs.

However, if you are the party host and this was your party that you invited them to, you will be expected to pay for the limo services. The exception to this basic guideline is a bachelor or bachelorette party, which is discussed further in Chapter 12.

Scavenger Hunt Party:

Scavenger Hunt Parties originated as teen parties but even adults enjoy the challenge. These are high energy, fast-paced hunts for items either about town, within the neighborhood or within a given building such as a church, school, etc. The best method for a scavenger hunts is to acquire fun photographs of the hunted items with the team members in the picture. That way, there are elaborate items to find and not just bottle caps, strings and leaves and you have a memorable photo of the task. Make a scrapbook of all of the teams' photos after the party for a great book of memories! There are hunts where the guests travel about town and look for items in the task list or others that ask you to stroll about on-foot in a neighborhood and hunt for items.

My Mystery Party also has a large selection of teen appropriate scavenger hunts available by instant download or as boxed sets so the host never has to see the task list and can play along with the rest of the group. These parties will typically take 30-40 minutes for the guests to arrive, divide into groups and listen to the rules. The actual hunts are typically two hours and then the judging period takes about 30-45 minutes.

Amazing Race parties are an upscale variation of a scavenger hunt party. You will need to recruit help for your various stations around your location that you choose to host your hunt (i.e. neighborhood, city, etc). You will set up stations with challenges for the guests to complete before receiving the envelope to go to the next location.   The challenges can be anything from a simple hula-hoop challenge to a complex riddle or puzzle. Be creative and change up the challenges from physical to mental to a combination of both so you even it out for the guests. Not everybody is an athlete and not everybody is a mathematician either! The winner will be the team that completes all challenges at all locations and crossing the finish line first.

As an alternative, eliminate the last team that makes it to each station to reduce the amount of teams as the race proceeds. If you do this, allow the disqualified players to follow along to the next station to watch the teams still in the race compete on the challenges. You wouldn't want to kick the disqualified players out of the game altogether! However, this way, you can have the more delicate and / or longer challenges at the final stations as you won't have as many teams participating and therefore, it won't take as long and your race can be completed within a manageable time.

Sole Survivor Party:

Divide your guests into two teams (i.e. tribes) by giving each team different colored bandanas (i.e. red and blue). Elect two captains and allow them to choose their own teams but this leads to the last person picked getting their feelings hurt and therefore, is not suggested. Either pre-select the teams, have every other person that arrives go on an opposing team or pull the teams at random from a hat.

Once the teams are set, have them go through various challenges such as obstacle courses or puzzles, etc. Maybe have a video game challenge (i.e. Rock Band or Super Mario on the Xbox) or a quick game of Go Fish with a deck of cards. The challenge can be essentially anything you choose. As each team loses a challenge, they have to vote someone off their team. As you don't want any guests being bored for the rest of the game, allow them to make a third team of cast offs (i.e. purple team). This cast off purple team will compete with the original two teams (red and blue) and if they win a challenge, both of the original teams must vote someone off their team. The cast offs never have to vote anyone off their team but ask them to sit team members out of various challenges so you can have equal number of players – depending upon the challenge. They cannot sit the same player out in two challenges, however, until everybody has sat out a challenge.

Once the original teams get to 50% of what they once were, you will combine the red and blue teams. For example, if you started off with 20 people with 10 players on each team (red and blue) and once 10 people have been voted off and are on the cast off team (purple), combine the original two teams (red and blue) into one team (choose either red or blue for this merged team) who will now go against challenges with the cast off team. Now when the cast off team wins a challenge, only one player from the opposing team needs to be voted off. However, if the cast off team loses a challenge, no players are voted off and the next challenge is played.

When you get down to three players on the original team, the cast off team can cast a vote for the winner of sole survivor.

One-Color Party:

No matter what other theme you may choose, always elect to have a one-color party. Every possible item is in one color from the invitations, guests' attire, décor, food, and anything associated with the party games should be in this color. Songs about this color should be played throughout the night and movies with the color in the title should be played on the television (or big screen) without the sound. *An alternative to this party is a Black and White Affair. Normally associated with a formal event, it can also be a casual party but make sure that you outline exactly the type of party on the invitation.

Chocolate Spa Party:

Who doesn't love to be pampered? Hire a few stylists, massage therapists and/or nail technicians or recruit some adult/teen volunteers and transform your living room into a day spa! Have stations for manicures, pedicures, massages (shoulder/neck/arm) hair and facials.

Serve tons of chocolates, strawberries dipped in chocolate and champagne cocktails for adults to get into the relaxed state of mind. Have the nail technicians use chocolate hand and foot masques and salt scrub for an additional chocolate aroma!

Kidnap Breakfast:

These parties are discussed in the teen section but if you wanted to pull this off with adults – feel free to do so! This would be a nice surprise for anyone!

In advance of your party, with kids or teens, you must call every parent to get permission and if you are kidnapping a married girl friend ask her husband for assistance to *kidnap* (i.e. pick them up without advance warning) the morning of your kidnap breakfast. Make the parents / husbands *pinky swear* that they will not leak a bit of news out about your surprise breakfast. With unmarried single adult friends, you will have to count on luck that they will wake up to answer the door for your kidnap and that they will not get ready prior to answering the door. You might not have a high success rate in these instances – you really need someone on the inside such as a parent, roommate or husband to assist with the success of your party.

Recruit enough drivers to carry all of your kidnap victims in advance of your party. Select a morning, preferably a Saturday morning, when you know that most of your friends will be at home in their beds. Make reservations at your local breakfast diner or have someone prepare a big delicious breakfast at your home while you are out kidnapping your friends.

One by one, you are to arrive at your friends' homes and wake them up and take them with you. They are not allowed to brush their hair, put on makeup or change clothes unless they are wearing something inappropriate, that is. Do not allow this person to text or try to call and wake up the guests you haven't picked up to give them a heads up that you are on your way as they will, no doubt, get ready for your breakfast party!

As you pick up the next guest, every guest that has previously been picked up is to help wake up the next guest…and so on. Be ready for some morning grumpies!

Enjoy breakfast and then either arrange for the parents / husbands to pick them up at the breakfast location or bring them home! Take plenty of pictures!

Pirate Party:

Another solid party theme is a pirate party. Play Pirates of the Caribbean (any of the series) on the television (or projector) without sound. Purchase the corresponding movie soundtrack and play it as ambiance in the background. Alternatively, purchase a sound track of the ocean and / or a creaking ship and play it as ambiance (although this can be repetitive and annoying after a while).

Send your invitation in a bottle with a little bit of sand in the bottom. Alternatively, simply use parchment paper and scroll the invitations that were printed on top of a faded treasure map template.

The party décor should be pirate themed (Old World Nautical) using ropes, nets with starfish on them and make a few Jolly Roger flags to fly throughout the party area.

Give each guest a copy of a pirate dictionary such as the one on www.partyhost411.com/pirate and encourage them to speak like a pirate during the party. Ask that they dress up like a pirate for the party.

For adults, rum-based cocktails are suggested, as everybody knows pirates loved rum. Pirates consumed a lot of dried meat (jerky) so skewers of smoked beef medallions and chicken would be appropriate as well as any food related to the Caribbean (i.e. jerk chicken).

The entertainment can be a Murder Mystery Party (i.e. Curse of Parrot Island by My Mystery Party) or a Pirate Scavenger Hunt Party (again, My Mystery Party has a pirate themed scavenger hunt), or simply host party games in a pirate theme. Most of our party games can be tweaked to fit a pirate theme.

Zombie / Vampire Party:

With the increasing popularity of both zombies and vampires, host these parties any time of the year, not just for Halloween anymore and not just for teens. Adults, especially the Partiers and Peter Pans (see Chapter 5) will love being a crazy monster for a night. Be careful in selecting either of these themes for a kid's party, as many parents won't appreciate the gore involved with these themes.

Send your gothic style invitations to your guests instructing them to dress in either zombie or vampire attire (depending upon which theme you choose). Maybe for a vampire party, ask half of your guests to dress up as werewolves and then that can be the dividing line for the party games! Werewolves vs. Vampires!

The party décor should be in a gothic theme. For vampire parties, use candelabras, coffins, and tons of spider webs. For zombie parties, make the party area look as run down as possible with tons of spider webs as well.

Food should be within the theme of the party. Blood fondue is a great choice for both themes (see the Party Cuisine chapter 17). Remember, with strong themed parties, the food is part of the décor!

The entertainment can be a Murder Mystery Party or a Scavenger Hunt Party (again, My Mystery Party has zombie and vampire themed parties), or simply host party games in a vampire or zombie theme.

My Mystery Party has a Zombie Themed murder mystery party (Chronicles of Zombie Town) that has YouTube.com videos and a published novel to go along with the story line. This is a way to get your guests fired-up about your party.

Prom Themes:

The following is a comprehensive list of possible prom themes. Feel free to use these for any event, however.

A Night in Tropical Paradise	A Stroll through Candy Land
Back to the Beach	Medieval Nights
Moonlight in Morocco	Parisian Paradise
Vegas, Baby!	Where Land Meets Sea
Enchantment under the Eiffel Tower	Fire and Ice
Shanghai Surprise	Enchanted Gardens
Fairytale Island	Castle in the Clouds
Plunder through Pirate Cove	A Night in the Royal Courtyard
Under the Sea	A Night of Grecian Fantasies
Pandora's Elegance	Dream Catchers
A Black Tie Affair	Evening in Tinseltown
A Mystical Masquerade	Totally Devoted to You
A Black and White Affair	Red Carpet Affair
Diamonds are Forever	Welcome to the Plaza Hotel
Stardust Fantasy	Wish Upon a Star
Circus Circus	The Sky is the Limit
Stairway to the Clouds	Funkytown Fantasy
Journey to Outer Space	A Night at the Sock Hop
Retro Rendezvous	Glorious Garden Adventure
A Walk in Wonderland	Rock n' Roll All Night
Arabian Nights	Romance & Red Roses
A Night in the Big Apple	Romance in Rome
A Stroll Down Memory Lane	A Taste of London
Kisses are Forever	Miami Dreamers
Glamorous Hollywood	Frozen in Time
Back to the Roaring Twenties	Amazon Rainforest Escapade
Enchantment Under the Stars	Journey through Space
Night on the Nile	Under the Rainbow
World of Memories	Step into the Magic Time Machine
Sunset to Sunrise	Candles in the Wind
Springtime in Paradise	It's a Magical World
Love at First Sight	Journey Around the Globe
A Night of International Flair	Moonlight Magic
A Night in Neon Paradise	Putting on the Ritz
A Stroll Down Broadway	Paint the Town Blue
African Safari	Famous Couples through Time
Paint the Town with School Spirit	A Night to Freeze in Time
A Night in Cabo	Forever Young
Welcome to the Wild West	Winter Wonderland
Flashback through the Decades	Out of this World
You Ought to be in Pictures	High School Musical
Mardi Gras Masquerade	Welcome to the Casino Royale
Chic Celebration	Teens Just Wanna Have Fun

Chapter 9

Era Themes

Any of the following era themes can be combined with the themes in the previous chapter or even with the holiday-themed parties such as Halloween, Christmas, Easter, etc. Why not have a Medieval Casino party, a Smashing '60s Pirate Party or a Totally Tubular Halloween Party? Mix it up and your options are virtually never-ending.

Medieval:

The Middle Ages, also referred to as the Medieval Era of European history, spanned from the fifth to the 15th century. During this time, the nobles and clergy reigned at the top of social ladder with scientists, fur and wool merchants and artisans harboring a mid-level status and the commoners and peasants working the land at the bottom. Most of the people worked as farmers and there were many improvements made to farming methods. The primary modes of transportation were horses and ships yet most people never traveled far away from where they were born.

Use a long rectangular table to set up for the medieval feast. Select a bright majestic purple (i.e. satin, velvet, taffeta) piece of fabric for a runner with a thinner, metallic-golden fabric piece on top. At a local party store or toy store, purchase some plastic shields and swords and hang them on the wall in the party room (swords crossed and the shields in front). Drape the same fabric as the table runner as banners on the wall with a medieval mace or other medieval inspired piece as the focal point of the banner.

Light plenty of candles (in safe places) throughout the party room and on the dinner table. Gothic lanterns are great and can add to the atmosphere.

Play the soundtrack from Beowolf, Braveheart, Monty Python's Search for the Holy Grail, or Camelot softly in the background. Also, play any of these movies without sound on a television in the party room or dining area.

As your guests arrive, have someone dressed as a court jester play the trumpet as they enter the party room. If possible, print name cards at the table setting for your guests on parchment paper to make them look more medieval. For the picture backdrop, create a coat of arms and include a funny saying (i.e. Bravery to those who dare to slay the Darmont Dragon, etc.). Surround it by gold and purple balloons (balloons look great as a backdrop in a picture).

Print off a Medieval Dictionary from the internet (www.partyhost411.com/medieval) and have it available for your guests. Instruct your guests not to skimp out on the *Alas, Thee,* and *Thou's* during conversation.

Serve roasted chicken as a main course and of course, skip the utensils! On the side, serve dragon soup (vegetable soup) to be slurped from the bowl and baked bread loaves to be torn by their hands. Roasted potatoes are not horrible to eat with thine hands but one might require a wet wipe before and after dinner.

Most of the party games in this book can be altered to a medieval theme.

Wild West:

The Wild West period spans from the mid 1830s to about 1920. This time frame encompasses the American Civil War period from 1861-1865. The American frontier slowly moved westward during this time and the *west* was always considered the edge of this expanding boundary.

A Wild West party is an easy to follow theme for a party. The guests should all dress in costume in the spirit of the Old West and your entertainment should be in the spirit of the Old West.

Show spaghetti Westerns on a television without sound, all décor should be western themed. All photos in the room should be black and white so print off some black and white photos of your guests (if you have them) and make some wanted posters of a few of them and frame them for a fun effect.

The music should be Wild West themed or make a sound track of songs that talk about the west like 'Wild Wild West by Will Smith.'

The entertainment can be a Murder Mystery Party (i.e. Gravestone by My Mystery Party) or a Wild West Scavenger Hunt Party (again, My Mystery Party has a western themed scavenger hunt), or simply host party games in a western theme. Poker was a popular pastime in the old saloons so feel free to host a Wild West Poker tournament.

The buffet table should be in a Chuck Wagon theme and food should be barbecue, potato salad and beans. Alternatively, for appetizers, have deviled eggs, beef and chicken skewers, and a trail mix.

Roaring '20s:

A 1920s party should have a twenties music ambiance with a '20s Jazz mix CD playing softly, decor in the time (i.e. silent movie posters, etc.), and silent movies playing in the background (i.e. The Great Gatsby, etc.) if there is a television in the party room.

The twenties included prohibition where alcohol was illegal to possess and consume. A speakeasy was a bar or nightclub where you could get a drink of low quality alcohol brought by the bootleggers.

The Great Gatsby was a very popular novel published by F. Scott Fitzgerald in 1925 and it might be worth it to get it on loan from the local library to get a real taste and flavor of the decade. Alternatively, check out an episode of *Boardwalk Empire* on HBO and take some good notes.

The primary colors should be black, white and gray to remind people that this was not a decade riddled with color as far as documentation goes (movie film, pictures, etc). Set the party in a speakeasy, an illegal gaming room, a gangster's home (i.e. Al Capone), a silent movie premiere, or maybe even a Jazz Club!

If you choose a speakeasy theme, give your guests a secret password on the invite and have someone greet them at the door and ask for the password before they can enter. If you have the time and money, drape red (velvet) fabric on the walls and change a lamp or two to a soft red light.

Costumes for girls should include long pearl necklaces with feathered headbands or cloche hats. Hair should be short (wig it) and finger waved or pin curls. A flapper dress with 1920's style Mary Jane pumps and a feather boa is perfect!

Costumes for the boys include zoot suits, fedoras and wing tip shoes. Go 1920's gangster and include a fake Tommy gun as an optional prop.

Party Games are necessary. Host a Charleston Dance Off. Have your guests watch a how to videos on www.YouTube.com and then play fun '20s style music for them to practice their routine. Then, have everybody perform their routines in front of the rest of the group and the host picks a winner!

Download a 1920s slang term dictionary from the internet (www.Partyhost411.com/1920) and ask that your guests speak in 1920s slang during the party.

Food choices are great. *Bathtub Gin* was the popular drink served at speakeasies so find some gin cocktail recipes. Of course, you don't have to limit yourself to gin cocktails! Add mint juleps to your menu as these were popular them back in that day. Mint was utilized mostly to mask the taste of the bad quality liquor, but mint lends a unique flavor to cocktails, nonetheless.

Purchase some plastic fedoras from a local party store and serve snack mix and chips inside. For other snacks offer olives, salted nuts and candied ginger. For more substantial foods, Waldorf salad, deviled eggs, tea sandwiches, cabbage rolls and barbecued ribs were all popular in this era. Rice pudding was a great dessert as well as coffee cake, pineapple upside down and angel food cake.

For entertainment, consider hosting a Murder Mystery Party. My Mystery Party offers an awesome 1920s Murder Mystery Party called the Murder at the Great Gatsby.

Host a scavenger hunt challenge or do fun party games in the theme of the night. Illegal gaming rooms were popular back then so a casino night would be appropriate.

A jazz band playing smooth 1920s jazz would be a nice addition to the night as well.

Nifty Fifties:

Create a 1950s ambiance with a 1950s CD playing softly and fun fifties décor. Purchase these items and other sock hop or '50s diner party gear at any local party store.

Fill turquoise, pink, black and white balloons with helium (at your local party store), gather bunches with balloon weights, and place them strategically throughout your party room.

Cut out circles for record albums out of cardboard, spray paint them with black paint, and dip in black glitter. Paint the center either turquoise or pink and sprinkle with the same color (i.e. pink, turquoise) glitter. Hang these from the ceiling with clear fishing wire or hang them on the wall throughout the party area.

Download a 1950s slang term dictionary from the internet (www.Partyhost411.com/1950) and ask that your guests speak in 1950s slang during the party.

For food, serve '50s diner foods such as burgers, fries and milkshakes. Cheese balls and crackers is a good starter as well as filled celery with cream cheese. If you want more of a formal dinner, serve meatloaf and mashed potatoes. This was extremely common on the American dinner table back in this era. For desserts, chiffon pies were the rave such as strawberry, chocolate, lime). If you can get your hands on some Tang beverage, you are definitely authentic '50s. The '50s was calorie dense and not too health conscious so this is not the party to have with a bunch of dieters! Obviously, there are plenty of low-fat alternatives to the popular fifties cuisine.

For entertainment, consider hosting a Murder Mystery Party. My Mystery Party offers a fantastic 1950s Murder Mystery Party called the East Side Story – a 1950s Murder Mystery Party.

Host a scavenger hunt challenge or do fun party games in the theme of the night. Sock Hops were the rave so hire a DJ to spin some fun '50s tunes.

Smashing '60s:

Create a '60s flower power ambiance with a '60s mix CD playing softly, '60s decor (i.e. '60s movie posters, etc.), and movies without the audio (i.e. Bonnie and Clyde, The Graduate,

Doctor Zhivago, etc.) if there is a television in the party room. Use peace symbols, brightly colored flowers, and lava lamps in your décor scheme. Tie-dye was popular back in the 1960s so don't be afraid to use it! Burn incense for a 1960s aroma. If you can get your hands on some beaded curtains – do it!

For fun smashin' 60's attire, the 1960s featured a variety of ultra-chic couture with vivid psychedelic mod prints and bright colors. This was a decade to put a stop to the traditional conservative fashion trends of the 1950s. Boxed shaped PVC dresses with go-go boots were a hit and the bikini surfaced to the scene after the movie *Beach Party* hit the big screen. The mini skirt appeared and then Jackie Onassis made the French manicure and false eyelashes a trend. The pillbox hat with dark, glittery eye shadows were also among popular choices. Women's hairstyles became shorter bobs and flips with backcombed crowns and bangs with thick headbands. Some opted for long straight styles that continued into the 1970s. Sixties fashion wonders are waiting for your discovery at your local thrift store!

Smashin' 60's music was all about fun. In the beginning, there was doo-wop to saxophone melodies but the '60s were ever changing in the music arena. Motown arrived followed by the British Invasion.

Here are some artists that were all the rave in the 1960's:

Elvis Presley	Simon and Garfunkel	Jimi Hindrix
The Miracles	The Beach Boys	The Moody Blues
Joan Baez	Nancy Sinatra	Rolling Stones
Marvelettes	The Seekers	The Byrds
The Four Seasons	Jefferson Airplane	Led Zepplin
The Beatles	Velvet Underground	The Yardbirds
Sherman Brothers	The Doors	Johnny Cash
The Supremes	Love	The Who

Serve a cool cucumber spread and crackers and some buttered nuts to start the party right. Popular dishes from the '60s include the iceberg wedge salad, fondues and steak Diane. Beef Wellington emerged along with Buffalo wings. Soul food broke the surface and the now traditional surf & turf was born. For dessert, look for the Pillsbury recipe for the Tunnel of Fudge cake, you'll be in the '60s in no time. Also, don't forget that the space drink Tang was still popular at this time.

Download a 1960s slang term dictionary from the internet (www.Partyhost411.com/1960) and ask that your guests speak in 1960s slang during the party.

For entertainment, consider hosting a Murder Mystery Party. My Mystery Party offers a super 1960s Murder Mystery Party called the Peace, Love and Murder – a 1960s Murder Mystery Party.

Host a scavenger hunt challenge or do fun party games in the theme of the night. Hire a DJ to spin 1960's songs for the night.

Groovy '70s:

So you're either having or going to a '70s disco party, huh? Let's do this! The '70s was laden with hippie culture with hoards of youth opposing the Vietnam War and Capitalism. The environmentalist movement took off after Rachel Carson got a ban on DDT in the '60s and the oil crisis causes by oil embargoes caused a recession. Technological progress included microwave ovens, very primitive personal computers and finally - consumer video games!

There was a rise of soft rock/pop rock music with artists such as The Carpenters, Ray Stevens, Elton John, etc. Seventies parties were more formal where youngsters were involved.

Play '70s disco music - access the XM Radio channel or your local satellite / cable television typically has a disco channel. Abba and the Bee Gees were a hit in the '70s. Alternatively, purchase a fun disco party mix. Play the movie Saturday Night Fever on the television without the sound for a fun ambiance.

For a birthday, make a round cake with yellow icing and use piping (black) to draw a smiley face.
Decorate with lava lamps, '70s posters (Farrah, Mr. Natural, etc.), beaded curtains, black lights, incense and do NOT forget to have a disco ball!

Download a 1970s slang term dictionary from the internet (www.Partyhost411.com/1970) and ask that your guests speak in 1970s slang during the party.

Guacamole, mini kabobs, stuffed celery and broiled pineapple, pineapple cheese ball and yaki tori were hits in the '70s. Bundt cakes were still popular in this era.

For entertainment, consider hosting a Murder Mystery Party. My Mystery Party offers a groovy 1970s Murder Mystery Party called the Panic at the Disco – a 1970s Murder Mystery Party.

Host a scavenger hunt challenge or do fun party games in the theme of the night. Hire a DJ to and have your guests doing the bump all night under the disco ball.

Don't forget that the nostalgic game Twister was released in the 1970s!

Radical '80s:

The '80s was a fun era so this is one of the most upbeat parties you can host! Create a '80s ambiance with an eighties mix CD playing softly, '80s decor (i.e. '80s movie or band posters, etc.), and movies without the audio (i.e. Pretty in Pink, Weird Science, etc.) if there is a television in the party room. Arcade games became the rave. If you lived in that era, you likely had an Atari or maybe a Nintendo Entertainment System as Nintendo had commanded most of the American video game market by the end of the decade!   Commodore 64 was another popular home item although it had minimal uses for home users so it was typically a novelty at the time and not a staple as computers are today.

Other popular things were Cabbage Patch Kids, My Little Pony, Smurfs, Ninja Turtles, Yoda and the start of the *Back to the Future* movie series.

The Music Scene was definitely unique as the use of keyboards came into play (new wave or Synthpop) and MTV hit the airwaves. The following artists were popular in the 1980s:

Madonna	Queen	Michael Jackson
Duran Duran	Prince	Motley Crue
Guns N' Roses	Bon Jovi	Joan Jett

Clothing was colorful to say the least. Sweatshirt dresses with matching bold-colored leggings, parachute pants, big plastic bangles, and Member's Only jackets were extremely popular! The girls also took to Madonna couture with black lace and tutus with leather jackets and teased hair. Pastel jackets with elbow rolled sleeves, as seen on Miami Vice, were the rave for guys.

Invitations for your party should be in Valley Girl slang, fer sure and designed with brightly colored shapes such as flashy pink, green, turquoise, and arranged into bold patterns. Use the following words and phrases: totally, gag me with a spoon, like, fer sure, radical, bodacious, and tubular.

Download a 1980s slang term dictionary from the internet (www.Partyhost411.com/1980) and ask that your guests speak in 1980s slang during the party.

Popular foods released in the '80s include Jell-O pudding pops, Pop Secret microwave popcorn, Snapple, Hershey Kisses with almonds. The '80s is going to be hard to tag with unique menu items as most everything available then is still served now. Reese's Pieces were featured the smash hit movie E.T. and Ronald Reagan's favorite snack was Jelly Bellies. Perrier sparkling water, Tab Cola, Kool-Aid and Capri Sun were popular beverages. A bowl of 'spiked punch' is totally tubular '80s but only for adults!

There are a few versions of '80s trivia-based board games available. If you have access to an Atari, have a tournament on these 2-D games! Most of the party games in this book can be twisted with a '80s theme.

For other entertainment options consider hosting a Murder Mystery Party. My Mystery Party offers two different radical 1980s Murder Mystery Parties called Like, Oh My Gosh - Murder and Gag me with a Spoon – the Totally Tubular 1980s Murder Mystery.

Host a scavenger hunt challenge or do fun party games in the theme of the night. Hire a DJ to and have your guests dancing '80s style all night.

Futuristic:

Watch a few episodes of the Jetsons and Back to the Future Volume III before you decide to tackle having a futuristic party. Whenever you host this party, add 50 years to the date and call it just that – the year of the party. For example, if it is 2011, call it a *Year 2061 Party*. Since there is not a lot we can predict about this time since it hasn't happened yet, the setting of the party is your oyster. People tend to associate the future with things that hover and things that are silver so make plenty of your décor (if not all) in silver and hang odd things from the ceiling with fishing wire (clear plastic) as if they are hovering three - four feet above the ground. However, be sure to put these hovering items away from the general traffic areas or you'll have them knocked down in no time.

As your guests to design their own futuristic couture and have a costume contest. For those guests who are less than creative and are stumped on futuristic attire, point them in the direction of the Jetsons' costumes.

Chapter 10

Murder Mystery Parties

This chapter gives an easy to follow breakdown for hosting a mystery dinner party for adults or teens. The best website for murder mystery and non-murder mystery parties is My Mystery Party (www.mymysteryparty.com) because they offer over 100 themes in the kids, teen and adult categories. They are conservative and you're safe with personal, corporate, church groups, family parties and more!   Select instant download options or party ready packs - the staff prepares your custom party kit and ships it to you! They are a proven, reliable five star internet merchant as well.

First, let's discuss what a murder mystery party or non-murder mystery party actually is:

What is a Murder Mystery Party?

You invite your friends, family, colleagues or any group you choose to any location where you will serve light snacks all the way to an elaborate fine dining menu. There is a lot of variation on how to host a murder mystery. Typically, these are inexpensive home parties but also host them in a private dining room of a casual or fine dining restaurant or even a hotel room (if it is large enough for people you will invite). All you need is one party area and a restroom – not only for your guests to use but to allow the victim to leave and become the victim (see below).

There are different kinds of murder mystery formats and most evolve around a dinner. However, with My Mystery Party's format, dinner is always optional. Some companies offer pre-printed boxed sets. These sets typically are only for 6-8 characters and come with booklets for each character that discloses everything the character needs to know within that booklet. The problem with these games are the limited amount of characters, the lack of flexibility with your invite list and the fact that there is no suspense that builds during the game because the characters are given all of their information up front so the murderer will know they are the murderer and the victim is likely to be disclosed prior to the party.

There are multiple companies to download games from the web and you will typically receive more for your money with these games over the ready-made boxed sets in stores. The downloadable games range from approximately $29 to over $39. Most of these games have a large number of characters available to play (the average is 15 characters) and some offer bonus games within the themes of the mystery. My Mystery Party at www.MyMysteryParty.com has unlimited amounts of characters available as there are set characters available for immediate purchase and you have the option to purchase custom characters to be written for your mystery! This way, your invite list can expand and have unique characters written with your guests' personality in mind! This service is definitely not offered with the ready-made boxed sets! There are mysteries available on My Mystery Party that have 40 unique characters ready for purchase. You will never find a ready-made boxed set with 40 unique players.

With My Mystery Party's format, a pregame is optional and implemented prior to the guests arriving to the party. This builds pregame excitement. The guests arrive ready to play the character role you have pre-assigned them and will undergo three rounds of game play. There is also a pregame guest invite site at Your Mystery Party (www.yourmysteryparty.com) that has, depending upon the mystery, fun facts about the characters, the town or location of the mystery, costume suggestions and vendors and a synopsis of the mystery. Some games even have downloadable news articles that give slight hints about the story line. This site will build pregame excitement for your party!

When the game begins, the host will pass out the interactive clue cards to the guests in three rounds and the characters are instructed to perform certain tasks and discuss their clues. The motives grow with each round until a murder occurs. Obviously, the murder is simply outlined in the story line but a victim will become the *pretend victim* and the investigation will ensue – typically in Round Two. The guests will investigate the crime, guess whodunit, and then accuse each other. In the final round (Round Three), they'll find out the solution to the mystery.

Clue Based vs. Scripted:

The games at My Mystery Party are highly interactive and are a hybrid between scripted games and clue based games. Due to experience, the format of My Mystery party games are a hybrid to direct the guests enough through the storyline but not give complete free improvisational reign where it becomes chaotic and the guests get lost and / or create their own story lines. The clue cards have partial instructions of what to do during each round (i.e. Character A will be instructed to tell Character B a certain clue, etc.) and then there are basic clues where the characters can use this information to mingle about with other characters and gossip about each other.

The strict clue based games lend to problems because your guests can become disoriented and the less outgoing guests will withdraw because they won't know what to do with these clues. The scripted games will end up being like a rehearsal for a play and the guests will lose interaction time between each other and most likely lose interest. It kind of ends up like a 9th grade reading class where students are taking turns reading passages. Boring!

The answer to the dilemma is to make a hybrid game where guests are told what to do and say but allowed some improvisation and can make their own decisions with what to do with their clues. They're also given, in some games, clues that are meant to be concealed, as the players should know more about their own character than the rest of the group so they know how to react to each other when confronted with issues.

Steps to Follow:

The following outlines easy to follow steps on how to host a murder mystery party:

1. Choose a theme of the mystery party that you believe fits your occasion and that your friends will be the most receptive to. If you have a set of friends that are easy going and love to dress

up (such as the Peter Pans or Partiers from Chapter 5)...then you should choose a party that includes elaborate costumes and boisterous characters such as a medieval-themed or a fun Mardi Gras mystery (i.e. Bumped Off on Bourbon Street) game.

However, if you have a more formal or more professional event in mind (such as the professionals from Chapter 5), select a game that focuses more on the mystery and less on the characters like a haunted manor theme (i.e. Anonville Manor) or a glamorous '50s Hollywood theme (Franklin Vinatra) or maybe even a wine tasting game (Fine Wine, Good Friends and a Wicked Murder).

2. After you've chosen your theme, you need to match the most appropriate game for your group. Clue-based mysteries are appropriate for groups
under 30-40 people. Above 40 people, you really need to hire actors to act out a script-based mystery or assign the guests to play in groups with one member of the group playing the actual character. If you tried to have more than 40 unique characters in the story line that had plot twists, it would be chaotic for the guests!

3. After you choose your game and your invite list is made, you need to assign the character roles. You have to fill in the required characters first with your most solid guests that will stick to their RSVP. Also, select the most outgoing guests for these roles, as they'll likely have the biggest part in the mystery. The victim and murder will be one of the required players and will consequently, have two of the biggest parts in the game. Then, fill the optional roles with those guests who may be tentative and /or your more shy and reserved guests. As the host, you do not have to know who is the victim or murderer prior to the game. Simply have someone assemble your kit for you that will not be at the party. My Mystery Party offers the Party Ready Pack where they will assemble your kit for an additional charge.

4. Send out the invitations and tell each guest what character you have selected for them to play. The worst thing you could do is not assign the roles and ask your guests to choose which

character they'd like to play - you are asking for problems! You know your guests' personalities so you should be able to match them up appropriately. 80-year-old Aunt Myrtle doesn't need to play the role of a vixen femme fatale and 85-year-old Uncle Roy doesn't need to play the role of a suave male supermodel! Games typically come with costume suggestions for each guest. Encourage your guests to select a costume that fits their assigned character, as the costumes will increase the excitement and fun! However, if you don't want to put your guests out, you can always skip the costumes and simply wear the nametags that come with the game to designate the characters.

5. Manage your RSVP list. If for any reason, one of the required characters cannot make the event, quickly switch one of the optional characters into their slot and notify that guest immediately. If they've already purchased their costume, try another guest and so on until you find someone who hasn't purchased a costume yet. Worst case scenario, allow the guest that you are switching into the role to wear the costume they purchased but put the missing required player's name tag on them for the night. Explain to the remaining guests what has happened and hopefully within your theme, you can make some sense of the switch with the story line.

For example, if your missing required player was a doctor and the optional player you are switching was dressing up as a school principal – no biggie! Your story is that the doctor is simply in their work attire they wear under the lab coat. No matter what – do not ask your guests who have purchased a costume not to wear the costume because you are switching them for the games' sake. That will cause hard feelings for sure! Just make it work! Once you have your invite list set in stone, send the pre-game clues and /or task sheets to your guests. These are always optional but build pre-game excitement.

6. The day of the party, decorate your party area in the theme of the mystery. You only need one room to play a murder mystery. For example, if you are having a '70s disco-themed party, decorate the room as a '70s disco, play '70s disco music softly

in the background and play Saturday Night Fever on the television without the sound. When you can, keep the food within the theme of the party as your party food can be an important part of your décor!

7. As the guest arrive, greet them with a cocktail and appetizers. Take their individual pictures and allow them to read the guest instructions along with the mystery synopsis and character list for them to review while they await the other guests' arrivals. Again, My Mystery Party has an invite site at Your Mystery Party www.yourmysteryparty.com where the guests can access character list without the required versus optional designations, a mystery synopsis and depending upon the mystery, there might be news reports, pictures of the location and more. You should encourage your guests to view this website prior to your party as this will build pregame excitement and they will arrive on game day – ready to sleuth the mystery!

8. Once everyone has arrived, take a group picture immediately. Your guests have taken the time to gather a costume together and everyone will want a picture of the group after the party! How often do you dress up, really? This might be a once in an adult lifetime event for some people and it is in your hands to provide for memories in the future.

9. Instruct the guests to remain in character the entire party. Even during dinner and bonus games – they are to be in character. Right after all of the guests have arrived, allow time for everyone to be acquainted with each other and ask any questions about the mechanics of the mystery party before you get started. Some hosts opt to ask their guests to stand up and introduce their characters in front of the group. If large portions of your group are shy/reserved people, they might not appreciate this type of icebreaker. However, in a group of close friends, this is a great idea.

10. To start the mystery party, pass out the Round One clue cards in sealed envelopes. During this round of game play, make sure that the party is flowing properly by encouraging your guests to mingle in character as they would in real life. Check to

be sure that they are using their clue cards for information to discuss with the other guests. There is typically some sort of icebreakers on the round one clue cards that the guests can break the ice with - like trivia questions or riddles within the theme of the party. This jump-starts your guests to start talking! Once you see that everyone has implemented all of the actions and topics on their clue cards, progress the game to Round Two. Round one should take about 45 minutes to an hour. Never rush this round! This is a rookie host mistake and can prove very confusing for the next round if clues were rushed during Round One. The clues and tasks from Round one will set up the mystery and lay the foundation of the characters' traits, past actions and their motives. Most games will have side bonus games within the theme of the mystery to play - these are optional but very fun and you should scatter them through the mystery to break up the game.

11. Round Two is typically when the murder occurs but first, you will want to serve dinner (which is always optional). During dinner, there might be a side bonus game to play or if not, instruct your guests to remain in character until dinner is over. Some games, albeit not many, have the victim already disclosed before the mystery party begins and the guests arrive knowing whom it was or who will be murdered. We have found that you can increase suspense and excitement by making one of your guests the victim. Most of the My Mystery Party games have one of the guests as the unexpected victim. This guest is notified via their clue card during this round to go to the nearest restroom and become the victim. It can be as simple as putting on a victim sign or the My Mystery Prop Emporium also sell props such as a victim t-shirt, white face makeup, crime scene balloons and authentic crime scene tape. It's hysterical when a party guest comes back into the room in full force as a victim!

After the victim arrives, the investigation begins so pass out the Mystery Investigation Sheets and pens to each guest who will now act as an investigator of this mystery.

Don't worry; the victim is not taken out of the game! The victim still plays the game but as a ghost of their character so they can only communicate by sign language or writing, (this is optional - you can also ask that they speak like a ghost). The victim always enjoys the attention and never feels slighted because they were the victim! They play along as usual for the remainder of the game.

Some games will have a forensic analysis report (as a story line, a certain guest called upon a favor from a detective friend) and other games might have additional evidence like emails, contracts, etc. that were found on the victim (the victim will have them in their hand when they return to the room as the victim). Once everyone has completed their investigation and filtered through the information, Round Three can begin.

12. Take up the Mystery Investigation Sheets from the guests when you decide that Round Two is over. At this time, serve coffee and dessert to the guests and ask them to sit in a circle. Serve an after dinner cocktail for adults or hot cocoa for teens. Dessert is not mandatory but if you served dinner, it is considered rude not to serve some type of dessert! If you only served appetizers at your party, offer sweet alternatives at this time.

One by one, allow the guests to accuse who they believe the murderer is and tell them to include the motive in their accusation. After the accusations, pass out the final clue cards for round three. These will typically have the solution in it and one-by-one; the guest will read their solution, which will contain any involvement that their character had with the murder. The murderer will confess at this time and will disclose all of the details. Yes, the murderers are always honest in the end – if not; there'd never be a solution to the mystery!

Play another bonus game to top the night's fun off and end it with a hilarious awards ceremony. Ask one of your closest friends to host the last bonus game while you decide on the awards for the night and fill in the award certificates. The awards ceremony can be as simple as giving one award certificate (or plastic trophy from a local party store) to the best sleuther of the night or as elaborate as having trophies made for multiple winners such as the best sleuther, best in bonus games, best costume, best actor, etc.

After that, your party is done and your obligations as the host are over!

Chapter 11

Sleepovers

Your first thought might be that this chapter fits perfectly within the kid's or teen's party chapter. However, you're not entirely correct as you can be 40-years old or more and host an awesome slumber party with your girlfriends! You're never too old to have a slumber party!

Who Hosts Sleepovers:

Kick the hubby out for the night and invite your girlfriends over for some all night fun! On the other hand, if you're single – even more reason to have a slumber party! The point is that you only live once and why do you have to give up slumber parties because you're not a young anymore. The answer is...*you don't!*

In addition, these are not limited to girls! If you are hosting a slumber party for boys to men, call it an *all night* party, as you don't want the stigma of the girly *slumber party* or *sleepover* on the invites. The games and activities are primarily associated with girls but masculine alternatives will be provided as applicable.

Guest List:

Your first task, of course, is the invite list. Make a master list of your friends and then consider whether your home or party location (i.e. hotel room) can accommodate that many people for an entire night. It's one thing to have a party for three - four hours and have multiple guests waiting for their turn in the restroom but to deal with it all night...well, that can be taxing as a host and for the guests.

On the other side, consider feelings and who will find out they were not invited to your party, as you don't want to make anyone sad. It is difficult to make a final guest list for slumber parties, as you typically cannot accommodate your entire set of friends for the night.

One method is to send a *Save the Date(s)* email to your friends and ask for an RSVP on the dates they are available. Explain that this is not the invitation and you are only considering hosting the event based upon the feedback from your friends. Give them the choice of multiple dates that you are considering for your event and ask them to respond with all dates that they can attend your party. Then, by seeing who is available on these respective dates, this might fix the problem of having to invite too many guests.   Then select the appropriate date to have your party by your preferred guests' availability. It's an honest hosting trick but can backfire if all guests are available on all dates you've chosen. Then, you'll need to go to Plan B…which is either accommodating everybody or trying it again later!

Invitations:

You already decided upon your budget and figured out your location. You made your final invite list and it's time to make the invitations. Slumber parties typically span from around dinnertime (~7PM) to breakfast time the following morning (~10 AM). You don't want to end the party too early as the guests have likely stayed up late and will want to sleep in a bit. However, you'll have a group of early-risers who will rise with the sun no matter what and you don't want these people to become bored and starve themselves, either. As a compromise, breakfast should be served between 8:00 and 9:00 AM. The guests that would have liked to sleep until noon can catch some Z's when they get home later.

Purchase readymade invitations, download a template on the internet or create your own using word processing software or scrap booking materials. Do your invitations within your theme. If you are having a chocolate spa party, brown background with pink polka dots is awesome. If you are having a fabulous fashion party, the invite can be in the shape of a mannequin with a brightly colored dress on it, etc. Instead of an envelope, grab a piece of felt, roll it up, and tie it like a sleeping bag with the invitation hidden inside! Put a reminder to bring a sleeping bag, pillow, pajamas, toothbrush and anything else they'll need for the night. Have fun with the invitation and throw confetti into the envelope before you seal it! Get the party started upon the invite!

Activity List:
Next, it's time to make your activity list. Some folks will want a scheduled itinerary to keep everybody on track and others don't like the constraints and will simply make a master activity list. Alternatively, maybe put all activities in a hat and have each guest draw the next activity as you go?

With whatever method you choose, you'll need to plan carefully and grab the props for all activities that you want to do during your party.

The following are some suggested activities but you can and should use any of the party games in this book!

FUN SLEEPOVER PARTY ACTIVITIES:

Fabulous Flip Flops:
This speaks for itself! On the RSVP of your invite, ask for the guests to RSVP with their shoe size. Pick up some inexpensive flip-flops at your local hobby and craft store or even discount stores have flip-flops at very reasonable prices. You should expect to pay under $5.00 for each pair. Then, head to the fabric store and purchase random swatches from the clearance fabric bin. You'll want a good assortment of colors, textures, etc. for your guests. Either pre-cut your fabric for the guests or allow them to cut their size of strips for their shoes but either way, you're looking at about 4.5" by 2" strips. Some guests might want their strips more broad / thin or longer /shorter so allowing them to cut the strips might be a better idea. So have plenty of fabric-worthy scissors available if you choose this option. If they are cutting their strips, allow for more time, however.

Offer rhinestones and sequins and fabric glue in case your guests want to bling their flip-flops.

As the guests arrive, have them start on their flip-flops by selecting their fabric/strips. Instruct them to tie the strips onto the straps from one end to the other. This makes a cute, puffy and comfortable strap of the flip-flop! Obviously, the guests can take this home as a party favor. You've just given them a fashionable pair of shoes for under $8.00!

Decorate Cork Bulletin Boards, Picture Frames, Jewelry Boxes:

Arts and crafts are perfect ideas and time fillers for slumber parties. If the guests have just completed a strenuous activity (i.e. relay race style party game), then it is time for a relaxing activity.

Give the guests an array of arts and craft items such as sequins, rhinestones, paints, markers, felt, aluminum foil, buttons, etc. Don't forget the glue!

Whatever substrate you choose (i.e. bulletin board, picture frame, jewelry box), have one available for each guest. At your local hobby or discount store, you should be able to find undecorated, possibly unfinished wooden items for your guests to decorate. Make sure to do this activity sooner than later so there is adequate drying time. You don't want your guests to have to transport wet-paint items in their cars!

Karaoke:

Even if you can't sing, karaoke is fun for most. In fact, when you can't sing is when it can be an absolute blast and add to the excitement of the party!

Just playing karaoke is fun but maybe have a solo, duo and group competition? In addition, there are some various party games involving karaoke machines in our party game section of this book and alter them to fit your group as needed.

Beware as karaoke is addicting and is likely to be a favorite of your guests that they will want to re-visit throughout the night. Be prepared for nixing an activity off your list because your guests want to do karaoke again!

Spa Party:

You probably know what it feels like when you enter a spa, as it is instant relaxation. You should try to recreate this with your party area. Use low lighting, a soothing relaxation-themed ambiance track playing in the background, mini water fountains running and place multiple plants in the party room, as nature is relaxing. On the invite, instruct your guests to come in spa attire and get ready to relax!

Think about what you would want to have done at your local day spa. Make a list by pulling up a menu from the web from your favorite spa. Then, make adaptations for doing it at home with your friends!

Start with mani and pedi's. You'll need at least half the amount of footbaths for your guests. Therefore, if you have ten friends, you'll need five home footbaths. You likely don't have that many in your home so it's all right to poll your friends to see who can bring their foot bath with them. You can still do it if you have1/4 of the amount of foot baths by having half the guests focus on manicures first and the other half doing pedicures. The guests should take turns being the nail technician. Partner your guests when they arrive and for uneven numbers, make a trio or two.

If budget is not an issue, consider hiring nail technicians from a local nail salon. They'll be able to bring the equipment and perform the services on your guests.

Allow everybody's nails to dry by taking a chocolate break! Serve various chocolates and allow the guests to mingle and relax while enjoying the treats! For adults, serve champagne and for minors, serve ginger ale with a strawberry garnish.

After nail drying, switch to facials.   get inexpensive face cleanser, exfoliator, clay (or other type of) cleansing masks, and moisturizer at your local discount store or spring for some good stuff at your local department store or even go to the spa and pick some up – they all sell what they use on you! Have your guests continue to take turns giving each other facials. Maybe switch up the pairs so your friends get a chance to mingle with everybody and don't become too cliquish. Have some chilled cucumber slices for covering their eyes during the facial.

Some guests might not want to mess up their hair and / or you might not have enough sinks to deal with the rinse outs but with small groups, do a hair conditioning and shine treatment. Purchase a deep conditioner and shine treatment and give everybody a hair treatment. Do this prior to the facial and they can keep the conditioner on during their facial and rinse it out immediately after. Be sure to have enough hair towels available for each guest, however.

With hair, nails and face feeling awesome, call your spa party complete or... go on to a fabulous makeover!

Makeovers:

Fabulous makeovers are a female essential. Girls love to be pretty and look glamorous! Purchase plenty of makeup and glitter, adhesive backed rhinestones and even some false eyelashes!

Pair your friends into groups of two and have them take turns making each other as glamorous as possible. If you choose to do hair as well, have plenty of curling irons, straighteners, crimping irons, blow dryers as well as hair accessories (i.e. rhinestone bobby pins, ponytail holders, fabulous barrettes, etc). After everybody is glamorous, it is an absolute must to take as many pictures in as many combinations of guests as possible! Everybody will want a glamorous picture of herself!

If you plan on taking your guests to dinner or maybe bowling or other activity – it would be great fun to look glamorous in public so do the makeover before you leave!

Scrap Book Pages:

Scrapbooking has become a favorite pastime by loads of folks across the globe. Go to your local scrapbooking store and purchase a wide variety of scrapbook papers, appliqués, glues, decorative paper punches and anything else you find that looks creative.

Instruct your guests on the invitation to bring a few pictures with them for scrapbooking. Have the scrapbook items available on a main table and give some additional help to those girls (or gents) who haven't done scrapbooking before. You don't want to serve food and drink at this time but have some snacks available with beverages (with small cups to discourage them from bringing their drink to the scrapbook table) on a separate table away from the scrapbook table. A spill of a drink can ruin multiple guests' creations at once and put a damper on your party for the meantime!

Drama Bag Game:

Get drawstring bags of any kind or even pillowcases for each group that will play this game. Divide your guests into teams of three to four players. One group will place four items into the bag or pillowcase and give it to another group. Have groups exchange with each other or put a member from each group in a circle and have them pass their drama bag to their right.

Each team will spread out and devise a two -minute skit based upon the items in the drama bag. The items can be absolutely anything that the guests can find. Give the teams' ample time to write their skit and rehearse.

When it is time, allow each team to perform their skit in front of the group. Be sure to video tape this performance as it is likely to be hysterical!

Talent Show:

On the invitation, disclose there will be a *Midnight Talent Show* or whenever you'd like to schedule it. Request that the guests RSVP with their talent routine so you can make a program. When you have all of your guests' talent routines, assemble them in a logical order depending upon what they are. All poem recites or monologue performers should be grouped together (as you don't need to do anything for them), musicians should be grouped together and see if you need any special accommodations for them in advance. If two are playing the electric guitar, maybe only one person needs to lug over their amplifier and they can both use it, etc. Dancers and other performers that need audio accommodations are grouped together as you'll need someone to control the music source.

Print off a copy of your program for each guest and a ballot sheet. One by one, the guests are to perform their talent in front of the group. The guests are to vote at the end of the show for their favorite routine but they are not allowed to vote for themselves, of course. The host can tally the votes and declare a winner! Choosing a winner is optional, by the way, and depending upon your group of friends – might lead to hard feelings. You know your group the best! With kid's parties, never single out a winner or a loser – make everybody an equal winner somehow. This way, it remains a positive experience for everybody.

Fashion Show:

On the invitation, disclose there will be a fashion show. Request that the guests bring a swimsuit, active wear and a glamorous evening outfit. Make a catwalk by lining an area with tape and streamers or maybe even balloon bouquets but not too tall to hide the models. Play a fashionable song, such as 'Work It' by Ru Paul and allow your guests to model their outfits according to the category.

Give your guests ballots so they can vote for the best model and best outfit in each category and you can have a mini awards presentation at the end of the fashion show.

Take loads of pictures and take a group picture with the guests dressed in their attire for each category!

Truth or Dare:

Truth or Dare is a timeless staple for slumber parties. Every person on the planet that has been to a slumber party is likely to have played some variation of this game.

The guests are to write down five truth questions and five dares in increasing difficulty, fold them and place them into a container – one for truths and one for dares - for the guests to take turns drawing from. Instruct the guests to consult with you before putting dares that require specific items in the home – such as a jalapeno eating dare. The dares should not be dangerous or cause any type of harm to the guests and if any of these types of dares are placed into the container and drawn by a guest, the host is to remove the dare from the game and allow the player to select another dare.

The guests take turns selecting whether they want to perform a dare or a truth and will select from the appropriate container. If the guests decides not to do their truth or dare, they can select from the opposing container but they cannot select another of the same. If any guest still refuses to do the second item that they pulled, they have to perform a punishment (i.e. call a boy they like and tell them they have a crush on them, do ten pushups over a whipped cream pie, a pie in the face, etc.). Disclose what the punishment will be up front before the game starts. If the guest still refuses to accept the punishment, they are disqualified and can simply watch the rest of the guests play the game. Make sure you have buy-in from all guests prior to starting the game or you'll end up in a peer-pressuring situation that you don't want to be in!

Play will continue until the guests have all had a turn or all had two turns or until everybody is tired of playing!

Nail Polish Color Spin:

Purchase multiple fun colors of nail polish and some nail polish remover for guests who may arrive to the party with polish on their nails. Have all guests remove their nail polish prior to this game.

Place the multicolored nail polish in a big circle. Either make a spinner out of cardboard or borrow one from a board game or use a bottle and place it in the center of the bottles of nail polish.

One by one, the guests are to spin the spinner or bottle and whatever bottle of nail polish the spinner/ bottle is pointing to, the guest must polish one of their nails that color. This continues until all guests have every nail polished.

Party Charades:

Following our awesome party charade rules in the party games chapter, use the following general charade topics for your slumber party!

Cellular phone	Swing set	Figure skater
A Principal	Science class	'Crank that'
Gymnastics	Monopoly	Movie star / Celebrity
Jonas Brothers	Pedicure	Hannah Montana
Rock star	Movie Theater	A trampoline
Television	Commercial	A dozen roses
A Blue Jay	A mime	Miniature golf course
A candle	Coach purse	Amusement park
Lip gloss	Ransom note	Corn on the cob
Ballet shoe	Swimming pool	Modeling Clay
Circle of Life	Juicy Couture	Limited Too (clothing store)

Create-a-Song:

The host selects a general topic and the guests sit in a circle. The host will start the song and corresponding melody by singing the first lyric. The song will continue to be built as the guests go around the circle in clockwise fashion, adding their lyric on to the song and singing the song in its entirety each time. When the song is complete, the guests are to perform it together!

PARTY FOOD / PARTY FOOD RELATED ACTIVITIES:

Candy Hunt

There's nothing like a midnight candy hunt to spruce up the evening. In the party area, the backyard or whatever boundaries you choose, hide candy that is not currently served at your party in various locations. When the host says go, the guests are to hunt frantically for the candy! Have some backup pieces available for guests who are unsuccessful at finding any candy.

Make Your Own Pizza

The guests have to eat and they have nothing but time on their hands so put all of the pizza making ingredients on a table and preheat the oven(s).

Give everybody personal pan-sized crusts to start with and in a buffet-line style, have the guests assemble their pizzas. Place as many in the oven as possible, cook and serve. You'll probably have to have some of your guests wait for the second batch of pizzas so have those guests act as the wait staff for the first group and then they will switch when it is time for the second group to eat.

Chocolate Fondue

After eating dinner, the guests will certainly crave for something sweet! Using a fondue pot or double boiler, heat up your favorite chocolate sauce according to the package instructions.

Prepare bananas, pound cake, marshmallows, strawberries, brownies, and whatever other dip-able item you can dream up and put them around the fondue pot. Give your guests fondue skewers and allow them to dip their selected items into the chocolate sauce! For added fun, make multiple types of chocolate sauces in multiple fondue pots! No double dipping!

Sleepover S'mores & Milkshakes

Best by the campfire but can be made in the microwave since there's nothing like a s'more! A s'more is a graham cracker sandwich with melted marshmallows and chocolate inside. Nothing goes better with a s'more than a milkshake!

Have the guests stack their own s'mores and heat them up in the microwave or hold the marshmallows over the campfire (or outdoor fire pit) with the appropriate tools. With minors, parents should definitely supervise kids by the fire!

There are a couple of milkshake recipes in the Party Cuisine chapter. Don't over serve the milkshakes, as with the s'mores, the guests are likely to satisfy their sweet tooth quickly!

Chips and Dip

You can't have a party without chips and dip and a slumber party needs a continuous supply of these party essentials. Serve fun dips – not just prepared bean dips and French onion dips. Make your own spinach dips, avocado dips, guacamole, cream cheese spreads and give them fun names! Running out of chips and dip is a slumber party violation!

Fruit & Veggie Trays

Fruit and veggie trays should be served twice. Once when the guests first arrive and again for a late night snack. This is a healthy alternative to the dips and candy as some guests might prefer a breather from all the fatty foods. Also, offer another fruit tray during breakfast.

Top your own Pancake

So what's for breakfast? You have to feed your guests in the morning unless you believe they'll stay up all night and leave the moment they wake up. However, it would be considered rude to let your guests leave hungry so you need to have some options – even if it is just a muffin and a banana on the way out the door.

However, if you want to make a fun time of it, cook pancakes and then have a buffet –line *make your own pancake creation*. Serve a variety of nuts (i.e. pecans, macadamia, almonds, etc.), whipped cream, strawberries, bananas, vanilla ice cream, chocolate sauce, and a variety of syrups, blueberries, and anything else that would be fantastic on a stack of pancakes. Oh, and don't forget the butter!

Breakfast Parfaits
Allow your guests to assemble their own breakfast parfait! Again, in buffet-line style, have yogurt, whipped cream, a variety of fruit and nuts, broken up cookies, muffins, pancakes, and anything else to add to their parfait. Allow them to add layer by layer in clear parfait glasses!

Chapter 12

Bridal Showers & Bachelorettes

Let's tackle the Bridal Shower first and then we'll move on to exciting Bachelorette parties. Bachelor parties are not covered in this book as the guys are pretty set in their ways on what they want – most are not looking for advice or traditions.

Who's the Host?

The Maid or Matron of honor is the host of the bridal shower. It is part of the job that you take on when you accept the honor. It is highly acceptable to ask for help, however, and appoint a co-host. In fact, have as many co-hosts as you'd like!

What if you are the bride and are not going to elect a maid/matron of honor? Then, it will default to your best friend. *No best friend to speak of?* Defaults to your sister. *No sister?* Well, if you're out of options - host it yourself, why not? But leave out the *hosted by* section on the invite to reduce awkwardness.

When to Host?

The best time to host a bridal shower is about a month prior to the wedding. Not that the bride's not sure about the wedding or the groom but unforeseeable things can happen. Therefore, don't host a bridal shower too far before the wedding, as it is very uncomfortable and a lot of hassle to send gifts back. Yes, the bride and groom-woulda-beens must send the gifts back if they do not end up tying the knot!

Gift Expectations:

Are guests expected to attend the shower, give a gift, and then give another gift at the wedding? Well, actually you are supposed to bring a gift to both. If you attended the bridal shower and are going to attend the wedding – keep that into consideration and either purchase a gift for the bride for the bridal shower and a gift from the couple's bridal registry to the wedding. Alternatively, purchase two items from the registry that fit within your budget.

That way, you don't seem like you are skimping out on anything. *If you cannot attend a bridal shower, are you expected still to give a gift?* Of course! It is what the shower is intended for, actually! The maid/matron of honor has the responsibility to keep track of *who gives what* to the bride and groom so your gift will not be overlooked or forgotten just because you were not there to represent it.

Invitations:

Invitations for the bridal shower should be done in a bridal theme. Go formal or informal but remember that this is part of this couple's history together and a copy of this invitation will be forever kept in their wedding book. Evites are not good for bridal showers as they are too informal and are tacky to ask the bride to print a copy to save it. If you want to make the shower invitations yourself, do an internet search for different styles of bridal shower invitations, as there are many great examples out there for you to follow. Swinging wedding bells, flowers, and a wedding cake are all popular shape cut outs as the basis for the invitation. Stick to white with silver or gold trim for a more traditional feel or go crazy with the colors of the wedding if you are more into the modern times and if the bride has selected her colors.

Next issue for debate is the *hosted by* line of the invitation. This is a good time to announce the wedding party and here is an example: *Hosted by: Lora Beginsnot, Maid of Honor and Frankie Scotter, Bridesmaid.* Let's say you had ten people as hosts. They should all be listed on the invitation in some manner. If you only listed five hosts and the other five have vital roles in hosting the event but don't get a mention – they will get their feelings hurt and the bride will definitely hear about it later. Do not do this by any means. Ink is cheap enough so reduce the font size and give everybody credit. Saying that there wasn't room on the invitation is not an excuse. Again, this is the couple's history and if you are giving effort (i.e. money, labor, etc.) for their bridal shower, you want acknowledgement. Don't leave anybody out if they have provided any type of monetary gift and / or services for this event. Now, if there is one or maybe two to three major hosts that are paying for a large portion of the event and doing most of the work, it is acceptable to put their names as the main hosts. In a smaller font below or in any location on the invitation, list the others who assisted with the party. This is a positive event and should remain positive on all fronts. Don't start any disputes and hard feelings prior to the event for goodness' sake!

Who Makes the Invite List?

Does a bridal shower have to be all female? Modern times are moving toward co-ed bridal showers. Most of the time nowadays, the presents are for the groom as well as most will purchase from the bridal registry. The bride is not the only one who is going to use the toaster, sheets and towels! Make it a celebration for everybody, why not?

Host fun party games, offer great food (typically appetizers) and of course, the gift opening ceremony is the focus. However, with large showers, save the gift opening for after the shower as this can be long and monotonous. The bride and groom will be the only ones interested that Aunt Myrtle bought them a sheet set. *Boring!* Basic guideline, if there are more than ten gifts to open, save it for later – your guests will appreciate it! If they want to watch you open their gift, that's fine but only if they ask and do it after the party is over!

The guest list should include all family members of the happy couple. If you are hosting an all-female event, then you will extend an invitation to the wives (not necessarily the fiancés or girlfriends) of the male friends. Only invite the fiancé or girlfriend of a male friend of the couple if she is an established friend of the bride and / or groom as well. Never invite her is she's never met them.

Your guest list will include strangers. As a basic guideline, if the couple (either the bride or groom) have not had a meaningful conversation with a potential (friend) guest over the course of the last calendar year, that guest is not obligated to attend so leave them off the guest list. We don't ask things of people that we do not have an active relationship with, as that is tacky and rude. If they haven't thought of this person enough to (at a minimum) send an email in an entire year to see how they are doing, do not expect this person to spend money on a gift or take the time to come to the shower! Family members of both parents-to-be are obligated but friends are another story. Play any of the *Sims* games and you'll see that even in video games, relationships fade over time and friends become strangers and you'll need to start over on the relationship. You don't start over by asking them to go out of their way to attend your bridal shower and buy you a gift! *Inviting them to the wedding is a different story, however.*

The exception to this basic guideline is friends of the couple's parents. If the parents are active friends with these folks (i.e. have spoken to them in the last year), extend an invitation to them as long as the parent's friends *know* the bride and /or groom. If they've never met the bride and /or groom, don't put them on the guest list.

Now that you have your guest list, you will need to manage the RSVPs as with any party. You might need to assist with travel arrangements and lodging for out of town guests. Ask for all special accommodations to be disclosed with the RSVP for the invited guests on the invite *(these potential special accommodations are listed in the Master Party Checklist in Chapter 2).*

Location, Location, Location:

Location of the party is as variable with any event but remember it is about the couple getting gifts to start their wonderful lives together. If they are young, they might not be as financially sound as in 20 years from now. For example, if you end up spending over $5,000 on the shower, you could have simply donated that money to the couple. Therefore, these showers are generally low budget. The host's home that is most centralized, largest and easily accessible is the one to select for your event.

Now, in the case of a young bride with a young bridesmaid who might not have access to a large enough home to host a bridal shower, it is 100% acceptable to ask the bride or groom's parents to use their home for the shower. Use your resources!

Décor:

Décor should be in white with silver and gold accents if you want to stick to tradition. If the bride knows her wedding colors, see if she wants to decorate in that color. You should allow the bride to give input unless she wants everything a surprise. Brides tend to have ideal scenarios in mind that they've dreamed of since they were young so you want to give her what she wants, if it is possible. Your local party store likely has a bridal shower section as well.

Decorate the appetizer table with unscented white candles wrapped in tulle and sprinkles with small confetti (silver, gold) centerpieces. White roses are an elegant touch and again, if the bride has selected colors for her wedding, either use décor in that color as an accent or as a focus. Sprinkle white rose petals and metallic confetti or glitter on the tables and buffet tables. Be sure they are not heavy aromatic roses as strong floral scents can be de-appetizing when you are serving food!

Party Cuisine:

Party food should be appetizers. A formal dinner is not necessary for a bridal shower.   Serve cocktails but don't make it the focus – especially for an all-female, during the day with the bride's family shower. If it is an evening co-ed shower, make cocktails a bigger part of the celebration but the guests' drinking and driving issue is your responsibility, remember. If your guests consume too much alcohol, it is your responsibility not to allow them to drive!

Upon Guest Arrival:

As the guests arrive, have them sign in on the bridal shower guest book. Give them a nametag and either pre-print the nametags to include their name and relationship to the couple. Some of the guests will not know each other so name tags are necessary! If you do not pre-print the nametags, ask the guests to write their name and relationship to either the bride or groom. Using self-adhesive nametags are preferred but you can purchase plastic name badges that have safety pins on the back or even use lanyards. Using nametags and disclosing the relationship on them gives an inherent icebreaker for your guests to mingle about as strangers will have something in which to start the conversation. *So... you're Julie's boss, huh? Is she fun to work with or what?* Yes, it is all right to have a sense of humor!

Drop Bys vs. Scheduled Events:

Drop by showers versus scheduled events have two different dynamics. Disclose on your invitation if this is a *drop by* shower (i.e. *drop by anytime between 2-4 PM*) or give a starting time only (i.e. *starts at 7 PM)* if it is a scheduled event and you expect your guests to be there the time it is scheduled for. If you put on the time line that the shower is from 2-4 PM but do not specify whether or not if it is a *drop by* shower, your guests will be confused so do either one or the other method above.

A drop by shower means that your invited guests can simply drop by for a few minutes any time within the shower time period and give the bride (or couple) their gift. Whatever type of party you decide to do, make sure it is clear on the invitation! Also, since the default shower is females only, if you want to have a co-ed shower, make sure to disclose it clearly on the invitation. Don't have your guests guessing – be up front with your intentions!

In addition, send one invite per household, and hand write the names of the guests in formal style *(i.e. Mrs. Jane Doe or Mr. and Mrs. John Doe)*.

Party Games:

Party games are essential for the scheduled event showers. With drop by showers, it is too difficult to schedule party games, as you will not know when enough guests will be present to play a game and this obligates those guests who planned to *swing by for a few minutes* to stay longer than they expected. Refrain from doing party games unless you have a scheduled event.

With a scheduled event, after all of the guests have arrived snap a group photo. This will be a great addition to the bridal shower guest book. After the guests have received their nametags, found the appetizers and beverages, it is time to start the party games. Bridal showers should only be two to three hours long but why not give your guests a memorable time? After all, this is a celebration of the upcoming union of a special couple!

BRIDAL SHOWER PARTY GAMES:

Which Groom Did This?
Game goal: to match the crazy event with the correct groom.

Game play: this game is great for a co-ed shower. In advance of the game, ask all of the married men for something crazy they've done in their past that most people would not know about. If none of the men are married, change it to Which Dude Did This? On a display board, either post a picture of each guy or their name and relationship to the bride/groom as well as this crazy thing they have done in a different place designated by a bolded text (and large font size) letter or number.

During the shower, the guests are to come to the board and match the groom (or dude) with the crazy thing and turn in their guess to the host of the shower. The host will score the sheets and declare a winner at the conclusion of the shower. Then, allow the guys to defend themselves and explain why they did the crazy thing they did. This game should bring about tons of laughs!

Game gear: pictures or squares of paper with the guy's names on them and separate numbered (or lettered) squares with the crazy thing they admit to have done in the past.

Game time: ~ 5-10 minutes and the duration of the shower.

Famous Couples Trivia:
Game goal: to guess the famous fictional, historical or celebrity couple from a few fun facts.

Game play: do an internet search for famous couples and write down five fun facts about this famous fictional, historical or celebrity couple. Print out decorative cards with this information along with the answer below the five facts.

Hand the guests a card with their famous couple. As the guests mingle about during your meet 'n greet, they are to quiz each other on their famous couple. The one who guesses the couple with the least amount of facts wins! Then, the guests are to go on to the next person and so on until everybody has had a chance to mingle and quiz every other guest. Each guest can decide the order to give the facts to their partner – it doesn't have to be in the order written on the card. *Examples of famous couples are Tom and Katie Cruise, Fred and Wilma Flintstone, George and Martha Washington, etc.*

Game gear: the cards with the five fun facts and the famous couple (the answer) stated below the facts.

Game time: ~ 10-15 minutes.

Don't Forget the Love Song Lyrics:

Game goal: to guess the most correct missing lyrics of the given love songs.

Game play: one by one, the host will recite a partial lyric to a love song. The guest must complete the line with the correct lyrics for a point. If the guest answers incorrectly, it goes to the first person that raises their hand and gives the correct answer. If someone blurts out the correct answer during a steal, nobody gets credit. The guests must raise their hand and the host has to call on them.

The guest who finishes the most lyrics correctly wins! To find lyrics for love songs, do an internet search for 'love song lyrics' and tons of sites with lyrics for you and ideas for love songs will be available.

Game gear: love song lyric sheet, score sheet.

Game time: ~ 10-15 minutes.

Who Loves Ya, Baby?

Game goal: to guess your mate with only a handshake.

Game play: this game is great with a coed shower. Line up the men in any random order. Blindfold one of the ladies and then instruct the men to change places in line to mix up their order. One by one, the lady is to shake hands with each of the men who are remaining quiet and the host announces the man's number during the handshake.

At the end of the line, the blindfolded lady is to announce which number is her mate by shouting his number. Should invoke some laughter if she gets it wrong – especially if it is the bride that misses! Continue and let each lady get a turn!

Game gear: blindfold.

Game time: ~ 10 minutes.

Pin the Ring on the Finger:

Game goal: to pin the ring closet to the target on the ring finger.

Game play: give each player either a picture or a toy diamond ring with adhesive attached to the back. Also, print off a giant sized hand with a target placed on the ring finger and affix this picture to a wall approximately chest level to most guests in the party area.

Blindfold guests, spin them around three times and hand them their diamond ring. Point them in the general direction of the hand on the wall. They are to use one hand – the one holding the ring – and cannot touch the wall in which the hand is taped. Where the ring hits the wall is where it stays. They cannot feel around the wall for the hand! Leave the ring there or remove it and place a small mark or initials of the person whose turn it was.

The guest who gets the closest to the target on the hand wins!

Game gear: hand to tape to the wall and multiple rings for each guest with adhesive on the back and a blindfold.

Game time: ~ 10-15 minutes.

Name That Lie!

Game goal: to figure out which fun facts are true about the happy couple!

Game play: prior to the shower, get at least five facts that nobody knows (or at least most do not know) about the bride and the groom. Mix these facts in with another five or so lies about each of them. Hand each guest a paper with the word *truth* on one side and *lie* on another. Alternating between truth and lies (in any combination you choose), give a fact about the bride or groom and the guests are to hold up either truth or lie on their truth/lie sheets. All players with the incorrect answer are to be removed from the game (i.e. stand against the wall).

Continue to read facts about the bride or groom until you are done with all truths and lies and the last person or people in the game are the winners!

Game gear: fun facts about the bride and groom, truth/lie sheets (preferably affixed to a paddle) for each guest and some lies about the bride and groom.

Game time: ~ 10-15 minutes.

Step Right Up and Guess the Happy Couple's Age:

Game goal: to guess the bride and groom's age at various times of their lives.

Game play: prior to the event, ask the bride and the groom for pictures of their childhood throughout various ages (i.e. newborn, one year, three years, five years, up through early '20s, etc). Post these pictures on a display board for the bride and one for the groom and don't be obvious as far as the chronological order goes.

If you really want to mix it up for a challenge, put them together and don't label which are the bride's pictures and the groom's – see if the guests can tell their baby pictures apart! Label the pictures by placing large, bold text squares with numbers below each picture. Make an answer sheet with the numbers of the pictures next to a blank. The guests are to fill in the blank with the appropriate age and whether it is the bride or groom next to the numbered picture. Make sure to make an answer key in advance of the party to make the scoring of the sheets quick. After you score the sheets, reveal the winner(s).

Game gear: numbered pictures of the happy couple of all ages throughout their lives, guests answer sheets, an answer key.

Game time: ~ 10-15 minutes.

Don't Forget to Pick this up at the Store!

Game goal: to remember all of the items that your spouse tells you to pick up at the grocery store!

Game play: assemble a table full of at least 15-20 common grocery list items such as milk, bread, cheese, butter, etc. Show the guests the table for a period of 30 seconds. Take the items away from the table (or cover them with a sheet) and give each guest a pen and paper and ask that they write all of the items down from memory. The guest, who can name the most items correctly, wins!

See how good of a spouse the bride and groom will be!

Game gear: multiple grocery items, a tray, paper and pen for each guest.

Game time: ~ 10-15 minutes.

Let's Make a Baby!

Game goal: to make the best baby out of the materials given.

Game play: divide your guests into groups of two to three. Assemble various crafty items (i.e. foil, newspaper, paper towels, toilet paper, sequins, buttons, markers, leaves, yarn, etc.) on a main table in the middle of the party room.

Assign glue, tape, staplers, etc. to each group. When the host says go, each team is to grab the items they need to make the perfect baby. Give the teams a designated amount of time (i.e. 10 minutes) to create the perfect baby out of the items given. When time is up, host will judge which team has created the perfect baby!

Game gear: various craft items.

Game time: ~ 10-15 minutes.

Don't Say it, Honey!

Game goal: to collect the most wedding rings.

Game play: when guests arrive at the shower, hand them a toy wedding ring. As the guests mingle and play shower games, etc., they are not to say a designated word such as *wedding*. Whenever anybody says the forbidden word, another guest has the right to take away his or her toy wedding ring. The game continues until the shower is over and the host calls for rings. Whoever has collected the most rings wins the game.

Game gear: a toy wedding ring for each guest.

Game time: ~ the duration of the shower.

Revealing Squares:

Game goal: to get to know the other guests! A great icebreaker!

Game play: ask that the guests sit in a circle around the party area. Pass around a roll of toilet tissue and have guests pull a random amount of tissue before you tell them what the challenge is about.

After everybody has pulled off their random piece of toilet paper, instruct each guest to reveal as many things about themselves to the group as they have squares of toilet tissue! Start with the bride and continue around the circle to her left.

As an alternative, have each guest tell something about the happy couple instead of about themselves or go around the circle twice.

Game gear: a roll of toilet tissue.

Game time: ~ 10-15 minutes.

The Price is Right, Honey!

Game goal: to guess the right price on the honeymoon items shown to the group.

Game play: the host is to assemble a variety of honeymoon items available for purchase. Depending upon where the bride and groom are going for their honeymoon will depend on the types of items you will select to show to the group. Some items can be shown via picture that you download from the web. For example, a tropical vacation would include sunscreen, bathing suits, etc. and a ski vacation would include a ski suit, goggles, etc.

One by one, the host is to show an item to the group and the players write down on their sheet of paper how much the item costs. When all of the items have been shown to the guests, the guests are to switch papers with someone beside them.

The host will then reveal the correct price of each item and the guests will score each other's answers. Any guess within $1.00 should be counted as correct. If the item costs $17.50 and the guess is anywhere from $16.50 to $18.50 – the guess is counted as correct. However, a guess of $18.51 is incorrect. The person who guessed the most items correctly is the winner!

Game gear: various honeymoon related items with their known prices on an answer key. Paper and pens for each guest.

Game time: ~ 10-15 minutes.

How Much Was It in _____?

Game goal: to guess how much each random item cost in the year that either the bride or groom's parents got married.

Game play: the host is to assemble a variety of random items available for purchase in the year that either the bride or groom's parents were married (alternate between years or if it's the same decade, then say the '40s or '50s, etc).

Use a picture for some items, as they might not still be available for purchase. One by one, the host is to show the item to the group and they are to write down on their sheet of paper how much the item cost in the specific year. After showing all items to the guests, the guests switch papers with someone beside them.

The host will then reveal the correct price of each item in that specific year and the guests will score each other's answers. Any guess within $1.00 is correct. If the item costs $17.50 and the guess is anywhere from $16.50 to $18.50 – the guess is counted as correct. However, a guess of $18.51 is incorrect. The person who guessed the most items correctly is the winner! Do an internet search on your random item of your choosing. There are plenty of websites dedicated to the various years to find out how much various retail items cost back then.

As an alternative to using the bride or groom's parents wedding dates, select any year in the past (i.e. 1960, 1970, 1980, etc).

Game gear: the random items available for purchase and their prices on an answer key. Paper and pens for each guest.

Game time: ~ 10-15 minutes.

Is your Palette Better than the Bride's?
Game goal: to be the one who can correctly guess the random food items – while blindfolded!

Game play: gather ten random food items of your choice. Select things with bold flavors such as cilantro, olives, barbeque sauce, etc. One at a time, bring in the blindfolded competitors to the contest room.

Using a small plastic sample spoon (or other utensil); ask the blindfolded guest to open their mouth and spoon in sample #1. They are immediately to guess the food item.

Record their guess on the sheet and then proceed to the next item. Allow them to drink water in between food items. Proceed until all ten food items are tasted and guessed before moving on to the next player. The bride is to go first and then all competitors will have a turn. Their goal is to beat the bride!

Each player that has already had their guesses at the ten items may remain in the room with you and assist you with the remaining players. The one who guesses the most items is the winner and *hopefully* it is the bride! In the event of a tie, a best two out of three rock, paper scissor tournament will decide the winner.

Game gear: random food items. Small plastic sample spoons, a blindfold, a chart to write your guests' guesses down with an answer key.

Game time: ~ 20 minutes.

What Wedding Thing Am I?

Game goal: to figure out the picture, word or phrase on the card that is on your forehead.

Game play: make cards (small paper squares) of wedding related items and affix them with tape or other adhesive that is safe for the skin to your guests. Make sure there are not any reflective surfaces in your party area before you begin.

The guests are to ask yes /no questions to the other guests in order to figure out what is on their head. They are only allowed to ask questions of one person until they say *no* to any given question. At that point, the person that was answering questions is allowed to ask the person that was asking questions first. The pairs will switch and find someone else for their next line of questions. This will continue until there is a winner and then the loser is the last one standing. You might not want to wait until there is one loser but call the last five people standing the losers. That way, you don't single one person out.
Try to get an even range of difficulty with the squares. Don't make someone's card be a *diamond ring* while someone else has a *gazebo in the backyard.*

Game gear: small paper squares with any random wedding item on it (word, phrase, picture), scotch tape.

Game time: ~ 15-20 minutes.

Brilliant Wedding Product Marketeers:

Game goal: to come up with the ideal marketing strategy for a common wedding item.

Game play: give your guests a common wedding product such as a wedding guest book. Give them the going price and any specs that are available for this product. The product can essentially be anything you choose – flowers, wedding dresses, wedding cakes, etc.

Divide your guests into teams of five or six players and allow them to reinvent the marketing strategy for this item. Then, they are to propose it to the group. The groups can raise or lower the cost of the product but they cannot harm the profit margin. The best and most convincing marketing strategy wins!

Game gear: pen and paper, researched costs and specs of a given wedding product.

Game time: ~ 20-25 minutes.

Fantastic Wedding Movie Challenge:

Game goal: to be the team that can come up with the most correct wedding-themed movies with the corresponding tag lines, movie synopses, and / or movie quotes.

Game play: divide your guests into teams of four (or whatever number you choose). Select wedding related movies from websites such as www.IMDB.com. On this particular site, there are quotes, tag lines, etc. to select from for all movies. Make a sheet with a blank next to your quote, tag line, etc. for the guests to fill out when the competition starts.

Give the teams 15 minutes (or more) to fill in the correct movie in the blank next to the tag line, quote or synopsis.

When the time is up and / or the guests are finished, collect the answer sheets and score them using your answer key.

Game gear: copies of your challenge sheets, answer key and pens for each team.

Game time: ~20 minutes.

Wedding Day Charades:

<u>Game goal:</u> to earn the most points by guessing the charades correctly!

<u>Game play:</u> one player draws a charade topic from a hat and acts it out for the other players. The first one to guess the charade topic correctly gets a point. Play continues until all of the topics are guessed correctly.

The actor of the charade may not speak, point to an object, or acknowledge the other players until they give a correct guess. Decide if the actor is allowed to hold up the amount of words in the phrase with their fingers before starting. Also, decide if they can cup their ear to act out words that 'sound like' other words. Whatever you choose, make it known before the game begins. *This game may also be played in teams.*

Example charade topics are as follows but you should choose charade topics within the theme of your party:

Diamond Ring	*Honeymoon*	*Preacher*
Altar	*Gazebo*	*Videographer*
Photographer	*Daddy's Little Girl*	*Momma's Boy*
Threshold	*Bridezilla*	*Wedding Gown*
Bridesmaid	*Best Man*	*Maid of Honor*
Flower Girl	*Wedding Bouquet*	*Unity Candle*
"I Do!"	*"I Object!"*	*Bridal Shower*
Rehearsal Dinner	*Bachelor Party*	*Limousine*

<u>Game gear:</u> paper strips, pen (or word processing program and printer), and a hat (or any container to hold the pieces of paper with the charade topics).

<u>Game time:</u> ~20 minutes.

Bridal Bingo

<u>Game goal:</u> to be the first one to Bingo by finding guests who can answer *yes* to the squares on your bingo sheet!

<u>Game play:</u> make bingo sheets with as many squares as you desire. A typical sheet will have either four by four or 5 by 5 format. Put a bride related event in each square such as 'has

been married at least ten years' or 'has a wedding dress in her closet' or 'has served as a ring bearer / flower girl.'

When the host says go, the guests will start asking each other questions on their bingo cards. If anyone says yes to a question, the guest that said yes is to sign the square on the bingo card. If they say no to the question, the one asking the question must first answer a question for the player they just asked and then they may move on to ask someone else. The first player to get five across, down or diagonal – wins the first bingo.

The game can continue with the first to get two lines across, down or diagonal and then the first guest to blackout. If at any time it is discovered that nobody at the party can answer yes to a question – everyone gets credit for it immediately. In the event of a tie on the first bingo, the tiebreaker will be the first one to get another square signed.

Game gear: bingo sheets and a pen/pencil for each guest.

Game time: ~ 5 -10 minutes.

Wedding Rap Off:
Game goal: to be the most awesome rapping duo at the party!

Game play: divide the guests into pairs. Give the teams ten minutes (or more) to create a unique 30-second rap routine about the upcoming marriage of the happy couple to be performed to the group. Play any rap beats repeatedly in the background so the teams have ample time to practice with the music.

There are instrumental rap beat tracks (mp3 format) available for purchase and instant download on My Mystery Party in the Mystery Prop Emporium (http://www.mymysteryparty.com/mypapr.html).

*As a fun and potentially hilarious alternative, don't allow any time for your guests to write lyrics and ask them to come to the microphone (microphone is optional)/ stand in front of the group and show how they can *lyrically flow.* When the time is up and / or the guests are finished creating their rap routines, one at a time, the guest duos are to perform their rap routines for the other guests. The host will judge or the guests will vote via a ballot for the best rap routine. The guests are not allowed to vote for their own duo. In the case of a tie, the host will be the tiebreaker. Please, by all means, video tape this and save it for the happy couple.

Game gear: any type of rap beats and a music source to play them.

Game time: ~ 30 minutes.

Unmentionable Declarations:

Game goal: to be the team to answer the most secret words correctly without saying the prohibited descriptive words.

Game play: divide your guests into two teams. One team chooses a member to draw a secret word card. The secret word cards should include a wedding related secret word (or phrase) in bold, large font at the top and then below it, a list of forbidden or *unmentionable* descriptive words in smaller, un-bolded font. For example, if you select the secret word *diamond,* the unmentionable words below should be ring, jewelry, engagement, finger, propose. Make at least five different secret word cards for each team.

Set the timer for 30 seconds. The player is to describe the secret word or phrase at the top of the card without using any part of the secret word or phrase or the unmentionable words at the bottom of the card. The team member cannot say any form of the word(s) s/he is describing or any form of the prohibited words on the card.

One person from the opposing team is allowed to monitor the player that is describing the word to ensure that the rules are followed and s/he hasn't accidentally (or intentionally) said a forbidden word.

A point is given when the guessing team members say the correct word - exactly how it written on the card - within the 30 seconds. Play alternates between teams until all cards are played.

<u>Game gear:</u> secret word cards placed in a pile face down. Any 30-second timer.

<u>Game time</u>: ~ 20 minutes.

Chapter 13

Baby Showers

The first issue to get out of the way is *who gives the mommy-to-be the baby shower? Does she host the event herself? Is it her mother? Does her sister take the reins? Best friend? Husband?*

Now, let's settle this debate for the last time and then talk about how to host the most fantastic and quite memorable baby shower. Don't be afraid to have a little fun – it doesn't have to be only about the presents, you know!

Who is the Host?

The answer to the above questions is *all of the above*! There is no right and wrong to host a baby shower. The days of strict baby shower etiquette are *over.* Nowadays, we are only concerned with the fact that the new parents need a little help and why not celebrate the occasion? If the mommy-to-be is without family and doesn't have a close enough girlfriend to step and take the lead, it is fine for her to host her own baby shower. Simply skip the *hosted by* section of the invitation to reduce any awkwardness.

In the case of the mommy-to-be having close friends and family, it should be a collaborative effort. If you are her mother or best friend, please don't assume that her sister that agreed to host the shower has it all under control so all you need to do is *show up.* Contact her sister and see what you can do to help! She might not want the help and that's fine but you need to check and do your duty!

Friend and family relationships are two-way streets and you should do for others *more* than what you'd expect of them in return! That way, you are always pleasantly surprising each other.

When do you Host?

When do you host the shower? Is it as soon as the pregnancy test is positive, after the baby is born or sometime in between?

There is no clear-cut answer to this besides the fact that hosting a baby shower when the pregnancy is still in the uncertain stages (i.e. first few weeks to one - two months) can lead to an uncomfortable time where the grieving parents are sending gifts back to the givers. Not only will there be a period of grieving of the loss of the baby, but also the parents will have to deal with the stress of telling everybody that was at the shower or sent gifts. It's best to have the shower at least 26 weeks into the pregnancy, as this is when the baby can survive on its own if a pre-term delivery should occur. It's best to host it closer to the due date but don't schedule it too close to the due date or she might not make it to the shower if she is delivering!

Some people have elected to have the shower after the baby is born and the shower doubles as a *meet the baby* event. During the first few weeks, if the mother is breastfeeding, the infant is afforded some protection through the mother's immune system. However, anything the mother is not immune to, the baby will not be immune to either. For example, guests harboring new strains of the flu might be infective to mother and baby. This is a delicate time for the infant so the risks should be considered for showers hosted after the delivery.

Invitations:

Invitations should be very charming and well thought out with the parent's wishes and the sex of the baby in mind. If she knows if it is a boy or a girl, go with either a pink or a blue invitation. If not, stick with something neutral so a boy doesn't have a pink invitation stuck in his baby book forever. If you want to do something really outrageous, use taped up preemie disposable diapers (as if they are dirty diapers) with small but very cute card invitations inside and fill (reasonably speaking) with brown confetti! How funny is that?

Evites are not acceptable for baby showers as this is going to be part of this baby's baby book and therefore his or her history! How can you save an evite, anyway? Print it off? Not acceptable! Do an internet search for different styles of baby shower invitations, as there are many great examples out there for you to follow. A bottle shape is popular, diaper shapes are a staple, maybe even get white felt and make a tiny diaper to stick on the invitation! Awww, how cute! Keep in mind that this is the child's permanent history.

Next issue for debate is the *hosted by* line of the invitation. First, if ten people are hosting, they should all be listed on the invitation in some manner. If you only listed five and the other five had vital roles in hosting the event but are not mentioned – they will get their feelings hurt and the mommy-to-be will definitely hear about it. Do not do this by any means. Ink is cheap enough so reduce the font size and give everybody credit. 'No room on the invitation' is not a valid excuse. Again, this is the baby's history and if you gave effort (i.e. money, labor, etc.) for his/her baby shower, you want the baby to know later! Don't leave anybody out if they have provided any type of monetary gift and / or services for this event. Now, if there is one or maybe two - three major hosts that are paying for a large portion of the event and doing most of the work it is all right to put their names as the main hosts and then in a smaller font below or in any location on the invitation, list the others who assisted in any way. This is a positive event and should remain positive on all fronts. Don't start any disputes and hard feelings prior to the event for Goodness' sake!

All Female or Coed:

Does a baby shower have to be all female? Modern times are moving toward co-ed baby showers. *Why not make it a celebration for everybody?* Have fun party games, great food (typically appetizers) and of course, the gift opening ceremony is the focus. However, with large showers, save the gift opening for after the shower as this can be long and monotonous. The parents-to-be will be the only ones interested that Granny Lee bought a stroller for little Johnny. Basic guideline, if there are more than ten gifts to open, save it for later. If someone wants to see you open his or her gift, wait until after the shower.

Guest list should include all family members of the parents-to-be and all close friends of the daddy and mommy-to-be. If you are hosting an all-female event, extend an invitation to the wives (not necessarily the girlfriends unless they know the mommy-to-be) of the male friends. Your guest list will include strangers.

As a basic guideline, if the either of the parents-to-be have not had a meaningful conversation with a potential guest (excluding relatives) over the course of the last calendar year, that guest is not obligated to attend so leave them off the guest list. We don't ask things of people that we do not have an active relationship with, as that is tacky and rude. At a minimum, if they haven't thought of this person enough to send them a low effort email in an entire year to see how they are doing…do not expect them to spend money on a gift or take the time to come to the shower!   Family members of both parents-to-be are obligated but friends are another story. However, shame on you if you haven't spoken with any member of your family for over a year!

Play any of the *Sims* games and you'll see that even in video games, relationships fade over time and friends become strangers and you'll need to start over on the relationship. You don't start over by asking them to go out of their way to attend your baby shower and buy you a gift!

The exception to this basic guideline is friends of the grandparents-to-be. If the grandparents are active friends with these folks (i.e. have spoken to them in the last year), extend an invitation to them as long as the grandparent to be's friends *know* the mommy or daddy-to-be. If they've never met them, don't put them on the guest list.

Now that you have your guest list, you will need to manage the RSVPs as with any party. You might need to assist with travel arrangements and lodging for out of town guests. Ask for all special accommodations to be disclosed with the RSVP *(these potential special accommodations are listed in the Master Party Checklist in Chapter 2)* for the invited guests on the invite.

Location, Location, Location:

Location of the party is as variable with any event but remember it is about the parents-to-be not only celebrating the upcoming birth of the child but also about getting gifts to help them raise their baby in the first years when they are so financially demanding. For example, if you end up spending over $5,000 on the shower, you could have simply donated that money to the couple. Therefore, these showers are generally low budget. The host's home that is most centralized, largest and easily accessible home is the one to choose.

Shower Décor:

Décor should be in traditional pastel colors and baby items should be the focus. The exception to the pastel color scheme is when the parents have selected primary colors for the nursery. Your local party store likely has a baby shower section. There is diaper and bottle confetti, small plastic baby bottles, large cutouts, etc. for you to decorate the party room. Grab some pink and blue balloons or if you know the gender of the baby, go for it in all pink or all blue décor. Grab some pastel lights in pink and /or blue or even clear white and decorate the baby gift table for a fun festive effect.

Decorate the appetizer table with baby bottle centerpieces. Take a large, glass baby bottle, wrap the bottom in tulle fabric and secure with a pastel colored ribbon. Remove the nipple from the bottle and add some white roses. Sprinkle glitter and baby shower confetti. Place these around the appetizer table with plenty of confetti sprinkled around.

Shower Cuisine:

Party food should be appetizers. A formal dinner is not necessary for a baby shower.   Serve cocktails but don't make it the focus. Maybe a nice mimosa, Bellini, or Chambord and champagne cocktail but no *shots at the bar*, please.

Upon Guest Arrival:

As the guests arrive, have them sign in on the baby book (if there is a baby shower section) or purchase a baby shower guest book and have a table or pedestal set up near the entryway with a pen for the guests to sign in as they arrive. Give them a nametag and either pre-print the nametags to include their name and relationship to either parent-to-be. A portion of the guests will probably not know each other so name tags are necessary! If you do not pre-print the nametags, ask the guests to write their name and relationship to either of the parents-to-be. Using self-adhesive nametags are preferred but you can purchase plastic name badges that have safety pins on the back. Using nametags and disclosing the relationship on them gives an inherent ice breaker for your guests to mingle about and gives the guests who don't know each other something to start a conversation about. *So... you're Frank's boss, huh? Is he a slacker or what?* Yes, it is all right to have a sense of humor!

Drop By vs. Scheduled Events:

Drop by showers versus scheduled events are two different shower animals. Disclose on your invitation if this is a *drop by* shower (i.e. *drop by anytime between 2-4 PM*) or give a starting time only (i.e. *starts promptly at 2 PM*) if it is a scheduled event and you expect your guests to be there the time it is scheduled for. If you put on the time line that the shower is from 2-4 PM but do not specify whether or not if it is a *drop by* shower, your guests will be confused so do either one or the other method above.

A drop by shower means that your invited guests can simply drop by for a few minutes any time within the shower time line and give the mommy-to-be their gift. Whatever type of party you decide to do, make sure it is clear on the invitation! Also, since the default shower is females only, if you want to have a co-ed shower, make sure to disclose a co-ed shower clearly on the invitation. Don't have your guests guessing – be up front with your intentions!

Drop by showers are more economical and are really more about the gifts as the focus and less on the celebration. If you are a host and on a strict budget, keep in mind that you'll need to serve less food and won't have to purchase party game props and prizes with this method. However, scheduled events are so much more memorable so get a co-host to split the cost and upgrade to a scheduled event if possible!

Party Games:

Party games are essential for the scheduled event showers. With drop by showers, it is nearly too difficult to schedule party games as you will not know when enough guests will be present to play a game and this obligates those guests who planned to just *swing by for a few minutes* to stay longer than they expected. Refrain from doing party games unless you have a scheduled event.

With a schedule event, after all of the guests have arrived snap a group photo. This will be a great addition to the baby book. After the guests have received their nametags, found the appetizers and beverages, it is time to start the party games. Baby showers should only be two to three hours long but *why not give your guests a memorable time during the shower?* After all, this is also a celebration of the upcoming birth of a child!

Prizes for games are always optional but highly suggested. You set the tone for the prizes depending upon your budget. Have simple award certificates (find a template on MS Word, etc.) and write in the winner(s) names. Alternatively, have trophies made at the local sporting goods store (~$8.00 each for the cheap ones).   Also, pick up award ribbons at the local party store. If you don't want to have award type prizes, start with candy bars or cute decorated jars of candy on up to gift certificates at Starbucks or the local mall for bigger games. There is no right or wrong when it comes to prizes because it's all about fun and the thrill of competition.

BABY SHOWER PARTY GAMES:

Famous Babies Trivia:

Game goal: to guess the famous fictional, historical or celebrity baby from a few fun facts.

Game play: do an internet search for famous babies and write down five fun facts about this famous fictional, historical or celebrity baby. Print out decorative cards with this information along with the answer below the five facts.

Hand guests a card with their famous baby. As the guests mingle about during your meet 'n greet, they are to quiz each other on their famous baby. The one who guesses the baby with the least amount of facts wins! Then, the guests are to go on to the next person and so on until everybody has had a chance to mingle and quiz every other guest. Each guest can decide the order to give the facts to their partner – it doesn't have to be in the order written on the card.

Examples of famous babies are: Stewie from the Family Guy Cartoon, Maggie from the Simpsons Cartoon, any of the Rugrats cartoon characters, the Gerber Baby, Simba from the Lion King, Baby Huey, Suri Cruise, etc.
*As an alternative, play this game with famous moms, famous dads, or even famous families.

Game gear: cards with the five fun facts and the famous baby (the answer) stated below the facts.

Game time: ~ 10-15 minutes.

What Child is This?

Game goal: to guess the most correct baby pictures of the shower attendees.

Game play: instruct guests to bring a baby picture to the shower. After the guests have arrived, assemble these pictures on a designated wall or create a board to display the pictures. Be sure to use gentle adhesive such as Scotch tape as the guests will want these pictures back unharmed! Don't stick a pin through them! Make an answer key prior to assigning a number to each picture to score them quickly and easily later.

At the guest's leisure, they are to come to the board and view the pictures. Number the pictures on the board display by placing a number below the picture (don't write on the pictures) and give each guest a guess sheet. They are to write down the guests' name according to the baby picture on their guess sheet by number and turn it in to the host when they are done. If not all guests brought a baby picture, stick a gold star on the guests' nametags that are participating in the challenge.

Game gear: baby pictures of the guests, a board or designated wall to assemble a picture display, answer sheets with answer key, pens for each guest. Gold stars for the nametags in case not every guest brings a baby picture.

Game time: ~ 10-15 minutes.

Don't Forget the Baby Lyrics:

Game goal: to guess the most correct missing lyrics of the given baby lullabies or children's poems.

Game play: one by one, the host will recite a partial line to each guest from a given nursery rhyme, poem or baby lullaby. The guest must complete the line with the correct lyrics for a point. If the guest answers incorrectly, it goes to the first person to raise their hand and give the correct answer. If someone blurts out the correct answer during a steal, nobody gets credit. The guests must raise their hand and the host has to call on them. The guest who finishes the most lyrics correctly wins!

To find lyrics for nursery rhymes and other baby poems and songs, do an internet search with keywords such as *Mother Goose Rhymes* or *Baby Lullaby Lyrics.* As an alternative, purchase the parents-to-be a nice Mother Goose book and read the lyrical lines straight from the book. The parents-to-be keep the book as a prize, of course.

Game gear: nursery rhyme / lullaby lyrics.

Game time: ~ 10-15 minutes.

You Suck! Baby Bottle Mayhem:

Game goal: to see who can suck the most out of a baby bottle in a given time.

Game play: you will need a baby bottle for each guest participating in this challenge. Fill the bottles with an equal amount of the beverage of your choice.

When the host says go, the guests are to race to see who can finish the beverage in the bottle the quickest by sucking it though the nipple. The first one finished, wins!

When the host gives the prize for the winner, they are to say in humor, *"you won because you suck the most!"*

Game gear: baby bottles for each guest participating in the challenge, beverage of your choice.

Game time: ~ 10 minutes.

Pin the Sperm on the Egg:

Game goal: to pin the sperm closet to the target on the egg!

Game play: cut out an egg from white felt or print off a picture of an egg. Make the egg nucleus from a smaller circle of light blue felt. Create sperm from pieces of felt or pictures of clip art of sperm found on the internet by searching the keyword *sperm clipart*. The sperm should also have a light blue nucleus. If you choose to make felt sperm, cut out a white circle, the smaller light blue circle and affix fun googly eyes on the circle. For the sperm tail, affix a piece of white yarn or pipe cleaner. Affix a piece of tape on the back of each sperm.

Blindfold each guest, spin them around three times and hand them their sperm with the adhesive on the back. Point them in the general direction of the egg on the wall. They are to use only one hand – the one holding the sperm – and cannot touch the wall in which the egg is taped with the other hand. Where the sperm hits the wall is where it stays. They cannot feel around the wall for the egg! Leave the sperm where it lands until the game is over or remove it and place a small set of initials of the person to keep track of the locations of sperm.

The guest who gets the closest to the target on the egg wins! When you award the winner the prize, you must say in humor, *"test results are in...you are the baby's daddy!"*

Game gear: egg to tape to the wall and multiple sperm for each guest with adhesive on the back and a blindfold.

Game time: ~ 10-15 minutes.

Pregnant Lady Relay Dash:

Game goal: to experience the frequent urination and water weight of pregnancy while working as a team and getting all members across the finish line first.

Game play: not just the pregnant mother has to experience a little discomfort and difficulty moving around! Let's give all of the guests a shot at it! Divide your guests into teams of two. Have each guest blow up a balloon and place it under their shirt to simulate being pregnant.

Half of the players on each team line up on opposing sides of the course. Give one side ping-pong balls and give the players on the other side water balloons. The nickel side players are the frequent urinaters and the water balloon side are the water weights. Guests are to hold their ping-pong ball or water balloon between his or her knees.

When the host says go, the first person in the nickel line is to waddle across the course to a bucket in the middle of the lane. This is the potty and they must get their ping-pong ball into the potty. If they drop their ball at any time, they must go back to where they started and start over. They cannot remove the balloon from their shirt to pick up the ping-pong ball. If their balloon pops at any time, they must blow up another one and put it under their shirt.

Once the ping-pong ball player gets their ping-pong ball into the bucket, they can run to the first water weight team member and tag them. They are to waddle with the water balloon in between their legs as fast as they can across the lane and tag the next nickel holder in line. This continues until a team successfully gets all members across the finish line!

Game gear: water balloons for half of the players, ping-pong balls (or substitute for uncooked beans, coins, buttons, etc.) for half of the players, a bucket for each lane (or a training potty), and balloons for each guest.

Game time: ~ 10-15 minutes.

Name That Lie!
Game goal: to figure out which fun facts are true about the mommy and daddy-to-be!

Game play: prior to the shower, get at least five facts that nobody knows (or at least most do not know) about both the mommy and daddy-to-be. Mix these facts in with another five or so lies about each of them. Hand each guest a paper with the word truth on one side and lie on another. It's preferable to put these on a paddle with truth on one side and lie on the other. Alternating between truth and lies (in any combination you choose), announce a fact to the group about each parent-to-be and the guests are to hold up either truth or lie on their truth/lie sheets (paddles). All players with the incorrect answer are to be removed from the game (i.e. stand against the wall). Continue to read facts about the parents-to-be until you are done with all truths and lies and the last person or people in the game are the winners!

Game gear: fun facts about the parents-to-be, truth/lie sheets (paddles) for each guest and some lies about the parents-to-be.

Game time: ~ 10-15 minutes.

Who's the Best Parent...to an Egg?

Game goal: to be the best parent of your egg.

Game play: give each player a hardboiled egg – without cracks! Allow them to make a picture of a face or whatever they choose on the egg with non-toxic markers.

When the host says go, the game begins. During the shower, the guests are to take extra-special care of their egg. If anyone leaves his or her egg unattended, another guest can kidnap it, smash it, or hide it. The last person standing with an intact egg without any cracks is the winner. A crack signifies neglect! If any guest sees another guest without their egg at any time, that guest is automatically out of the game as this guest has most likely hidden their egg – which is child-egg abandonment and is against the baby shower law!

If a guest gently sits their egg down but the egg is still in view – they are still in the game. However, if the guest is not actively protecting it, another guest can smash it.

Declaring a winner: if there are multiple people with intact eggs at the end of the shower, have everybody give each other a big applause, as they are all egg-cellent parents!

Game gear: a hardboiled egg for each guest, markers.

Game time: ~ 10-15 minutes.

Step Right Up and Guess the Mommy's Age:

Game goal: to guess the mommy-to-be's age at various times of her life.

Game play: prior to the event, ask the mommy-to-be for pictures of her childhood throughout various ages (i.e. newborn, one year, three years, five years, up through early '20s if she is there yet). Post these pictures on any display board in any order (don't be obvious as far as the chronological order goes).

Number the pictures by placing large, bold text squares with numbers below each picture. Make an answer sheet with the numbers of the pictures next to a blank. The guests are to fill in the blank with the appropriate age that the mother was in the picture. Make sure to make an answer key in advance of the party to make the scoring of the sheets quick.

After you score the sheets, reveal the winner(s).

Game gear: numbered pictures of the mommy-to-be of all ages throughout her life, guests answer sheets, an answer key.

Game time: ~ 10-15 minutes.

Pregnant Dude Challenge:

Game goal: to be the first pregnant man to tie his shoes.

Game play: have the men at the shower (obviously this is for a co-ed shower) blow up their respective balloons to a nine-month pregnancy belly size. They are to slip their balloons under their shirts. Any guy that has a shirt too tight to house a pregnant belly should 1. be teased for wearing a skinny shirt to a baby shower and 2. be provided an XL (or larger) t-shirt to participate in this challenge.

Tie a piece of yarn around their feet (they are to take off their shoes) but do not tie it into a bow. If every guy happens to have on laced shoes with equal difficulty in tying them, skip the yarn and simply allow them to tie their own shoes. You use the yarn to equalize the difficulty and in case someone is wearing shoes without laces.

When the host says go, the men are to tie both strands of yarn on both feet into a bow without popping their balloon or removing it from their shirt. If a player pops a balloon, they are to blow up another balloon of the same size and start over.

The first pregnant man to have both pieces of yarn (or shoelaces) tied into *complete* bows without popping their balloon, wins!

Game gear: balloons for each male guest, two strands of yarn long enough to tie around their feet into bows like shoelaces (optional to purchase shoelaces for each male guest); extra balloons in case they pop.

Game time: ~ 10-15 minutes.

Baby Sock Hop Challenge:
Game goal: to match up the baby socks in the fastest time.

Game play: purchase multiple pairs of baby socks in all colors and patterns (these will be given to mom and dad-to-be after the shower). Take them out of the package and put them into a drawstring bag.

When the host says go, set a timer and each guest is to assemble the socks into correct pairs. The guest who has the fastest time wins! *If any of the socks are incorrectly paired, the time doesn't count.*

Game gear: two draw string bags, at least five pairs of baby socks (but more than ten is suggested), a timer.

Game time: ~ 10-15 minutes.

Remember! A Baby Item Memory Challenge:
Game goal: to remember all of the baby items on the tray.

Game play: assemble a tray full of at least 15-20 baby items such as nail clippers, pacifier, diaper, etc.

Show the guests the tray for a period of 30 seconds. Take the tray away, give each guest a pen and paper, and ask that they write all of the items down. The guest(s) who can name the most items correctly wins!

Game gear: multiple baby items, a tray, paper and pen for each guest.

Game time: ~ 10-15 minutes.

Guess What's in the Diaper Bag!

Game goal: to use your psychic abilities and guess the items in a full diaper bag. *(This diaper bag is later given to the mom-to-be!)*

Game play: bring in a diaper bag stuffed full of goodies. Give each guest a paper and pen. Allow them ~five minutes to write down all of the items in the diaper bag. When time is up, they are to switch papers with another guest. One by one, pull out an item from the bag and the guests are to score each other's papers. The guest(s) who guesses the most items correctly wins!

Game gear: a diaper bag full of goodies, pen and paper for each guest.

Game time: ~ 10-15 minutes.

How many Pacifiers?

Game goal: to guess the number of pacifiers in a jar.

Game play: obtain a medium sized jar and place as many pacifiers inside as possible. As the guests arrive, have them guess how many pacifiers are in the jar. At the end of the shower, pull them out and count them (or count them in advance and reveal the correct number). The one who guesses the closest or gets it right, of course, wins!

Game gear: ballot sheets, a glass jar with multiple pacifiers inside.

Game time: ~ the duration of the shower.

Birthday Squares

Game goal: to purchase the squares with the correct birthday of the baby on it.

Game play: this is an optional betting pool on the delivery date (aka: birthday) of the baby. Alternatively, if this is a scheduled delivery, bet on the exact time of birth. You decide how much you want each square to cost but it has to cost the same for each square. Grab a large envelope to collect the funds and you will keep this envelope until the baby is born. You will give the winner the envelope once the baby is born.

As the guests purchase squares, allow them to sign their initials on your square sheet that *does not have* the columns and rows labeled yet.

An example square sheet is below:

	BLM	PBQ	FSJ	ABL	PBQ
	LRH	KCB	PBQ	BLM	YRG
	KCB	JTH	ABL	YRG	FSJ
	KCB	KCB	ABL	BLM	YRG

On strips of paper, write the potential delivery dates of the baby – obviously including the due date as it is scheduled now. If the baby is due on May 31st, maybe start with May 29th and end with June 2nd so go as early and late as you choose around the due date. Fold these strips of paper and put into a hat.

Once all guests have filled in their initials and paid their money per square, draw the various calendar dates from a hat. Draw these strips and place in the exact order that you draw on the tops of the column as shown in the figure below.

Make separate strips for the hour of delivery and place into another container in which to draw the folded strips. Repeat with the hour of the day or put the hours into groups (i.e. 12:00 AM to 5:59 AM, 6:00 AM to 11:59 AM, etc.) to minimize the number of squares on the sheet (as there are 24 hours in a day and baby can come at any time).   Make this square sheet as extensive as you want but you will need to collect money for each square. Draw for the row titles next and fill in the blanks in the exact order in which you draw them.

Example labeled square sheet:

	May 29	May 30	May 31	June 1	June 2
12:00 AM - 5:59 AM	**BLM**	PBK	FSJ	ABL	PBK
6:00 AM – 11:59 AM	LRH	KCB	PBK	**BLM**	YRG
12:00 PM – 5:59 PM	KCB	JTH	ABL	YRG	FSJ
6:00 PM – 11:59 PM	KCB	KCB	ABL	**BLM**	YRG

Selecting a winner: for example, if the baby were born at 3:00 PM on May 31st, the person with the initials ABL would be the winner (in the gray-highlighted square above). If everybody put in 2.00$ in this example betting pool for each square, the winner would collect $40.00! Once the baby is born, the winner is selected via their square and the prize money is theirs!

Game gear: an unlabeled column and row squares sheet as shown above, strips with the potential due dates and separate strips with the potential hours for the host to draw from, pens for each guest to initial the squares. A large envelope to collect the money for the squares. In addition, a designee (i.e. the host) who will hold on to the square sheet and prize money until the baby is born. Give the award in the hospital during visiting hours!

Game time: ~ 10-15 minutes.

Dirty Diaper Door Prize
Game goal: to be the one with the lucky poo in your diaper!

Game play: with white pieces of felt, fold ~ 1" diapers and affix a safety pin to the back of them. In one of the diapers, put melted chocolate and allow drying prior to folding the felt into a diaper.

Alternatively, if you want to be less realistic and more on the cuter side of baby poo, purchase some brown sequins or brown glitter and glue inside one of the diapers.

As the guests arrive, affix a diaper to each person's shirt and instruct them not to touch it until the end of the shower. At the end of the shower, allow the guests to unfold the diaper and the guest with the dirty diaper gets the door prize! The door prize can be anything – such as a movie theater gift certificate, etc.

Game gear: white felt for dirty diapers, a small piece of chocolate (melted) or brown sequins/glitter, glue to secure the folds and the safety pins.

Game time: ~ the duration of the shower.

Babies & ABCs:

Game goal: to be the first team to come up with a baby related item for each letter of the alphabet.

Game play: divide your guests into groups of two to four. Give each team a pen and a sheet that has the letters of the alphabet with blanks beside them.

When the host says go, each team is to name a baby-related word for each letter of the alphabet. The first team to shout 'Babies and ABCs Now Everyone Must Freeze' will cause everybody to stop playing.

Freezing consists of every team turning their sheet over and putting their pen down. The host will read the shouting team's sheet and verify that all letters have a real word relating to a baby next to it.

For fun, read the words aloud to the rest of the group but get ready for disputes. As long as the word is *somewhat* related to a baby, let it count as this is a game that's just for fun! If there is absolutely no relation to a baby (i.e. rollercoaster) on one or more words or if one letter is blank, the game is back on and opens for any team to win. The false-announcing group, however, is disqualified and must remain a peaceful audience until there is a real winner. The game continues until the first team has a verifiable win!

Game gear: sheets with the letters of the alphabet and blanks beside the letters and pens for each team.

Game time: ~ 10-15 minutes.

Let's Make a Baby!
Game goal: to make the perfect baby out of the materials available.

Game play: divide your guests into groups of two to three. Assemble various crafty items (i.e. foil, newspaper, paper towels, toilet paper, sequins, buttons, markers, leaves, yarn, etc.) on a main table in the middle of the party room. Assign glue, tape, staplers, etc. to each group.

When the host says go, each team is to grab the items they need to make the perfect baby. Give the teams a designated amount of time (i.e. ten minutes) to create the perfect baby out of the items given. When time is up, host will judge which team has created the perfect baby!

Game gear: various craft items.

Game time: ~ 10-15 minutes.

Don't Say it, Baby!
Game goal: to collect the most pacifiers.

Game play: when guests arrive at the shower, hand them a pacifier. As the guests mingle and play shower games, etc., they are not to say a designated word such as *baby*. Whenever they say the forbidden word, the guest that hears it has the right to take away their pacifier. The game continues until the shower is over and the host calls for pacifiers.

Whoever has collected the most pacifiers wins the game. Of course, the pacifiers go to the mommy-to-be at the conclusion of the shower! A run in the dishwasher and they're good to go!

Game gear: a pacifier for each guest.

Game time: ~ the duration of the shower.

Revealing Squares:

Game goal: to get to know the other guests! A great icebreaker!

Game play: ask that the guests sit in a circle around the party area. Pass around a roll of toilet tissue and have guests pull a random amount of tissue before you tell them what the challenge is about.

After everybody has pulled off their random piece of toilet paper, instruct each guest to reveal as many things about themselves to the group as they have squares of toilet tissue! Start with the mommy-to-be and continue around the circle to her left. *As an alternative, have each guest tell something about the mommy or daddy-to-be instead of about themselves or go around the circle twice.*

Game gear: a roll of toilet tissue.

Game time: ~ 10-15 minutes.

How Many Squares?

Game goal: to select randomly how many squares of toilet tissue will go around the pregnant mother's belly.

Game play: ask that the guests sit in a circle around the party area. Pass around a roll of toilet tissue and have guests pull a random amount of tissue before you tell them what the challenge is about. *(Revealing Squares can be done back to back with this challenge to throw the guests off on why they are pulling off squares of toilet tissue.)*

When everybody has pulled off a random amount of toilet tissue squares, have the mommy-to-be stand up in the middle of the circle. One by one, guests are to attempt to wrap their toilet tissue piece around the mommy's belly at the biggest point (where her belly button is). The guest with the closest toilet paper piece to her belly size wins! Allow mommy to keep the toilet paper piece for the baby shower book!

Game gear: roll of toilet paper.

Game time: ~ 10-15 minutes.

Diaper Changing Challenge Relay Race:

Game goal: to change the baby's diaper the fastest!

Game play: designate multiple baby changing areas as the diaper changing stations or just one if this challenge is done one by one. Do this challenge either simultaneously or all at once, depending on how many babies and changing accessories you have available. If you do it individually, use a timer and a whiteboard to keep track of the best times. This challenge is hysterical at a co-ed party when men compete against each other.

When the host says go, the players are to change their baby doll's diaper in the fastest time possible. The baby doll should have a dirty diaper with the same amount of chocolate pudding inside as all other contestants. The players have to remove all traces of chocolate pudding from the baby doll with a wipe, dispose of the wipe and diaper properly and add diaper rash ointment and baby powder to the baby's tender areas and put on a new diaper correctly in the fastest time possible. The host is to inspect each newly changed baby doll to determine if all pudding was removed, the waste disposed of properly and the ointment and powder applied properly. Any doll that still has pudding inside is considered a *diaper rash waiting to happen* and the player gets an additional 10 seconds added to his/her time.

The player that can change a diaper the fastest wins!

Change it up and substitute pureed carrots or avocados instead of pudding as you never know what you're gonna get in a baby's diaper!

Game gear: baby dolls, chocolate pudding, baby wipes, newborn (or doll sized) diapers, ointment, baby powder, a waste receptacle for the dirty diapers and wipes. A timer or a cell phone can be used as a timer.

Game time: ~ 10-15 minutes.

Dress the Baby Relay Race:

Game goal: to change the baby doll's clothes and get her ready for bed in the fastest time.

Game play: designate multiple baby changing areas as or just one if this challenge is done one by one. Do this challenge either simultaneously or all at once, depending on how many babies and baby clothes you have available. If you do it individually, use a timer and a whiteboard to keep track of the best times. This challenge is hysterical at a co-ed party when men compete against each other.

When the host says go, the players are to change their baby doll's clothes in the fastest time possible. The baby doll should be fully dressed and pajamas should be folded neatly by the changing station. The contestant is to remove the clothes and replace with the pajamas in the fastest time possible. The host will inspect to ensure that the pajamas are put on correctly and the time will be recorded. The player that can change the baby's clothes the fastest wins!

Game gear: baby dolls, baby doll clothes (regular day outfit and pajamas), a timer.

Game time: ~ 10-15 minutes.

The Price is Right, Baby!

Game goal: to guess the right price on the baby items shown to the group.

Game play: the host is to assemble a variety of baby items available for purchase. One by one, the host is to show the item to the group and they are to write down on their sheet of paper how much the item costs. When all of the items have been shown to the guests, the guests are to switch papers with someone beside them.

The host will then reveal the correct price of each item and the guests will score each other's answers. Any guess within $1.00 should be counted as correct. If the item costs $17.50 and the guess is anywhere from $16.50 to $18.50 – the guess is counted as correct. However, a guess of $18.51 is incorrect. The person who guessed the most items correctly is the winner!

Game gear: various baby items with their known prices on an answer key. Paper and pens for each guest.

Game time: ~ 10-15 minutes.

How Much Was It in 1950?
Game goal: to guess how much each baby item cost in 1950.

Game play: the host is to assemble a variety of baby items available for purchase in 1950. Use a picture for some items, as they might not still be available for purchase. One by one, the host is to show the item to the group and they are to write down on their sheet of paper how much the item cost in 1950. After showing all items to the guests, the guests switch papers with someone beside them.
    The host will then reveal the correct price of each item in 1950 and the guests will score each other's answers. Any guess within $1.00 should be counted as correct. If the item costs $17.50 and the guess is anywhere from $16.50 to $18.50 – the guess is counted as correct. However, a guess of $18.51 is incorrect. The person who guessed the most items correctly is the winner! Do an internet search on your baby item of your choosing. There are plenty of websites dedicated to the 1950s to find out how much retail items cost back then.
    As an alternative, select any year in the past (i.e. 1960, 1970, 1980, etc).

Game gear: 1950's baby items available for purchase and their prices on an answer key, paper and pens for each guest.

Game time: ~ 10-15 minutes.

Is your Palette Better than a Baby's?
Game goal: to be the one who can correctly guess the ten random baby food items – while blindfolded!

Game play: gather ten random baby food jars of your choice. Choose both straight flavors such as baby food carrots or baby food that has combinations of flavors such as Hawaiian Delight or Peas and Carrots. One at a time, bring in the competitors and blindfold them.

Using a small plastic sample spoon (or other utensil); ask the blindfolded guest to open their mouth and spoon in sample #1. For example, if you choose Hawaiian Delight as baby food item #1, you will give them a spoon full of Peas and Carrot baby food to taste. They are to guess the *main ingredients* in the baby food item (i.e. peas and carrots).

Record their guess on the sheet and then proceed to the next item.   Allow them to drink water in between food items. Proceed until all ten baby food items are tasted and guessed before moving on to the next player. Each player that has already guessed the 10 items may remain in the room with you and assist you with the remaining players.

The one who guesses the most items is the winner! In the event of a tie, a best two out of three rock, paper scissor tournament will decide the winner.

Game gear: random baby food jars. Small plastic sample spoons, a blindfold, a chart to write your guests' guesses down with an answer key.

Game time: ~ 20 minutes.

What Baby Thing Am I?

Game goal: to figure out the picture, word or phrase on the card that is on your forehead.

Game play: make cards (small paper squares) of baby related items and affix them with skin-safe tape or other adhesive that is safe for the skin to your guests. Make sure there are not any reflective surfaces in your party area before you begin.

The guests are to ask yes /no questions to the other guests in order to figure out what is on their head. They are only allowed to ask questions of one person until they say *no* to any given question. At that point, the person that was answering questions is allowed to ask the person that was asking questions first. The pairs will switch and find someone else for their next line of questions. This will continue until there is a winner and then the loser is the last one standing. You might not want to wait until there is one loser but call the last five people standing the losers. That way, you don't single one person out.

Try to get an even range of difficulty with the squares. Don't make someone's card be a *diaper* while someone else has a *case of colic.*

Game gear: small paper squares with any random baby item on it (word, phrase, and picture) within the theme of your party, scotch tape.

Game time: ~ 15-20 minutes.

Brilliant Baby Product Marketeers:

Game goal: to come up with the ideal marketing strategy for a common baby item.

Game play: give your guests a common baby product such as a disposable diaper. Give them the going price and any specs that are available for this product. The product can essentially be anything you choose – diapers, baby rash ointment, pacifiers, etc.

Divide your guests into teams of five and allow them to reinvent the marketing strategy for this item. Then, they are to propose it to the group. The groups are allowed to raise or lower the cost of the product but they cannot harm the profit margin. The best and most convincing marketing strategy wins!

Game gear: pen and paper.

Game time: ~ 20-25 minutes.

Fantastic Baby Movie Challenge:

Game goal: to be the team that can answer the appropriate baby-themed movie with the corresponding tag lines, movie synopses, and / or movie quotes.

Game play: divide your guests into teams of four (or whatever number you choose). Select baby related movies from websites such as www.IMDB.com. On this particular site, there are quotes, tag lines, etc. to select from for all movies.

Give the teams 15 minutes (or more) to fill in the correct movie in the blank next to the tag line, quote or synopsis.

When the time is up and / or the guests are finished, collect the answer sheets and score them using your answer key.

Game gear: copies of your challenge sheets, answer key and pens for each team.

Game time: ~20 minutes.

Babyriffic Charades:

Game goal: to earn the most points by guessing the charades correctly!

Game play: one player draws a charade topic from a hat and acts it out for the other players. The first one to guess the charade topic correctly gets a point. Play continues until all of the topics are guessed correctly.

The actor of the charade may not speak, point to an object, or acknowledge the other players until they give a correct guess. Decide if the actor is allowed to hold up the amount of words in the phrase with their fingers before starting. Also, decide if they can cup their ear to act out words that 'sound like' other words. Whatever you choose, make it known before the game begins.
This game may also be played in teams.

Example charade topics are as follows but you should choose charade topics within the theme of your party:

Diaper Rash	Baby Shampoo	Baby Crib
Terrible Twos	Play Pen	Babysitter
Cutting Teeth	Baby Bottle	Breast Feed
Potty Train	Gerber	Nap Time
Sterilize	Disposable Diaper	Grandmother
Grandfather	Sibling	High Chair
Soy Milk	Colostrum	Nipple

Game gear: paper strips, pen (or word processing program and printer), and a hat (or any container to hold the pieces of paper with the charade topics).

Game time: ~20 minutes.

Baby Bingo:

Game goal: to be the first one to bingo by finding guests who can answer *yes* to the squares on your bingo sheet!

Game play: make bingo sheets with as many squares as you desire. A typical sheet will have either four by four or 5 by 5 format. Put a baby related event in each square such as 'has given birth to a boy' or 'knows how to change a diaper' or 'used to be a babysitter.'

When the host says go, the guests will start asking each other questions on their bingo cards. If anyone says *yes* to a question, the guest that said *yes* is to sign the square on the bingo card. If they say *no* to the question, the one asking the question must first answer a question for the player they just asked and then they may move on to ask someone else. The first player to get five across, down or diagonal – wins the first bingo.

The game can continue with the first to get two lines across, down or diagonal and then the first guest to blackout. If at any time it is discovered that nobody at the party can answer yes to a question – everyone gets credit for it immediately. In the event of a tie on the first bingo, the tiebreaker will be the first one to get another square signed.

Game gear: bingo sheets and a pen/pencil for each guest.

Game time: ~ 5 -10 minutes.

Baby Rap Off:

Game goal: to be the most awesome rapping duo at the party!

Game play: divide the guests into pairs. Give the teams ten minutes (or more) to create a unique 30-second rap routine about the upcoming baby to be born to be performed to the group. Play any rap beats repeatedly in the background so the teams have ample time to practice with the music. There are instrumental rap beat tracks (mp3 format) available for purchase and instant download on My Mystery Party in the Mystery Prop Emporium (http://www.mymysteryparty.com/mypapr.html).

As a fun and potentially hilarious alternative, don't allow any time for your guests to write lyrics and ask them to come to the microphone (microphone is optional)/ stand in front of the group and show how they can *lyrically flow.*

When the time is up and / or the guests are finished creating their rap routines, one at a time, the guest duos are to perform their rap routines for the other guests. The host will judge or the guests will vote via a ballot for the best rap routine. The guests are not allowed to vote for their duo. In the case of a tie, the host will be the tiebreaker. Please, by all means, video tape this and save it for the baby!

Game gear: any type of rap beats and a music source to play them.

Game time: ~ 30 minutes.

Unmentionable Declarations:

Game goal: to be the team to answer the most secret words correctly without saying prohibited words.

Game play: divide your guests into two teams. One team chooses a member to draw a secret word card. The secret word cards should include a baby or child related secret word (or phrase) in bold, large font at the top and then below it, a list of forbidden or *unmentionable* descriptive words in smaller, un-bolded font. For example, if you select the secret word *bottle,* the unmentionable words below should be drink, beverage, liquid, hold, and feed. Make at least five secret word cards for each team.

Set the timer for 30 seconds. The player is to describe the secret word or phrase at the top of the card without using any part of the secret word or phrase or the unmentionable words at the bottom of the card. The team member cannot say

<u>any form</u> of the word(s) s/he is describing or <u>any form</u> of the prohibited words on the card.

One person from the opposing team monitors the player that is describing the word to ensure that the rules are followed and s/he hasn't accidentally (or intentionally) said a forbidden word.

A point is given when the guessing team members say the correct word - exactly how it written on the card - within the 30 seconds. Play is alternated between teams until all cards are played.

<u>Game gear:</u> secret word cards placed in a pile face down. Any 30-second timer.

<u>Game time</u>: ~ 20 minutes.

Seasonal Festivities

Chapter 14

Halloween Party 411

The best time of the year for parties is the fall and winter. The season kicks off with festive and hauntingly fun Halloween parties! Halloween is a festive holiday annually celebrated on October 31st. The most likely origin of Halloween is the Celtic festival of *Samhain* and the Christian *All Saints Day*. The Celtics started the tradition of dressing in costume on Halloween to ward off spirits passing between this world and the spirit world. The 16th century name Halloween is derived from the Scottish *All Hallows Eve*, which is the night before All Hallows Day (i.e. All Saints Day). All Saints Day is November 1st and is a Christian holiday honoring the Saints.

Modern day Halloween is a worldly tradition filled with fun customs such as trick or treating, watching scary movies, pulling pranks, haunted hayrides, murder mystery parties, pumpkin carving, Halloween dance parties, and of course the nefarious spine-tingling haunted houses. The most popular type of Halloween party is a Murder Mystery Party but by no means is the only type of party!

Have a Halloween dinner party, set up a haunted house in your home or rent a party room to make a haunted house, host a dance party, or simply invite your friends over to watch scary movies and play fun Halloween party games!

Halloween themed food is definitely part of your party decor! Make sure to do this right and display all of your yummy and festive treats on a spooky Halloween-themed buffet table! Make fun note cards and place in front of each dish to show the ghoulish names to your guests!

HALLOWEEN PARTY IDEAS:

Halloween parties can be hosted at home, at a restaurant private dining room, a hotel ballroom, a hotel suite or even rent a limousine or a party boat! Wherever you choose to have your party, be sure to have loads of spooky décor and plan out a fun night of activities. The following are some suggested types of Halloween parties. However, use any of the party themes and games in this book and make your own combination for the perfect Halloween party.

Costume Ball:

If you have the budget, this is the way to go. Everybody should host or at least attend one costume and /or masquerade ball in their lifetime! Costume Balls are typically hosted in a hotel ballroom but by all means…have one at home. A Ball is more formal than traditional costume house parties, however, and your guests will be expected to *go all out* for their costumes. The host will be expected to make a more formal style party ambiance as well. (Costume and Masquerade Balls are discussed in more detail in Chapters 6 and 8.)

There is a costume ball murder mystery party available for purchase on My Mystery Party (Walgrave Astoria Costume Ball Murder Mystery) on www.mymysteryparty.com.

Costume Party:

A scaled down and much more laid back version of the Costume Ball is the traditional costume party. Host these anywhere but are normally hosted at home. You've probably already hosted tons of these shindigs so make sure you're not doing the same ole' thing you've done every year. Switch it up as far as the décor and the night's activities go. If you have always done party games, try a dance party. If you've switched off those two types of parties, maybe try a murder mystery party or scavenger hunt challenge. There are endless possibilities so be creative! Your guests should never expect what will come next. The only common theme you should have is the costume contest. If your guests have gone to trouble to assemble a costume then the best costume should be awarded!

Masquerade Ball:

The same traditions apply like the Costume Ball and everybody should experience a Masquerade and /or Costume Ball at least once. To host a traditional Masquerade Ball, you would instruct your guests to wear traditional Masquerade Ball attire such as a Victorian floor length gown and suits and elegant Venetian style masquerade masks. However, feel free to host a less formal version in your home! Host a masquerade party and ask your guests to wear masks and normal attire! (Costume and Masquerade Balls are discussed in more detail in Chapters 6 and 8.)

There is a masquerade ball murder mystery party available for purchase on My Mystery Party (Abby Manor Masquerade Ball Murder Mystery) on www.mymysteryparty.com.

Zombie Party:

Why not have a more themed version of a costume party? Instruct all of your guests to come as zombies! Decorate the party area as if it is a rundown town taken over by zombies, such as from the novel *Chronicles of Zombie Town.*

At your Halloween buffet table, don't forget the brains (i.e. Jell-O / gelatin recipes can be found on the internet), assorted fingers, and ghoulish head centerpieces as décor. There is a zombie themed murder mystery on My Mystery Party (Chronicles of Zombie Town Murder Mystery) as well! (Zombie/Vampire parties are discussed in more detail in Chapters 6 and 8.)

Monster Party:

Here's another alternative to a themed costume party – have your guests dress up as their favorite monster! Decorate the party area as if it is a secret underground cave for monsters. For the buffet centerpieces, grab some various monster masks and make stuffed heads to put them on. There is a monster themed murder mystery (Daunting Night of Monsters and Murder) on My Mystery Party as well!

Haunted House Party:

The Haunted House party is an exciting crowd pleaser! If your home is large enough a route can be created for your guests to travel through without breaking everything you own, why not set up a few rooms as a haunted house? Recruit some close friends to play the roles of the various rooms in the haunted house such as an alien invasion room, a Phantom of the Opera room, a serial killer room, a Bride of Frankenstein room, etc. When the guests arrive, have someone dressed as a grim reaper escort them through the show and into the party room. Be sure to have someone waiting at the front to put the guests in a line in case you have a lot of guests show up at once. The guests should go one-by-one in a home haunted house. If you allow multiple guests at once there will be more accidents as far as breaking pictures, sheetrock, etc. Remember – you live there!

Once everybody gets into the party room, ask if anyone would like to go through again – why not? You went to a lot of trouble to create the Haunted House! Then, the guests can relax and have fun with party games, dancing or whatever activities you have planned for them next.

There is a Haunted House themed murder mystery party available (*Homicide on Halloween at the Chamber of Screams*) on the My Mystery Party web site.

Murder Mystery Party:

Halloween is the #1 time for murder mystery parties. At least one Halloween in your lifetime, you have to host a murder mystery party! However, be careful as they can be quite addicting! (Chapter 10 discusses Murder Mystery Parties in further detail.)

Limousine Halloween Party:

Plenty of establishments around town will be hosting Halloween celebrations on Halloween night. Gather up your friends dressed in their best Halloween costumes and rent a limousine! Split the cost as long as you disclose this up front on the invitation!

In advance of your party, do an internet search and create the perfect schedule to hit as many of the costume contests and other fun Halloween festivities around town. First, go to dinner in your Halloween costumes! To get the party started, give a detailed itinerary to your limo driver and party on!

Party Game Extravaganza:

Either with or without costumes and in any location - have the primary focus of the night center around Halloween party games. You can't go wrong with Halloween party games and there are many games to choose from in the Party Game section of this book. There is a dedicated Halloween party section (Chapter 29) but any of the party games can be transformed into a Halloween themed game by sticking the word monster, spooky or scary in front of the title!

For a Halloween party game extravaganza, decorate your home in spooky décor, ask your guests to dress up in their best Halloween costumes, serve fun party food and have a slew of games ready to go! Have an itinerary of the night's fun or allow the guests to draw from a hat for the next party game. Prizes are expected, but always optional. You can pick up cheap prizes anywhere such as the grocery store, local party store, etc. by going to the Halloween aisle.

Halloween Slumber Party:

Halloween slumber parties (aka: sleepovers) can be a real blast! A slumber party should start around dinnertime and end the next morning after breakfast. Follow our fun suggestions for sleepovers (Chapter 11) but put a Halloween twist on everything.

Once the late night hours arrive, it is time for telling ghost stories and watching scary movies. The point of a Halloween slumber party is to get scared and try not to go to sleep!

It's probably best not to require your guests to dress in costume as they'll be sleeping over and some guests might require a shower to get their makeup off or have expensive costumes that need special care. Therefore, ask that they come in the most festive Halloween pajamas!

Scavenger Hunt Party:

Scavenger hunt parties are high energy and very challenging events.   Do an about town hunt, a neighborhood hunt or a building hunt. (Chapter 6 covers Scavenger Hunts in further detail). My Mystery Party carries all varieties of Halloween Scavenger Hunts – both about town and on foot hunts made for the Halloween season and Halloween night.

Haunted House / Hayride Party:

If you have a haunted house and / or haunted hayride in your area, you have to do it at least once! Get your guests together and make a night out of hitting the haunted hot spots around town! With this type of party, you *must* disclose what you are planning to do on the invitation. Some guests do not enjoy being scared and will not want to endure a night of peer pressure from the other guests!

Commercial haunted houses & hayrides are definitely not for everybody and peer pressure is not good at a party! In fact, it can cause massive hard feelings against you as the host. Extend the invite – but don't force it with anyone.

Halloween Camp Out:

Contact your local campground and reserve a camping site. Nothing is spookier than being in the open nature around a campfire on Halloween night! Tell ghost stories by the fire as you roast marshmallows!

Adult supervision is essential and mandatory with kids around a campfire and in the great outdoors in general so have a good adult to child ratio if you have a party with minors at a campsite.

Backyard Tent Party:

Can't rent a campsite? Well, don't do the bonfire but still set up a tent and grab some flashlights to tell ghost stories all night in the backyard!

Halloween Casino Party:

Have your guests all come as monsters, zombies, or witches and host a Casino Night! (Chapter 8 covers casino parties in further detail.)

HOMEMADE DECORATING PROJECTS:

Cardboard / Styrofoam Tombstones:

Now is the time to use those old boxes in the garage! Transform cardboard into a variety of cool things for Halloween. For tombstones, cut out tombstone shapes and paint them a deep gray color by using spray paint or any other type of paint. If you're a budding artist, shade the stone and paint the weathered cracks, making it look authentic!   No Halloween tombstone is complete without a whimsical saying on the front (i.e. *Here Lies Uncle Buck. He Lost a Battle with a Mack Truck*) on the front with black paint, allow thorough drying and tape them to or set against the wall for a fun cemetery effect.

If you desire a more authentic, 3D effect with your tombstone or want to create a mock cemetery instead of propping or taping to a wall, switch to Styrofoam instead of cardboard. You'll want to make a double layer and glue them together but put in metal or wooden stakes in between prior to gluing. If you put a furrow into one of the layers on the inside, you'll have a nice place for these stakes to lie and you won't have any bulging once glued. First, allow the glue to dry and then paint as you did with the cardboard. Stake these tombstones into your front lawn and make a cemetery. To create an ultra eerie scene, add dry ice in inconspicuous places! (Follow all directions for handling and using dry ice.)

Cardboard Flying Bats:

Using cardboard, cut out bat shapes of all sizes, paint them black and hang from the ceiling with translucent fishing wire in various heights. Glue on googly-eyes (pick some up at any craft store) for a fun effect!

Flying Trash Bag Ghosts:

Purchase white trash bags, paper towels, markers, translucent fishing wire. Stuff the bottom of a trash bag with a few paper towels and tie at the neck with the fishing wire. Draw two hollow eyes on the face region and be careful not to tear the bag. Attach the fishing wire to the neck and hang from the ceiling.

Spider Webs:

White or gray yarn or crepe paper are both good for creating giant spider webs. Only do this if you already have these items, as the store bought spider webbing is very cheap and easy to use...and will look more authentic. If you had a bunch of cotton balls or cotton batting, also use this as spider webs by stretching it out carefully.

Scary Trick or Treater Greeter:

Grab your old clothes and stuff them with other old clothes. Put on a pair of shoes with stuffed socks and create a trash bag head by stuffing it with old clothes or paper towels. Put a wig on the trash bag head and slap on a scary mask (i.e. an old grandpa with a scary face). Sit this spooky effigy on your porch in an old rocking chair to greet the Halloween Night trick or treaters!

Alien Eggs:

Make a small hole in the top, bottom of an egg by using a small pin, and with your middle finger and thumb, slowly and carefully spin the pin back and forth. Gently blow out the egg's contents by blowing on the top and allowing the contents to come out of the bottom (make scrambled eggs – why not?) Then, very carefully paint the shells green, gold or silver and place them in a nest on your porch. Make a nest out of anything (twigs, hay, etc.) – just like birds do! Put a fun sign next to the nest that says...*Beware! Alien Eggs: Scheduled to Hatch on Halloween Night!*
As an alternative, paint plastic Easter Eggs.

Shrunken Apple Voodoo Heads:

Shrunken voodoo heads are a staple as far as easy to make Halloween décor is concerned! You'll need to start this project at least two weeks prior to Halloween! Purchase as many apples as you want heads, a few grains of rice, one cup of lemon juice and a few teaspoons of salt. Peal the apple, coat with lemon juice and sprinkle with salt. This will prevent oxidation and browning of the exposed apple flesh.

Carefully, with a paring knife or other tool of your choosing, carve the face: eye sockets, a nose, a mouth and if you wish, make some ears. No details are necessary (i.e. dimples, wrinkles, etc.) as when the apple heads dry out – you won't see them.

Use the rice grains as teeth by sticking them into the apple head's mouth gently. Make some heads have missing teeth, of course! Pick up some cloves or other material for the eyes but this is optional, as they'll look fabulously wicked as simple apple heads!

Place the apples, preferably on a wire rack so the bottom can dry out properly, in a warm, dry location for about two weeks.

Covered Furniture:

What comes to mind when you think: old, abandoned haunted mansion? White sheets on the furniture! Hey, for your Halloween party, this décor will double as furniture protection - so throw some white sheets over your furniture for an old, abandoned and massively haunted mansion ambiance!

Shadow Silhouettes:

Purchase some large, black butcher paper or black plastic from a home goods store. Cut out silhouettes of eerie Halloween shapes such as bats, cats, witches or even normal people. Tape the silhouettes to the wall or windows and they will look like shadows!

Acorn, Marble, Rock Pumpkins:

Do you have extra acorns, marbles or round rocks lying around? Grab some orange and black acrylic paint and paint fun pumpkin creations on them. Allow them to dry and then assemble them in a small, decorative glass dish for a fun pumpkin-inspired piece.

Hatching Snake Egg:

Blow up a white 8" balloon about 2/3 filled with air. Use paper mache or you can use an Elmer's glue and water mixture (~1:1 ratio) with gauze to cover most of the balloon. Use a bowl to prop the balloon as you cover it with the soaked strips of gauze, leaving a section at the top that is jagged and peeled back to put your newly hatched snake. While the opening is drying is a great time to start the peeling back effect. You'll need to keep working on it as it dries to get the full effect of the shell break.

When the paper mache egg is completely dry, pop the balloon and remove it. Paint the egg in a snake egg pattern (do a web search for images of snake eggs) and purchase a large plastic or toy stuffed snake and assemble the snake inside of the egg as it is hatching. This will terrify your guests! Make an entire nest of these creepy hatchers!

As an alternative to snakes, use dinosaurs or other creepy crawlies.

Hatching Spider Cocoon:

Purchase a large toy tarantula or black widow and set aside.

Blow up a white 8" balloon about 1/4 of the way with air. Make an Elmer's glue and water mixture (~1:1) and dip strips of white gauze into the mixture. Wrap the balloon with the strips and allow drying. As an alternative, use paper mache for this project but white gauze will look more as enlarged spider silk fibers and you won't have to paint it afterward.

Use a bowl to prop the balloon as you cover it in the gauze. At the point of the balloon tie, leave an opening and do not put any gauze. Also, leave a few more gaps in random places on the balloon and this is where you will attach the spider chains after it dries completely.

Using translucent fishing wire, string together various lengths of small plastic spiders (purchase at any local party store) by tying the wire to a leg and adding more spiders every 2-3 inches.

When the gauze egg sack is completely dry, pop the balloon and remove the balloon. Use one of the open holes to insert fishing line to hang from the ceiling.

Attach the spider chains to the top by tying to the fishing line at the base (top) of the egg sack. They will cascade down and over the egg sack as if they are newly hatched. Attach the mother spider to the top of the egg cocoon with glue. Arrange her to look down upon her hatching spiders *and* at your guests below. Allow the baby spiders to dangle beyond the egg sack as if they are falling to the ground. Your guests will certainly avoid this scary sight!

Mini Pumpkin Black Cats:

Purchase mini pumpkins (any color), black paint, white paint, green paint, felt, small boa and tooth picks. Paint the pumpkins black and allow drying. Paint festive cat eyes on the front of the pumpkin. Cut out small triangles of felt for the ears and glue a black-painted toothpick onto the back of the felt with the pointed side of the toothpick down.

Insert the ears with the toothpick in the appropriate locations on top of the pumpkin. Cut the mini boa for the tail (as long as you want it to be) and glue another painted toothpick to the string in the middle of the boa (or tie this onto the toothpick if the string is small enough. Then, insert the toothpick for the tail in the back.

Creeptastic Votives:

Purchase clear votive holders, black paint, green (or red) paint, and a small paintbrush. Paint the votive holder black but do not paint random sets of holes for eyes. Once the paint dries, add a clear coat over the votive for a shiny and finished effect. Where your eyes (blank holes with the glass exposed) are located, draw tiny green irises and a black (or red) pupil with the paint and the small brush. Do not take up the entire exposed glass, as you need the light to shine through and cast eerie eyeball shapes onto the wall! Allow to dry, place a votive candle inside and enjoy your creepy ambiance.

Ghostly Chair Covers:

Using white pillowcases or white sheets and if you have high back chairs around a dining table, create ghostly seats! Slip the pillowcase (or sheet) around the high back chair and glue felt eyes (long, oval shapes) and a misshaped mouth. With gauze, fasten either the sheet or the pillowcase at the base of the chair and tie loose knots to secure it at the bottom. Allow the gauze to drape to the floor. Add multiple strands of gauze to make a jagged, flowing effect. For a cutesier ghost, make them smile and substitute the gauze for white tulle.

STORE-BOUGHT DÉCOR SUGGESTIONS:

Hit the Sales:
Many stores will start sales one week prior to Halloween. In the case of a party, this might be the economical way to go. However, you won't get to enjoy the full month of October with your eerie delights or pick from the full selection! Good news is you will have these items for next year! Remember to hit the after Halloween sales! If you wait until after Halloween to hit the sales, you should be first in the door as these aisles can clear out within one day!

Lighting:
Change out your porch light with a black light for a fun effect on Halloween night. For an inside party, lighting should be low. Change out the bulbs for low watt bulbs or darker / colored bulbs.

For adult parties, switch out for candles but follow safety guidelines with candles! Candles at parties can be hazardous if not handled appropriately. One guest throws their coat on top of a tabletop candle…you have a *party killer* on your hands! There are fake candles that run on batteries available for purchase at most home décor stores and party stores that look very realistic. Using these fake candles is a highly suggested alternative! Plus for economy's sake think of a few cheap batteries versus repurchasing candles each year – *which do you prefer?*

Ghoul Head Buffet Centerpieces:
On your Halloween buffet table, create a few gruesome heads looking at the food. Not very appetizing, but Halloween shouldn't be *appealing* – it should be scary and part of the décor! However, the food should taste fantastic. Remember this is a party and your guests need something to munch on that is delicious!

Create a gruesome head centerpiece by putting a Halloween mask on a Styrofoam wig head. As an alternative, use modeling clay over the Styrofoam wig head with acrylic paints, a wig and marbles for eyes. Put a fake blood pool around the neck of the head as if it burst through the table. Add stitches to the face, fake blood and scabs (see homemade effects below). If you don't have a Styrofoam wig head, stuff a trash bag with paper towels. It might take a bit to get the right shape, however. However, either way…oooooh, scary buffet!

If you have the budget and have a willing participant, have a person sit with their head poking through the buffet table. You will need a disposable table to insert a hole large enough for the person's head to get through very comfortably. Then, drape the tablecloth over, with a corresponding hole cut out for their head to poke through comfortably. You are set - a *real live* ghoul head on your buffet table! Have them ghoul-ify their face, of course! Give this person a beanbag chair or some form of support under the table if you expect them to remain with their head through the buffet service.

Again, the party menu as well as the buffet table *is* part of the décor. Check out our menu suggestions, prepare spooky food, and label it with gothic-inspired cards with the eerie names.

Crime Scene:

Purchase authentic crime scene barrier tape, preferably authentic and not the cheap party tape. Rope off an area close to your porch to warn trick or treaters and party guests not to contaminate the crime scene. Why not grab some chalk and make a body outline and add to the gruesome scene?
(The My Mystery Party Mystery Prop Emporium sells authentic crime scene barrier tape at a reasonable price:
http://www.mymysteryparty.com/crscbata.html).

Porch Frights:

Decorating the porch / front walkway is imperative as it sets the mood for your party. If you don't decorate here, your guests will wonder if they have the correct date and house address! This also gives a fun atmosphere for the trick or treaters on Halloween Night.

Line the walkway with illuminated carved pumpkins as you don't want to scare them right away! Use fun pumpkins lining the walkway as a lure to get your guests and trick or treaters to the spooky front porch.

As outlined above, stage a stuffed dummy with a mask and / or an alien egg or hatching snake nest and hanging spider-hatching cocoon right by the front door. A smoking carved pumpkin (by placing dry ice and a flash light inside) is an awesome eerie effect.

The smoking witch's cauldron never gets old. Place a flashlight with a colored piece of saran wrap on the end (preferably green or red) and dry ice inside of the cauldron. Tape the flashlight away from the dry ice so it doesn't freeze and ruin the flashlight. Direct the flashlight beam towards the back of the cauldron so the indirect light will shine through the top.

PUMPKIN CARVING:

First, let's discuss how to carve a pumpkin! Either at the pumpkin patch or the local grocery store – shop for and choose your pumpkin carefully! Select the freshest, most colorful pumpkin in a nice, rounded shape or if you prefer tall and oval – go for it!

With a thin marker, draw a circle around the stem. Make sure it is large enough to fit your hand through it. Carefully cut through your guide with a pumpkin-carving tool with extra caution as to not cut your hand (these are usually available in the grocery stores by the pumpkins or at pumpkin patches).

Remove the stem and scoop out the pulp and seeds from inside with a large spoon! Trim your stem cap of the extra seeds and pulp that is hanging on. The less pumpkin flesh you have to rot, the better off you'll be!

Either using a template (download free templates from the web) or using a free hand template, draw a pattern for the face (or other Halloween shape). If you do a face, make the eyes and nose large enough so cut all of the way through safely and remove the pieces. With great care and caution, follow your pattern all the way through. From the inside, gently pop out the pieces to the front and discard them.

On Halloween night, place some dry ice (adult supervision as dry ice damages the skin and can asphyxiate if used in a small space) and a flashlight inside. Again, dry ice in an enclosed area can be dangerous as it liberates carbon dioxide constantly so try to place it in large open spaces. As an alternative light source, a simple votive candle will do for an eerie glow!

You always have the alternative of not carving the pumpkin to make it last longer. Paint a cute or scary face with acrylic paints for a fun, festive Halloween effect.

HALLOWEEN COSTUME IDEAS:

The following is a list of possible costume ideas for you and your guests. Stray from the norm of what you typically select for a costume and be something entirely different this year!

Most of the following costumes are available for purchase in various costume stores but with a touch of creativity, you can make your own costume for a lot less money!

Magician	Pizza Man	Witch
Medic	Zoo Keeper	Vampire
Soccer Player	Sumo Wrestler	Gravedigger
Football Player	Paperboy/Girl	Pilot
Baseball Player	Custodian	Goblin
Golfer	Repairman	Grim Reaper
Swimmer	Chimney Sweep	Devil
Hair Dresser	Construction Worker	Superhero
Artist	Bullfighter	Wolf Man
Nun	Car Hop	Corpse
Stadium Vendor	Referee (Blind)	Mad Butcher
Chef	Supermodel	Dark Angel
Swat Team	Photographer	Witch Doctor
Monk	Show Girl	Lizzie Borden
Painter	Detective	Bat
Secret Service	Flight Attendant	Skeleton
Carpenter	Drag Racer	Mummy
Teacher	Fisherman	The Munsters Cast
Lumberjack	Animal *(Various)*	Car Salesman
Salesman	Insect *(Various)*	Zombie
Gondolier	Tarantula	Beast
Waiter	Black Widow	Medusa
Proctologist (Dr. Ben	Psychic	Cancan Dancer
Dover)	Warlock	Geisha Girl
Executioner	Shopper	Hillbilly
Guitar Hero	Belly Dancer	Aerobics Girl
Harem Girl	Bride / Groom	Mime
Biker	Protester	Hula Dancer
Clown	Gypsy	Skateboarder
Hiker	'80s Valley Girl	Bandito

Gambler	Gymnast	Alien
Beauty Queen	Bank Robber	Emo Teen
Jailbird	Shiek	Lion Tamer
Scarecrow	Bowler	Mr. Monopoly
Rap Artist	Olympian	Juan Valdez
Prom Queen	Boy Scout	Ice Skater
Morton Salt Girl	Army Soldier	Breakdancer
Old Lady	'50s Greaser	Snowboarder
Dead Prom Queen	'20s Mobster	French Maid
Eskimo	'60s Mod	Fraggle Rock Cast
Barbie	'70s Disco	Addams Family Cast
Jersey Shore Cast	'80s Breaker	Wild West Cowboy/girl
Greek Goddess	Sesame Street	Boxer
Charlie's Angels	Potato Head	Ghostbuster Movie Cast
Unicorn	Spartan	Matador
'50s Sock Hopper	Butler	Indians
Welder	Plastic Surgeon *(Carry*	Raggedy Ann
Coal Miner	*Plastic Wrap)*	Absent Minded Professor
Lifeguard	Movie Characters	Fictional Characters
Maid	Weatherman	*(Various)*
Spy	Priest	Dead Man Walking
Mad Scientist	Fireman/Woman	Video Game Character
Train Conductor	Judge	*(Various)*
Veterinarian	Mechanic	Martial Artist *(Ninja)*
Dj	Undercover Cop	Marathon Runner
Mario	Ballerina	Hunter
Can-Can Dancer	Sheriff / Cop	Wendy From The
G.I. Joe/Jane	Construction Worker	Restaurant 'Wendys'
Dead Prom Queen	Cartoon Characters	Crash Test Dummy
Disney Characters	*(Various)*	Baby
'20s Flapper	The Jetsons Cast	Boxer Ring Girl
Smurf	Muppets Cast	Chiquita Banana Lady
Wizard Of Oz Cast	Glamorous Celebrity	Girl Scout
Mermaid	Zebra	Reality TV Star

EASY HOMEMADE COSTUMES:

A few cheap accessories might need to be purchased from your local party store to make these costume creations complete.

Computer Nerd:

You'll need a very small short-sleeved button up shirt. Button it to the top button and wear a bright colored bowtie. Fasten suspenders to pants. The pants must be too short (i.e. high waters) with white tube socks and black dress shoes showing. Pull pants up high and fasten with the most un-cool belt you can find. Add a pocket protector with maybe a handy protractor, glasses with a taped bridge and apply a bunch of fake pimples on your face. Grease your hair back to look extra nerdilicious.

Celebrity:

You've probably been to prom, a dance, or some other formal or semi-formal event before. Take out the outfit, dust it off and be as glamorous as you can be (i.e. sunglasses, hair styled glamorous, ultra-glamorous makeup, etc.) for an easy Hollywood Celebrity costume.   Carry a sharpie marker for autographs.

Rock Star:

Select a brightly colored, tight-fitting shirt. Jeans (or shiny spandex leggings if you have them) and tons of bandanas. Tie the bandanas in your hair, around your wrists, and legs. Boots are great. Tease your hair as high as it will go or wear an out of control longhaired wig.

Tourist:

Hawaiian shirt, zinc oxide on the nose, sunglasses, large-rim hat, Bermuda shorts and flip-flops! Grab a map, fruity cocktail with an umbrella straw and a camera as optional props!

Crazed Groupie Stalker:

Wear trendy clothing as you are trying to get the eye of the Celebrity you are stalking. Have a fake tattoo of the celebrity's signature anywhere on your body. Carry tons of pictures, posters and other memorabilia of your iconic celebrity and be sure to show and tell!

Pirate:

Tie a bandana around your head with the long pieces to one side. If you have boots, great, and if not, grab a piece of black fabric and wrap it around tight-fitting pants on top of black shoes. Wear a loose fitting shirt with a vest (make a vest by cutting an old shirt) and wrap a piece of fabric (or two) around your waist as a belt.

Make a pirate eye patch out of felt and a piece of elastic. Wear one hoop earring on the side opposite the long bandana tails. If you happen to have a stuffed parrot, attach it to your shoulder with Velcro or attach a piece of dark, long fabric to it and tie it around your shoulder. Get ready to say *Arrrrrrrr!*

Cowboy:

Grab some jeans, western (or flannel plaid) shirt, cowboy boots with a Western belt and large belt buckle. Cowboy hat, lasso and a bandana tied around the neck make great touches. Chaps and a vest (leather preferably) are perfect!

Traveling Hobo:

Ragged, tattered clothing. If you're done with some clothes that aren't good enough to go to Goodwill or other charity, rip them up a bit and add dirty blotches on them. Dirt smudges on the face (use eye shadow). A stick with a bandana tied on the end and stuffed with a fake can of food.

Zombie:

Ragged, tattered clothing. Purchase a zombie makeup kit from the local party store. Using white makeup as a base, cover your exposed skin. Add green and blue eye shadow (or face makeup) on top in random patterns and add tons of fake scabs and scars. Add blood streaks wherever you feel like it.

HOMEMADE CREATIONS FOR COSTUME FX:

Fake Blood (Non-toxic):

2.5 cups of corn syrup
~10 drops of red food coloring
~1-2 drops of blue food coloring
3/4 cup of water
Chocolate syrup to thicken, deepen color
How to prepare: mix the ingredients above and allow thickening at room temperature. This fake blood is non-toxic but *very sticky!* If you get it into your hair, be careful and wash it out thoroughly! Clean the skin before applying the fake blood with skin cleanser. Vampires and zombies – take a swig of this in your mouth and allow to gently seep (i.e. drool) out of your mouth for a cool effect. Wait at least 10 minutes before touching the blood tracks.

Because of the food coloring and chocolate syrup this can stain white fabric, carpet, furniture, etc. so remain in a protected area while drying thoroughly!

Fake Burned Skin:

Liquid latex (theatrical supply store) or other type of adhesive safe for the skin
Fake blood (from above or other fake blood)
Cotton balls or cotton quilt batting
Black face / body makeup
How to prepare: clean the skin where you want to apply your fake burn with skin cleanser. Adhere long strands of cotton to the skin with liquid latex or other skin adhesive according to the directions. Continue to apply the cotton strands in an irregular, criss-crossing fashion until a large enough burn area is achieved. Allow the adhesive to dry completely. Pour fake blood over the burn and again, allow drying. With a makeup applicator, apply the black makeup in random splotches, especially in the raised areas to simulate charred skin.

Fake Scabs:

1 cup gelatin
1 cup water
Fake blood (from above or other fake blood)
How to prepare: clean the skin where you want to apply the scabs with skin cleanser. Prepare the gelatin per the package instructions. Allow the gelatin to cool until warm but not solidified. Testing the temperature first to be sure you do not burn the skin, apply the warm gelatin on the cleaned area of skin before it gets to room temperature. The gelatin will solidify quickly once it gets on the skin in a thin layer. Color the scabs with the fake blood.

Bruises:

Red, burgundy and purple crème theatrical (or cosmetic) makeup
Makeup sponge
Powder (either compressed makeup or baby powder)

How to prepare: clean the skin where you want to apply the bruises with skin cleanser. Using the makeup sponge, start with the red crème and make the outline of the bruise. Don't apply too much at once, keep it light and smooth and pat the makeup very lightly for even coverage. In the case of a bruise – less is more – you want very bare coverage! You want the skin to show through the makeup.

Next, use the burgundy and lightly go over most of the red section. Again, you want the red makeup and the skin to show through. Then, do the darkest purple color in an area of the bruise – again, doing it light enough to where the red, burgundy and the skin shows through.

Last, set with powder! You always have to powder crème-based makeup or it will wipe off, sweat off and look disgusting in mere moments!

Chapter 15

Winter Holiday Parties

The most expensive and elaborate parties are traditionally hosted in the fall and winter seasons. Corporations tend to host their end of the year banquets, galas and balls in the winter season. Friends and families host holiday parties and of course, everybody in the world celebrates New Year's Eve!

Chances are that this year, you either will host or be invited to an event this winter holiday season.

Non-denominational Holiday Parties:

With most countries, especially in the U.S., which is a melting pot of various cultures and traditions, non-denominational holiday parties are on the rise. Especially if hosted by a corporation that is tasked with keeping everything on an even playing field for all employees. You don't want to host a Christmas party for your employees when you might have a large portion of employees who do not celebrate Christmas. Put yourself in their shoes and see how you'd feel if you were asked to attend a party celebrating a holiday you never celebrated. It would feel awkward so don't expect a multi-cultural group of people to all appreciate a holiday party centered around a religion and / or traditions they are not all a part of. Be sensitive to everybody's traditions, culture and religion when you are hosting a non-denominational party so leave any specific religious holiday traditions out of the plans.

On the other hand, if you elect one representative from each religion, combine all religions and traditions and have a multi-denominational party. However, do not leave anyone out! You'll need to poll your employees first to be sure everybody's religion and customs are represented equally. For ease, let's focus on the non-denominational events.

First, you have the décor to consider. Going with a winter theme is safe as everybody experiences winter. Whether it is cold or not, you have those months and certain things are associated with December and January even in hot climates. White and gold are safe alternatives but can look a tad too much like a wedding. If you add an accent color such as green to symbolize the evergreen trees of winter, that's very elegant and stately looking. Avoid red and green or the silver and blue combinations as those lean toward specific holidays.

Select any type of party theme for a non-denominational holiday party. Celebrate the season as a whole and not the holiday. Focus on the reason for your event. If it is for a company party, then focus on the company's accomplishments and type out the positive events of the year on stately cards and place them around the room for the guests to view. The décor should be festive with loads of winter flowers, tulle and ribbon and of course, never forget the candles.

Christmas Parties:

If everybody on your guest list celebrates Christmas, by all means, host a Christmas-themed celebration for your company, family and / or friends. Christmas parties can range from renting an elegant hotel ballroom for thousands of dollars to a simple home party in the living room. All of the same rules for guest lists and invitations apply to Christmas parties.

Make centerpieces and buffet displays out of festive evergreen twigs and chestnuts with red and green tulle and satin-wired ribbons. It is preferred to use wired ribbons so you can shape the perfect holiday bows.

Create an archway with a large sprig of mistletoe hanging from a satin ribbon about seven feet from the floor. Arrange holly bouquets throughout the room with festive ribbons tied around them. With the holly bouquets since they are smaller, use smaller, unwired satin ribbon with long ties to drape down.

Play a festive Christmas party CD in the background such as *Party of 2's Ultimate Merry Christmas Dance Party Mix.* For more elegant affairs, purchase a classical mix of the traditional Christmas songs and play softly as guests arrive and mingle.

If there are kids invited to the party, consider hiring a Santa Claus performer to take their wishes and dreams for Christmas this year. You will need to create a backdrop and rent/make a chair suitable for Santa to sit in to speak to the children. Call the local petting zoo companies to see if they have reindeer available to visit your event for an hour or two for an ultra-festive addition!

Have a Secret Santa gift exchange! Prior to your party and once you have the RSVP'd guests, draw names out of a hat and assign the guests to purchase one gift at a minimum and maximum price range (i.e. $15.00 to $20.00). They are to bring the gift to the party and sneak it on a table at the front. Have a gift opening ceremony during your event and watch the surprised faces glow! Be careful with guests who RSVP and then later do not show up. It might be wise to have a backup present or two in case this happens!

Host a murder mystery party or non-murder mystery party alternative (there are tons of Christmas themes on My Mystery Party at www.mymysteryparty.com) or host a Scavenger Hunt party (again, available for download or as a boxed set on My Mystery Party).

Another alternative is to hire a DJ and have dinner and dancing or play fun party games. Alter the party games in this book to fit your Christmas theme.

For an ultra-subdued party, have your guests come in their favorite pajamas and watch the movie Polar Express (or other Christmas movie) while enjoying eggnog and hot cocoa by the fire!

New Year's Eve Parties:

Nothing tops off a party like screaming *Happy New Year!* Besides weddings, a New Year's Eve party is most likely one of the more expensive parties you will ever attend or host. This is the time of the year to be elaborate if you are going to have a sophisticated and costly event!

Masquerade Balls, Costume Balls as well as Black Tie Affairs and other High Society Galas and Charity events are the rave on New Year's Eve. Restaurants spike up their menu prices and typically offer some form of entertainment for the night as well.

When hosting your own New Year's party, play a festive party mix CD in the background as the guests arrive. Decorate the party room in festive colors. Traditional New Year's Eve colors are silver, black and purple but modern times dictate *anything goes.* Without the sound playing until it's time, have the closest time zone to New Year's television station on (if you are not in it) on the television screen so your guests can watch the celebrations in advance of your time zone as well as any celebrations after your time zone.

For a few laughs, hire a performer to play the role of Father Time for your event for a hilarious and fun addition to the night.

For the midnight countdown, hold up balloons with netting on the ceiling for your own personal ball drop when the clock strikes midnight! Moreover, get the champagne glasses ready for a toast at midnight! For good luck for the upcoming year, give your guests a shot of black-eyed peas and cabbage! Black-eyed peas are for overall health and good luck and cabbage is for luck with money! Of course, there are variations to this tradition all over the place!

Murder Mystery Parties are always a hit for New Year's Eve. As with all seasons, My Mystery Party at www.MyMysteryParyt.com has a great selection of New Year's Eve games.

Chapter 16

Other Seasonal Holiday Parties

Just because the fall season is filled with Halloween followed by the unmatched winter holiday festivities doesn't mean the party is over for the year! There are plenty of reasons to celebrate throughout the year! Let's take these events in approximate order (as some events change dates such as Mardi gras) throughout the year.

Mardi Gras Parties:

This is the party of the year in old New Orleans! However, don't forget that Mardi gras certainly didn't originate in New Orleans and is celebrated nearly across the globe! It's a festive time to enjoy life, party, and have a great time!

The Carnival season commences on January 6th, which is also referred to as the Twelfth Night. Carnival season ends on Fat Tuesday, which is the official Mardi gras. This is the day before Ash Wednesday, which is the first day of Lent. Lent is seven Wednesdays prior to Easter.

A Krewe is a general term for all of the Carnival organizations in New Orleans and was coined by the original Mystic Krewe of Comus - the first Carnival secret society formed in 1857. Each Krewe is a private society and hosts individual celebrations throughout the Carnival season. Each Krewe designs and creates a parade float for the parade in a unique theme that changes each year.

If you are having a Mardi gras celebration, have any type of Mardi gras celebrations ranging from informal home parties to a formal Bal Masque in a hotel ballroom. A Bal Masque is a traditional Ball held for the Krewe and their guests within the theme they have chosen for the year. The royalty of the Krewes are presented during the Ball that includes dramatic performances, dancing, great food and fun music.

Mardi gras décor is flamboyant and is in three basic colors: green, purple and gold. The more glitter, feathers and beads you have, the better. Throw in a few fun masks and you've got a party started!

Consider playing fun party games with beads as prizes, host a masquerade ball but with a Mardi gras theme, do a murder mystery party, a scavenger hunt party or even do a fun movie night. The underlying theme of a Mardi gras party is to celebrate life and have fun!

My Mystery Party has both murder mystery parties and scavenger hunts in Mardi gras themes available for purchase as instant downloads or boxed sets.

Valentine's Day Parties:

Valentine's Day is meant to be a day to celebrate love. Lovers should unite to appreciate what they have in each other and to show each other how much they are in love. The modern day Valentine's Day is a two-way street as both males and females are expected to surprise each other with a thoughtful gift. Valentine's Day gifts don't have to be expensive diamonds or watches as you can show your love by a dozen roses or even make your loved one a card. Sometimes the little things mean the most!

However, what if you want to celebrate with friends and family? Well, that's fine! Host a Valentine's Day celebration with friends and family that are couples! Go to a nice dinner, invite everyone back to your home, and watch a romantic movie while nibbling on delicious chocolates!

Nevertheless, you don't have to be in a relationship to celebrate Valentine's Day! In fact, gather up a bunch of single friends and have an 'anti-Valentine's Day party!' Have an Ex-orcisim and ask all guests to bring pictures of their 'ex' and burn them all in a safe yet ceremonial mini-bonfire.

As a positive alternative for a singles V-day party, play matchmaker, invite all of your single friends, and tell them to invite a set number of *their* single friends. Then you'll have a bunch of people who are willing to meet new people! How cool would it be if someone ends up meeting at your party and stays together for the next sixty years!

Party ambiance should be low lighting with loads of candles, soft love songs playing in the background and the smell of roses in the air. Scatter rose pedals on the guest tables and buffet tables. Valentine's Day traditional décor is pink and red hearts as the central focus followed by chocolates, cupids and roses. Accent with silver and throw in some feathers and sequins.

Party food for Valentine's Day is rich and delicious! Today is the day to indulge and savor love so have a hearty steak with luscious lobster and potatoes for dinner followed by a *to die for* chocolate cake! If you are having a party serving appetizers, serve rich foods such as bacon wrapped beef medallions or scallops, crab cakes, and lobster stuffed mushrooms. Of course, don't forget the chocolate truffle tray, chocolate covered strawberries or the chocolate fondue!

St. Patrick's Day Parties:

St. Patrick's Day is a celebration held annually on March 17th in honor of his St. Patrick's death around the year 460 A.D. – at least this is one possible reason of the origination of the holiday. St. Patrick is believed to have been the one to teach Christianity to the Irish. Most accounts of St. Patrick's life are overstated and the fine details of the chronology are in essence, a mystery. In Ireland, St. Patrick's Day is a religious observance of a Roman Catholic holiday. Now it is a secular holiday held in honor of Irish customs throughout the world.

The traditional color of St. Patrick was actually blue but over the years, it has morphed into green as the traditional color. There are no snakes in Ireland and St. Patrick is credited with their removal. It's probably a myth but feel free to use this as a fun bit of trivia at your party! Why not hide plastic snakes around the house and have a St. Patrick snake eradication scavenger hunt!

Party food should be fun finger food and turn *everything* green! If this is for adults, serve light beer and turn it green with 1-2 drops of food coloring. Serve white cheese fondue and white chocolate fondue but add 1-2 drops of food coloring to turn it green! Have a relish tray complete with all green items.

Party décor should be very green and very festive. Use tons of green confetti, green feather boas, green beaded necklaces, and of course – as many shamrocks as you can stand! Don't forget to have a Blarney Stone (a large rock) which is thought that once it is kissed, it gives the kisser the *gift of gab!*

Easter Parties:

Easter is a religious holiday typically celebrated on Easter Sunday, which is two days after Good Friday. Easter marks the end of Lent, which was a period of 40 days prior and involves fasting and atonement for sins.

Modern secular traditions include the Easter Bunny and Easter Egg Hunts and are celebrated by most everyone regardless of their religious beliefs. These are spring celebrations and are not necessarily tied to the Christian holiday by traditional standards.

If you are planning to host a party for Easter with a large amount of guests, keep in mind that not all of your guests may be Christian and celebrate the religious aspects of Easter. Stick to the spring celebration aspect of Easter and plan for the modern traditions such as Easter egg decoration, Easter egg hunts, and fun Easter-themed party games.

Party décor should be fun spring colors and include baby chicks, baby bunnies, the Easter Bunny and loads of colorful Easter eggs. In addition to confetti, use green plastic or metallic Easter basket shred as filler in the table centerpieces and buffet table centerpieces. The party ambiance should be lively and fun as this is the time of the year to celebrate life.

The party entertainment focus should definitely have an Easter-theme. There is an Easter Party Game & Hunts (Chapter 40) in this book, which has plenty of fun Easter themed games.

As guests arrive, have them decorate Easter eggs for an Easter egg contest. Start with a Top Chef Deviled Egg or Egg Salad Challenge (see the Party Game section) to make use of the hardboiled eggs. Adapt the memory game to include Easter related items or the human bingo game to include Easter related questions such as have you ever held a bunny, etc. Without a doubt, host an Easter Egg hunt. Whether it is simply hiding eggs around the house for your guests to find or doing a more organized style scavenger hunt (see Easter Party Games & Hunts Chapter). My Mystery Party also has tons of scavenger hunts to choose from with riddles to be solved to find the next egg in the chain. Do a neighborhood or an about town scavenger hunt party as well.

A mystery party can be done for any occasion and Easter is no different. However, some occasions should not be celebrated with a *murder* mystery and Easter would be one of those occasions. There is a family friendly Easter (non-murder) Mystery Party available for purchase as an instant download or boxed set on My Mystery Party.

Party food should be mostly egg dishes such as a few flavors of deviled eggs, egg salad sliders, and petite quiches. Be sure to decorate the buffet table with plenty of decorated hardboiled eggs in cute Easter baskets. Have small waste receptacles decorated in an Easter them on a table for the guests to peel Easter eggs and throw away the shells.   Salt and pepper should be available as well.

Cinco de Mayo Parties:

Cinco de Mayo is a day celebrated all over the world annually on none other than May 5th! In México, families, friends and neighbors get together to have a colossal party (aka: fiesta) in honor of the day. This celebration honors the May 5, 1862 victory of Mexico over the French (Battle of Puebla).

The invitations should be ultra-festive and within the central theme of a Mexican Fiesta. Consider sombreros, chili peppers, and even a tortilla chip as fun themes and shapes for your invites! Use a fun, festive slogan such as *Margaritas & Fajitas* or *Forget the Siesta, Let's Have a Fiesta!* Festive confetti in the invitation envelope is a pre-party for your guests and is highly suggested!

The party décor should be in bright, Mexican-themed colors such as green, yellow and red. Celebrate Mexico and use maps of Mexico in your décor. Decorate your party area with mini cactus plants, paper flowers, small sombreros filled with red-hot candies or large sombreros filled to the brim with warm tortilla chips next to a festive colored dish (or dishes) of spicy salsa. Break out the red and green Christmas lights as they'll look spectacular here or if you have chili pepper lights – even better! Add bouquets of red, white and green flowers and scatter fun toy maracas throughout the room. In any corner of the party area, stick bouquets of helium-filled red, yellow and green balloons. Play a festive Mexican party mix CD in the background as the guests arrive and for adults, serve Margaritas. Purchase fun sombreros, Mexican decorated bandanas and /or adhesive mariachi mustaches and hand these festive items to your guests as they arrive to get into the spirit of your fiesta.

The party food should be spicy and delectable. Mexican food is required. Serve margaritas to adults and frozen virgin margaritas for teens. Serve hot sauce and queso with chips as appetizers on a buffet table. You should never run out of salsa and chips at a Mexican Fiesta! Have a make your own burrito bar and as appetizers, serve mini quesadillas, mini tacos, and a mountain of nachos as a buffet statement piece.

A Mexican Fiesta is not complete without a piñata game, pin the tail on the donkey, a Mexican hat dance and other fun party games (see the party game section). Simply alter the titles and themes of any of our party games to fit your Fiesta theme. Why not hire a dance instructor to teach your guests how to Salsa?

Memorial Day / Labor Day Parties:

Both Memorial Day and Labor Day are great holidays for backyard barbecues and lazy days by the pool, lake and / or ocean – whatever body of water you have access to.

Memorial Day is a U.S. Federal Holiday in observance of U.S. soldiers that have died while serving their country, originating with those soldiers who died during the Civil War. Memorial Day is the last Monday of May and marks the start of the summer season with Labor Day marking the end of summer. As of Memorial Day, fashionably speaking, you are allowed to wear the color white.

Labor Day is also a U.S. Federal Holiday observed the first Monday in September. The Central Labor Union of New York established this holiday in 1878 in honor of trade and labor organizations' workers and families. Labor Day also marks the last fashionable day to wear the color white!

With either of these days, remember to observe with your family and friends what the meaning of the day is about, especially Memorial Day. It's not only about getting together and having a great time with your loved ones but also to remember those who gave their lives for our country.

Party décor for Memorial Day is a red, white and blue patriotic theme. Labor Day can be anything – either a summer theme to signify the last bash of summer or as a fall theme to signify the new beginning of the fall season. In either case, the décor should be casual, minimal and more on the conservative side.

Everything about these events should be casual from the party invitations (great even to use evites) to the guests' attire. It would not be a bad time on either holiday to host a luau, either. Do the cooking outdoors, as the weather is likely to be outdoor weather - depending upon your location, of course. Hamburgers, hotdogs served with chips, potato salad and baked beans are essential party staples on these occasions.

Independence Day Parties:

Also known as the Fourth of July, Independence Day is yet another U.S. Federal Holiday. July 4, 1776 marks the day that the U.S. gained independence from the Kingdom of Great Britain. July 4th celebrations are typically backyard barbecues, parades, firework shows, concerts, baseball games in honor of this exciting federal holiday.

Party décor for these events must be in patriotic colors – red, white and blue. Any type of décor with a U.S. flag is expected and awesome. Red, white and blue balloon bouquets filled with helium should be in abundance. Why not purchase a gigantic Mylar eagle balloon?

Fireworks are a staple but is probably best if you visit a location that is hosting a show. There are plenty of free shows and you are likely to be able to see one from your own backyard. If you live in a legal area to shoot fireworks, why not host your own show? Make sure that all minors have adult supervision while around or handling fireworks and that all adults know what they are doing and follow the strict instructions on the fireworks' packages to avoid any injuries or accidents. There are many emergency room visits on this day and a large portion is due to dehydration as well as fireworks injuries. Safety first!

Make a mix CD with American themed songs such as proud *to be an American, the Star Spangled Banner*, etc. to play in the background as patriotic ambiance and crank it up during the fireworks show!

Party Cuisine 411

Chapter 17

Universal Party Cuisine

Plan your menu – either with your caterer or if you plan to prepare the food yourself - according to the majority of guests that will attend and to your theme. Do any of them have special accommodations or allergies? If you do not know your guests well enough to know food restrictions or allergies, it might be worth it on the invite to put a line underneath the RSVP line asking the guests to let you know of any special food accommodations they have.

Party Themes:

As far as themes go, if you are having a strong themed party (i.e. Mexican fiesta, pirate, zombie, Halloween, Mardi Gras, Medieval, etc.), your food is part of your décor and should match the theme of the party. You wouldn't want to serve hamburgers and fries at a Mexican Fiesta or modern day food at a medieval party, now would you? If you do, expect a barrage of comments from the peanut gallery of guests as they snack on the ill-fitting themed foods. No matter how good they taste, if they don't fit the role, don't serve it!

In the case of a strong themed party, such as the Radical '80s, Zombies or Pirates, include fun nameplates or cards in front of each dish and make the buffet line a fun event and a conversation piece. This keeps the excitement of the party theme continuous throughout dinner. If it is a sit down dinner, have the servers announce the name of the dish in the theme of the party such as in the case of a pirate party, have them announce when the *Swashbuckler Salad* is served.

Only Appetizers:

It is acceptable to serve only appetizers during an event. However, put this on the invitation! Disclose it up front! You don't want your guests to expect to be served dinner and then be disappointed that they have to fill up on appetizers. You should have both sweet and savory appetizers available. If they expect only appetizers, they'll be able to make the decision to eat dinner prior to their arrival at your party or not. Also, make sure you do not run out of appetizers! Also, if you are going to serve only say a pickle tray, bowl of snack mix and a bowl of M&Ms, which isn't suggested but it does happen, then you should put on the invitation *'light snacks will be provided.'* Which means in a nice way to your guests – *don't come starved!* A complete disaster ensues when a party runs out of food. That's a party killer for sure. *No food, party over!* Have a backup plan in case your guests are hungrier than you realized and you *do* run out of the planned appetizers – even if it is bags of snack mix or popcorn, have 'something' on hand as a last resort.

Finger Foods or Sit Downs:

Next, consider what your guests will be doing during the party and make the food optimal. Consider taste but almost equally as important is the ease of eating the foods. Don't serve foods that require a knife and fork if the guests don't have a formal table in which to eat. In this scenario, keep it finger foods and foods with toothpicks (put small trashcans for toothpick disposal around the party area unless you want to pick these up for days).

If you are having a formal sit down dinner or even a buffet style dinner that is served at a set time, the guests are likely to arrive famished. Serve light appetizers as soon as they arrive – don't expect them to wait one to two hours for dinner to be served! It is a *mutant party foul* to serve dinner and not desserts so pony up for some sweets and plan your menu correctly! Have as many courses as you'd like but appetizers (typically with cocktails), dinner (either buffet or served) and dessert (with coffee or after dinner drinks) are required at a minimum for a formal dinner party.

MENU RECIPES FOR POPULAR PARTY FOODS:

There are more recipes within the individual party theme chapters.

BEVERAGES:

Swamp Juice

How to prepare: with a large pitcher of apple or white grape juice, add a drop of green food coloring inside. Go to any fish store and purchase seaweed to float in the pitcher (wash it thoroughly with soap and water first!)

Use this method on St. Patrick's Day to make green beverages of any clear or light colored liquid, however, skip the seaweed!
Makes 1 pitcher.

Fiesta Margaritas

(Omit this recipe for teens and offer any green or red beverage instead – place 1-2 drops of green (or red) food coloring in a clear soda or apple juice for a fun Fiesta effect!)

1 6-ounce can frozen limeade concentrate
6-ounce tequila
2-ounce Triple sec
Crushed ice

How to prepare: Pour the ingredients into a blender with crushed ice and mix until smooth. Pour into glasses and serve with a salted-rimmed glass and a lime wedge garnish.

*For superlicious strawberry margaritas, add 8 ounces frozen sliced strawberries in syrup and reduce to 4 ounces of limeade.

Flagtastico Cocktail

4-ounce Hypnotic® liqueur
2-ounce coconut rum
2-ounce pineapple juice
Cherries for garnish
Sugar (red sugar optional) for the rim of the glass

How to prepare: combine all ingredients over ice in a cocktail shaker and shake well. Strain into a martini or cocktail glass and serve. With a red sword toothpick, garnish with cherries.

Festive Fiesta Ending

0.75-ounce Godiva liquor
0.75-ounce Bailey's Mexican cream liquor

Fill the coffee mug with 1/2 coffee and 1/2 milk or half & half (warmed) to taste

Green food coloring

Top with whipped cream (put 1-2 drops of green food coloring into the whipped cream and top with red sprinkles)

How to prepare: mix the liquors together in a shaker and strain into a coffee mug. Fill the mug with coffee and milk to taste and top with green whipped cream and red sprinkles.

Perfect Citrus Punch

1 12-ounce can of frozen orange juice

1 2-liter bottle of ginger ale

1 12-ounce can of frozen pink lemonade

1 quart of orange sherbet

1 quart of pineapple sherbet

1 quart of vanilla ice cream

Fresh cherries (no pits)

Thinly sliced orange slices (into rings)

How to prepare: using a medium to large punch bowl, add the sparkling water and the concentrated juice and mix thoroughly. Place sherbet and ice cream into the bowl in small scoops and allow to float in the punch. Float the orange slices on top of the punch (or as an alternative, use pineapple) with the cherries (stems removed) in the center like flowers. *Makes 1 punch bowl.*

Sassy Strawberry Punch

2 2-liter bottles of fruit punch, chilled

1 2-liter bottle of lemon-lime soda, chilled

2 quarts of strawberry sherbet

8-10 large fresh strawberries

How to prepare: using a large punch bowl, mix the fruit punch and soda thoroughly. Add the sherbet with an ice cream scoop and float into the mixture. Slice the strawberries into thin slices and float on top of the punch. *Makes 1 punch bowl.*

Spicy Apple-Cranberry by the Fire

2 12-ounce cans of apple juice concentrate

2 Tablespoons of maple syrup

1 12-ounce can of frozen cranberry or cranapple juice

10 cups of water
6 sticks of cinnamon
4 whole cloves
1-teaspoon of ground nutmeg
3/4 cup of sugar
How to prepare: using a large pan, combine the ingredients above and bring to a boil on the stovetop. Cover, reduce the heat and cook for 15 to 20 minutes. Serve warm in coffee mugs. *Makes ~14-15 cups.*

Non-alcoholic Champagne

1-liter bottle ginger ale, chilled
1-liter bottle sparkling water or lemon-lime soda, chilled
~24-ounce bottle of white grape juice, unsweetened and chilled
How to prepare: using a large pitcher, combine the above ingredients and pour into champagne flutes. If you want to make less, use equal amounts of ginger ale and sparkling water.   *Makes ~15 cups.*

Sweet Ending Hot Cocoa

3/4 cup granulated sugar
1/3 cup unsweetened cocoa powder
1/4 cup of chocolate sprinkles
1/4 cup of chocolate sauce (optional)
1/4 cup of caramel sauce (optional)
1/3 cup boiling water
3 1/2 cups milk
3/4 teaspoon vanilla extract
1/2 cup half-and-half cream
Whipped Cream to top the cocoa
How to prepare: combine the cocoa, sugar and salt in a medium sized saucepan and carefully add the boiling water. Bring this mixture to a boil and stir frequently. Reduce the heat and simmer while stirring frequently for 3 minutes. Turn off the heat and stir in vanilla, milk. Pour into mugs and top with whipped cream and chocolate sprinkles to the tops of the mugs and serve! Drizzle the top with caramel &/or chocolate sauce. *Makes ~7-8 cups.*

Magnificent Milkshake

3 pints softened cookies and cream ice cream
3/4 cup milk
½-teaspoon vanilla extract
How to prepare: Add the above ingredients into a blender and mix at medium speed until blended thoroughly. Add 2-3 Oreo cookies to make a more cookie-licious shake!   *Makes ~7 cups.*

Yummy Banana Milkshake

3 bananas – diced
5 cups of whole milk
1/2 cup of softened vanilla ice cream
1 cup of ice cubes
1/2 cup of sugar
1 strawberry (for garnish)
How to prepare: Throw the above ingredients into a blender (minus ice cubes) and blend for a few seconds on medium. Add ice cubes and blend until mixed thoroughly. Slice the strawberry and make a slit into one side. Add the strawberry as a garnish. *Makes ~6-7 cups.*

APPETIZERS AND SNACK FOODS

Beetles in a Blanket

1 16-ounce package of Lil Smokies
1 can refrigerated dough for croissant rolls
How to prepare: flatten the croissant roll dough, cut each piece into 4 pieces. Place the lil' smoky on the center of the dough and wrap the dough around to cover the lil' smoky. Place on a cookie sheet and bake same temperature as the package of croissants instructs. The beetles in a blanket are done when the croissant is lightly browned. Can dip in ketchup or mustard. *Serves 10-12.*

Nut-tastic Apple Slices

2 medium-sized apples
3-4 tablespoon of smooth peanut butter
2-tablespoons of granola
1 teaspoon of cupcake sprinkles

How to prepare: Wash and core apples. Slice crosswise into 1/3-inch slices. Spread a moderate layer of peanut butter over apple slices and sprinkle granola over top. For a festive look, add a dash of cupcake sprinkles! *Recipe yield will depend upon the size and how thick you slice the apples.*

Party Munch Mix
1/2 cup of M&M's candies
1/2 cup of cheese-it crackers
1/2 cup of gummy candies
1/2 cup of medium-sized marshmallows
How to prepare: mix in a medium sized bowl and serve!
Makes 2 cups.

Big Bash Snack Grab
1/2 cup of jelly beans
1 cup of Chex cereal
1/2 cup of pretzel sticks
1/2 cup of marshmallows
How to prepare: mix in a bowl and serve! *Makes 2.5 cups.*

Party Time Deviled Eggs
6 hard boiled eggs, chilled
3.5-tablespoons of mayo
1-tablespoon of sweet relish
2-tablespoons of honey mustard
Black pepper and salt to taste
Garlic powder to taste
Paprika shaker
How to prepare: boil eggs, allow to cool, chill for 1 hour in the refrigerator, peel and cut in half. Remove egg yolks from eggs, cut them up into small cubes and put them into a mixing bowl, smashing egg yolks with a fork. Add in mayonnaise, mustard, relish, black pepper, seasoning salt and garlic powder. Mix all ingredients together until well combined. Taste mixture and add more seasoning if desired. Place mixture into a piping bag and pipe into the open egg-white shells. Make a piping bag by putting the mix into a plastic sandwich bag and snipping the corner of the bag and squeezing the mix through the hole.

Sprinkle the top of the eggs with paprika. *Makes 12 deviled eggs.*

Stufflicious Mushrooms

1/2 cup garlic bread crumbs
1-teaspoon Worcestershire sauce
1 package of large whole mushrooms with the stems removed and diced
1/2 cup of cooked, crumbled Italian sausage
1 egg
2-tablespoons of butter
How to prepare: cut the stems from the mushrooms and carefully scoop out the tops without breaking them apart and dice the stems.
Place the mushroom caps with the scooped side up on a baking sheet. Combine the remaining ingredients with the diced stems and mix thoroughly.
Fill the mushroom caps with the mixture (save a little bit of the breadcrumbs for the top), sprinkle with breadcrumbs, and drizzle melted butter over the top.
Cook at 350 degrees until lightly browned (approximately 20-30 minutes).
* Substitute sausage for diced lobster. *The recipe yield depends upon how many mushrooms are in the package.*

Italian Delights

1 large fresh French bread
1 bottle of prepared pizza sauce
1/2 cup of cheddar cheese, grated
1.5 cup of mozzarella cheese, grated
1/4 cup of butter
¼-teaspoon of garlic powder
Any other pizza toppings you desire (mushrooms, onions, etc.)
How to prepare: slice loaf of bread lengthwise, butter one side, sprinkle with garlic powder and place butter side down on a cookie sheet. Spread the other side with pizza sauce. Mix the shredded cheeses and place a thin layer over the sauce. Bake at 350°F until cheese melts. Cut into serving sized pieces. **
Add optional bacon pieces, pineapples, ham, etc. before baking.

Recipe yield will vary depending upon how you slice the bread when it is ready.

Super-Sized Party Mushrooms

1 large package of large portabella mushrooms
1 pound of ground beef (or ground turkey)
1/4 cup of a diced sweet yellow onion
1 shallot clove, minced
3 cups of grated mozzarella cheese
1/4 cup butter
Salt and pepper to taste
Garlic powder to taste

How to prepare: clean the mushrooms and scoop out the stems. In a medium skillet on medium-high heat, cook ground meat very thoroughly. Add chopped onions, shallots, and seasonings to the turkey meat and stir. Remove from heat and drain / discard all juice. Add 2 cups of cheese and mix. Spoon mixture into mushrooms and place them in a baking pan. Top with reserved cup of cheese and a dab of butter. Place in 350 f oven for about 25 minutes, or until cheese is melted and mushrooms are soft. *The recipe yield depends upon how many mushrooms are in the package.*

Fruitilico Salsa and Cinnamonico Chips

8 ounces of fresh raspberries
2 red apples, peeled & diced
2 pounds of strawberries, diced
4 kiwis, peeled & diced
4-teaspoons of sugar
1 cup of cool whipped topping
10-12 flour tortillas
1/2 cup of butter
2 cups of cinnamon sugar

How to prepare: mix the fruit, sugar, cream and chill while covered in the refrigerator for 1 hour. Preheat oven to 350°F and coat each side of the tortillas with butter. Cut the buttered tortillas into potato chip-sized wedges and coat with cinnamon sugar. Bake in the pre-heated oven for 8-10 minutes. Allow to cool for 15 minutes before serving. *Makes about 4 cups of fruity salsa.*

Turkeylicious Meat Balls

1-pound ground turkey meat
1/2 diced yellow onion
1/2 green bell pepper
2-tablespoons flour
½ cup of ketchup
1-teaspoon Worcestershire sauce
2-tablespoons of Mayo
1 egg
2-tablespoons garlic flavored breadcrumbs
Salt, pepper and garlic powder.
Canola oil

How to prepare: place turkey meat into a mixing bowl. Add finely chopped onions, bell pepper, seasonings, flour and garlic flavored breadcrumbs. Roll into bite-size balls. Preheat skillet pan, add oil. Pour a thin layer of garlic-flavored breadcrumbs onto a plate, roll the meatballs into the crumbs, shaking the excess off, and then place into skillet. Cook on all sides until meatballs are lightly browned. Place in a baking in pan in a 350-degree oven for about 20 to 30 minutes. *The recipe yield depends upon the size of meatballs but will range between 10 large and 25 small meatballs.*

Super Snackin' Popcorn Balls

2 quarts of popped popcorn
1/4 teaspoon vanilla
1 cup of sugar
1/3 cup corn syrup
1/3 cup water
1/4 cup butter

How to prepare: Preheat oven to warm (~200°F) Put popcorn in a deep buttered baking dish in the preheated oven. Combine other ingredients in a medium saucepan and stir over medium heat until the sugar is dissolved. Remove warm popcorn from oven and carefully pour syrup mixture over popcorn, stirring the mixture completely. Form popcorn carefully into balls and allow cooling before serving. *Makes about 8 cups.*

Delicious Puppy Chow Mix

1 6-ounce bag of sweetened milk chocolate chips
1/4 cup of smooth peanut butter
6 cups of Crispix cereal
3/4 cup of powdered sugar

How to prepare: melt the chocolate chips in the microwave in a microwave-safe bowl on high for 1 to 1.5 minutes and stir until melted thoroughly. Add the peanut butter and mix thoroughly. Add the cereal and fold until covered and do not break cereal pieces. In a large sandwich bag, add a portion of the powdered sugar. Put in handful portions of the coated cereal in the bag and gently shake until coated with the powdered sugar. Store in the refrigerator until you are ready to serve. *Makes 6 cups.*

ENTREES AND MAIN COURSES

Spicy Chicken Soup

2 quarts water
2 cans of chicken broth
1 can cream of chicken soup
8-10 skinless, boneless chicken breast halves
Salt and pepper to taste
1-teaspoon garlic powder
1-teaspoon onion powder
1-2 bay leaves
2 shallot cloves, minced
1 onion, minced
5 chicken bouillon cubes
3-tablespoons virgin olive oil
2-teaspoons dried parsley
3 cloves garlic, minced
1 16-ounce jar chunky salsa
2 12-ounce cans peeled and diced tomatoes
1 12-ounce can whole peeled tomatoes
1 12-ounce can tomato sauce
3-teaspoon chili powder (more or less to taste)
1 15-ounce can whole kernel corn, drained
2 16-ounce cans chili beans, undrained
1 8-ounce container sour cream

Salt and pepper to taste.

How to prepare: over medium heat, in a large pot combine water, chicken, seasonings, bouillon cubes. Bring to a boil, reduce and cover. Simmer for about 1 hour or until chicken is done (check with a poultry thermometer). Remove chicken and shred or dice. In a separate large pan, sauté the onion and garlic in olive oil until brown. Stir in the remaining ingredients (including shredded / diced chicken) and then add the 5 cups of broth from the chicken pot. Simmer 30 minutes until done, removing bay leaves prior to serving. *Makes about 3 quarts.*

The Other Nut Salad

1 pound of mixed salad greens
1/2 red onion, thinly sliced
4 ounces crumbled blue cheese
1 green apple, cored and thinly sliced
1 cup raspberry vinaigrette dressing
1/2 cup sliced almonds
Salt and pepper to taste.

How to prepare: mix the ingredients together and drizzle the dressing on top. *Makes about 1.5 pounds of salad.*

Festive Fiesta Nachos

Velveeta cheese – 1 package
Rotel tomatoes and green chilies (2 cans, drained)
Ground turkey – browned and drained
1 Taco seasoning package
2 bags of tortilla chips.

How to prepare: add the taco seasoning to the turkey meat per the instructions, stir thoroughly, and drain. Add the meat to the melted cheese in a saucepan. Add both cans of rotel and stir thoroughly. Serve on the side with chips. *Makes about 8-10 servings.*

Crazy Meatball Subs

1 pound ground beef (or ground turkey)
1/2 cup of garlic-flavored bread crumbs
1 egg
1-teaspoon of seasoned salt
1/2 cup ketchup

1/2 cup marinara sauce
1 cup grated mozzarella cheese
1 package of hoagie buns
How to prepare: mix together ground beef, breadcrumbs, egg and seasoning. Shape into 1 ½ inch sized balls. Brown in skillet over medium heat. Add in marinara sauce and ketchup, heat thoroughly. Spoon meatballs and sauce onto split rolls, sprinkle with cheese and serve.
Makes about 8 servings.

Magnificent Mackin' Cheese Casserole

3 cups of elbow noodles
4 cups of cheddar cheese, grated
2 cups of jack cheese, grated
1 cup of evaporated milk
3 cups of whole milk
3 eggs
Salt and pepper to taste
1/4 teaspoon of garlic salt
1/4 teaspoon of onion powder
1 teaspoon of Worcestershire sauce
How to prepare: in salted water, bring elbow noodles to a boil and cook via the package directions. Mix cheeses with 1 cup of milk, eggs and salt, pepper, garlic salt, onion powder and Worcestershire sauce. Drain noodles and place a bottom layer of noodles into a buttered dish (9x12). Sprinkle cheese mixture over noodles. Repeat the layers until the casserole reaches near the top of the dish. Top with a layer of cheese. Pour the rest of the milk over the casserole, do not overflow the pan and allow for room to boil. Place pan on a cookie sheet. Bake at 350°F for approximately 45 minutes. *Makes about 6-8 servings.*

Fabulously Stuffed Chicken

2 cups of cooked jasmine white rice
1/2 cup chopped mushrooms
1 can cream of mushroom soup
~3/4 stick of butter
1/2 cup chopped green onion
1-teaspoon Worcestershire sauce

Salt and pepper to taste
4 tenderized chicken breast fillets
1 cup garlic flavored breadcrumbs
How to prepare: mix the white rice, cream of mushroom soup, Worcestershire sauce, sautéed onions and mushrooms, butter, salt, pepper, and garlic breadcrumbs.
Cut each chicken fillet into two equal sized pieces. Tenderize the chicken fillets with a meat tenderizer. At the edge of one end of the chicken fillet, place about 1/2 cup of the rice mixture and roll the chicken fillet around the rice. Place the chicken fillet into a baking pan with the free edge facing down. Microwave the remaining butter for 10 seconds and drizzle over the chicken breast. Lightly sprinkle salt, pepper and the garlic-flavored breadcrumbs over the buttered breast.
Cook at 375°F until done (approximately 40 minutes). Check with a meat thermometer to determine if the meat is done.
Makes 8 servings.

Cheesy Broccoli Casserole

2 bags of frozen broccoli
1 tube of Kraft garlic cheese
1/2 cup jalapeno jack cheese
2 cans of Campbell's cream of mushroom soup
1 can of Campbell's cream of celery soup
1/2 diced onion
1/2 stick of butter
1/2-teaspoon of garlic powder
Salt and pepper to taste
How to prepare: thaw out the frozen broccoli and drain the water. Melt the cheeses in a saucepan and add the creamed soups. In a separate pan, sauté the onions with the butter until golden brown. Add the browned onions to the cheese mixture. Pour the cheese mixture over the broccoli in a 9 x 12 baking dish. Sprinkle garlic breadcrumbs over the top of the casserole, cover and bake for 1 hour and 15 minutes at 350°F or until browned and bubbling. Allow to cool on the counter for at least 10 minutes before serving. *Makes about 8-10 servings.*

Teriyaki Chicken Wings

10-15 chicken wings / drumettes
1/2 cup soy sauce
1/4 cup brown sugar
1/6 cup vegetable oil
Dash of garlic powder.

How to prepare: cover wings with the sauce by placing in a large plastic sandwich bag with soy sauce, garlic powder, brown sugar and oil and shake until coated. Spread evenly on baking sheet and bake at 420° F until poultry is well done (check with poultry thermometer). *Have individually wrapped disposable hand-wipes available if you serve these. *Makes 10-15 chicken wings.*

Almond-Crusted Chicken Fingers

1 pound of fresh chicken tenders
Canola oil cooking spray
1/4 cup sliced almonds
1/2 cup flour
1 1/2-teaspoon paprika
1/4-teaspoon garlic powder
1/4-teaspoon onion powder
1/4-teaspoon salt
1/8-teaspoon black pepper, finely ground
1 1/2-teaspoon extra-virgin olive oil
4 eggs
Ranch dressing or honey mustard for dipping

How to prepare: in a food processor, add the dry ingredients and process until the mixture is a fine blend for the crust. Add the olive oil and process until mixed. Coat the chicken tenders with whisked eggs and add the chicken to the almond batting mixture in a shallow dish, turning to coat evenly. Add even pressure across the chicken tenders to ensure even coating. Place battered chicken on the baking sheet and bake at 450°F until golden brown. Turn mid-way through cooking (about at 12 minutes) - it should take around 25 minutes. (Check with a poultry thermometer to determine doneness.) Serve with cups of ranch dressing for dipping. *Recipe yield will depend upon the amount of chicken fingers in the package.*

Fantastic Teen Party Potato Casserole

8 large white potatoes - peeled & sliced thin
3.5-tablespoons of butter
1 small onion, finely chopped
1 package of Lil' Smokies cut into 1/2" slices
1.5 cups of shredded American cheese
Bacon bits or pieces
Salt & pepper to taste
How to prepare: melt butter in large non-stick skillet. Add potatoes and onions. Cover and cook over medium heat until potatoes are lightly browned and tender. Make sure to stir frequently to cook evenly. Add sausage slices and continue cooking until sausage slices are lightly browned. Cover entire top of potato mixture with slices of American cheese and sprinkle with bacon. Cover and continue cooking until cheese is thoroughly melted. *Makes about 8-10 cups.*

Funky Spunky Fondue

1 can of cheddar cheese soup
1 cup of finely chopped ham
1 can of Rotel tomatoes
1/4 cup of Monterrey Jack shredded cheese
1-teaspoon of oregano
1/4-teaspoon of garlic powder
1/4-teaspoon of sugar
1/4-teaspoon salt
1/8-teaspoon black pepper, finely ground
1 2-inch piece of pepperoni, finely chopped
1 loaf of fresh bakery bread, cut into squares
How to prepare: blend all of the ingredients together in fondue pot. Heat until it simmers. Reduce heat and serve with fondue forks and bread. Dip bread into hot dip with fondue forks.

DESSERTS:

The Cherry Smasher

1 large box cherry-flavored Jell-O gelatin mix
1 can or package of whipped cream
1 can cherry pie filling
1 small can crushed pineapple (keep juice.)

1 package of pecans (optional), diced.
1/2 package of marshmallows (optional)
How to prepare: put Jell-O into large bowl and add half of the water per the directions. Stir in cherry pie filling, pecans, marshmallows and pineapple (along with the pineapple juice). Refrigerate overnight. To serve, spoon into bowls and top with whipped cream and a cherry. *Makes about 4-5 cups.*

Bug Island

Small plastic sand pails (washed, sterilized)
Small sand shovels (washed, sterilized)
2 packages of butterscotch pudding
** Any ingredients necessary on the pudding cover (typically milk)
1 box of vanilla wafers
Gummy bugs *this depends on the type of party you are having.*
How to prepare: prepare the butterscotch pudding by the directions on the package.
Put ½ cup into each plastic sand pail.
Top with crumbled vanilla wafers to look like sand.
Add the gummy bugs as decoration on top and serve with the small sand shovels instead of spoons. *Alter the recipe for pirate parties, luaus and more!*

Carrot Cake Smoothie

2 cups of carrots, pureed
1/2 cup of sugar
1/2 cup of chunked pineapples
1/3 cup of pineapple juice
4 graham crackers
3/4 cup low-fat vanilla yogurt
1-teaspoon of honey
Ice as needed
How to prepare: place the carrots into a food processor and puree until smooth. Add the pineapple chunks and process until mixed thoroughly. Add the juice and then the remaining ingredients. Continue to puree until smooth, adding more ice if necessary. Add sugar to taste and should be as thick as a milkshake. *Makes about 4.5 cups.*

'Don't Spare the Calories' Tasty Bars

1/2 cup of butter
1 cup of flour
1/2 cup of brown sugar
1 egg
1/2-teaspoon of vanilla extract
1/2 cup of chocolate fudge sauce
1/4 cup of caramel sauce
1/2 cup of chopped nut ice cream topping
1/2 cup of flaked coconut
1/4 cup of sprinkles

How to prepare: mix the dry ingredients first, followed by the rest of the ingredients in a mixing bowl and stir well. Spread in a buttered 8-inch pan and bake at 350°F for 20 minutes. Set aside and cool for 10 minutes. Beat an egg white and fold into a mixture of the fudge topping, nuts, and coconut. Spread this fudge mixture over the cooled bars. Bake at 350°F for an additional 15 minutes. Remove from oven, cool for 10 minutes, drizzle caramel sauce on top, shake sprinkles and cut into squares. *Makes about 3 cups, the amount of squares will be determined when you cut them.*

Scrumptious Birthday Cake

1 1/2 sticks of unsalted butter, softened
1 1/2 cups sugar
2 cups all purpose flour
2 teaspoons baking powder
1/4 teaspoon salt
6 large egg whites (3/4 cup)
3/4 cup milk
2-teaspoons vanilla extract
Frosting – any type you choose

How to prepare: butter the bottom of two 9-inch rounds or one 9x12x2 baking dish. Grease the bottom of the pan with butter and dust with flour to prevent sticking.

In a large mixing bowl, beat butter and sugar for about 6 minutes on med-high speed until light and fluffy. Stir together flour, baking powder and salt and set aside. Combine egg whites, milk and vanilla extract and mix thoroughly. Add 1/3 of the flour mixture to the butter mixture then add half the milk mixture. Continue to add the ingredients in this order while mixing thoroughly.

Pour the cake batter into the prepared pan(s). Bake cake(s) about 25 to 30 minutes or until a toothpick or fork inserted in the center comes out clean.

Cool the cake for at least 20 minutes, remove from the pan(s) and then continue to cool completely. Never put frosting on a warm cake! When cool, frost the cake and write a festive message on top. Purchase fun figurines for your theme party at the local party store or bakery for added festivity.

Chapter 18

Halloween Party Cuisine

Monstrous Mini Pizzas

1 package of English muffins or bagels
1 jar of pizza sauce (any brand)
1 pound of Italian sausage - crumbled, cooked, drained.
2 cups of shredded mozzarella cheese
Optional ingredients for the faces: black olives,
sweet red peppers, capers, green bell peppers, green olives
How to prepare: preheat the oven to 425°F. Split the
muffins/bagels and toast each slice. Place each toasted
muffin/bagel on a cookie sheet. Spread the top of the
muffin/bagel with pizza sauce and top with cheese. Sprinkle the
Italian sausage on top of the cheese. With the optional
ingredients, make monster faces. Bake pizzas for
approximately 6 minutes or until cheese is melted. *Recipe
yield will depend on the amount of muffins or bagels you use.*

Witch's Brew Ingredients:

2 3 ounce packages of lime gelatin
1/2 cup of sugar
1 cup of boiling water
3 cups of cold water
2 quarts of lemon-lime soda (chilled)
2 quarts of limeade (non-carbonated)
How to prepare: dissolve gelatin and sugar into the boiling
water and stir until dissolved. Add the cold water and transfer
the mixture into a large punch bowl. Stir in the lemon-lime soda
and limeade. *Makes about 5 quarts.*

Happy Halloween Snack Bowl

2 cups of Chex Mix
1 cup of honey-roasted peanuts
2 cups of Honey Nut Cheerios
1 cup of raisins
2 cups of orange and black M&M candies
1/2 cup of peanut butter chips
1/2 cup of white chocolate chips
How to prepare: mix into a bowl, stir carefully and serve!
Makes 9 cups.

Ghoulish Eyes Hot Chocolate

8 cups of milk
1 cup mint chocolate chips
1 cup instant white hot chocolate mix
12 large marshmallows
12 chocolate M&M candies - assorted colors
Green food coloring
How to prepare: prepare the hot chocolate according to the directions and include the melted chocolate chips and stir until thoroughly dissolved. Heat the mixture. Drop 1-2 drops of green food coloring to get a nice green color. Cut out a depression in the top of each marshmallow and insert the M&Ms into the depression. To keep the candies in place, heat up the marshmallows for a few seconds in the microwave - but do NOT overheat! Carefully float the marshmallows on top of the tasty beverage. *Makes about 8 cups.*

Anti-Vampire Pumpkin Seeds

1-tablespoon olive oil
1/2-teaspoon celery salt
1/2-teaspoon garlic powder
1/2-teaspoon Cavender's seasoning
2 1/2 cups of fresh pumpkin seeds
1 dash of paprika
How to prepare: combine the ingredients into a mixing bowl and then add the pumpkin seeds. Mix thoroughly and make sure that the seeds are thoroughly coated. Spread on a baking sheet and cook at 300°F until golden brown (~ 45 minutes).
Makes about 2.5 cups.

Worms Crawl In, Worms Crawl Out
Spaghetti Pumpkin Peppers

10-12 orange sweet bell peppers
1 package of spaghetti noodles, cooked.
1 pound of ground turkey (or ground beef) cooked, drained
1 jar of spaghetti sauce

How to prepare: remove the tops of the peppers (and set aside) and remove the seeds and pulp from inside of the peppers. Carefully carve a fun pumpkin face in the side of each bell pepper.   Bake the peppers to soften in a 375F oven for 25 minutes.

Cook the spaghetti noodles according to the package directions. Brown the turkey meat and drain. Add the turkey meat to the spaghetti sauce and heat in a saucepan. When the noodles and spaghetti sauce are done, mix them in a large bowl to coat the noodles with the sauce. Spoon the mixture into each pepper and pull out the noodles from the top as well as the face of your pumpkin pepper. Put the pepper top back on and serve warm! *Makes 10-12 pepper servings.*

Sea Water from the Black Lagoon

How to prepare: get a pitcher of apple juice or white grape juice and add a drop of blue food coloring inside. Go to any fish store and purchase plastic seaweed. Clean it thoroughly with hot water and soap and let it dry before adding it to the pitcher for a cool effect. *Makes about 1 pitcher.*

Fingers in a Blanket

1 package of Lil' Smokies
1 can refrigerated dough for croissant rolls
Sliced almonds

How to prepare: Flatten the croissant roll dough, cut each piece into 4 pieces. Place the lil' smoky on the center of the dough and wrap the dough around to cover the lil' smoky. Place on a cookie sheet and bake same temperature as the package of croissants instructs. The fingers in a blanket are done when the croissant is lightly browned. Add the sliced almonds as fingernails. Can dip in ketchup or mustard. *Makes about 10-12 servings.*

Halloween Munch Mix

Makes 2 cups of snack mix ~ 8-10 light snacks
1/2 cup of orange jelly beans.
1/2 cup of Gold fish crackers
1/2 cup of mini marshmallows
Directions: Mix in a bowl and serve!

Moonlit Milkshake

3 pints vanilla ice cream -- softened
3/4 cup milk
1/2 teaspoon vanilla extract
How to prepare: Put ingredients into a blender and mix
thoroughly. Could be mixed with 1/4 cup chocolate or strawberry
syrup. Also, add 2-3 cookies, or 10 oz. fresh fruit to the blender
to make a more flavorful shake! With fruits, puree and strain
before adding to the blender. *Makes about 8-10 mini
milkshakes.*

Goblintastic Nachos

Velveeta cheese – 1 package
Rotel tomatoes and green chilies (2 cans, drained)
Ground turkey – browned and drained
1 package of taco seasoning
2 bags of tortilla chips.
Green food coloring
How to prepare: add the taco seasoning to the turkey meat
per the instructions, stir thoroughly, and drain. Add the meat to
the melted cheese in a saucepan. Add both cans of Rotel and
stir thoroughly. Add food coloring to get a nice green color –
worthy of a goblin. Serve on the side with chips. *Makes about
8-10 servings.*

The Chocolate Witch

2 cups whole milk
2/3 cup of heavy cream
2/4 cup of sugar
10-ounce bag of semisweet chocolate, chopped
1/2 bag of marshmallows
Whipped cream

Chocolate sprinkles or chocolate powder (cake décor or coffee aisle)

How to prepare: simmer the milk, cream and sugar together until just boiling. Stir in the chocolate until melted, not allowing it to boil. Add to mug and top with marshmallows, whipped cream and chocolate sprinkles/powder. *Makes about 8-10 servings.*

Coffin Cake

1 1/2 sticks of unsalted butter, softened
1 1/2 cups sugar
2 cups all purpose flour
2-teaspoons baking powder
1/4-teaspoon salt
6 large egg whites (3/4 cup)
3/4 cup milk
2-teaspoons vanilla extract
Chocolate frosting. Black squeeze frosting for the lining and orange squeeze frosting for any messages (i.e. *Happy Birthday ___, Happy Halloween*, etc.).

How to prepare: set rack at the middle level in the oven and preheat to 350 degrees F. Butter the bottom of a 13 by 9 by two-inch rectangular pan and dust with flour to prevent sticking. In a large bowl, beat butter and sugar for about 5 minutes, until light and fluffy. Stir together flour, baking powder and salt. Set aside. Combine egg whites, milk and vanilla extract. Add 1/3 of the flour mixture to the butter mixture then add half the milk mixture. Continue to alternate beginning and ending with flour mixture. Scrape the bowl and beater often.

Pour the cake batter into prepared pan(s), ensuring top is smooth. Bake cake(s) about 25 to 30 minutes, or until a toothpick inserted in the center emerges clean.

Cool in pan on rack for 5 minutes, then turn out onto a rack, remove paper and let cool completely. Put into the freezer for about 20-30 minutes, remove and then cut the rectangle in the shape of a coffin. Cover the cake with the chocolate frosting; line the coffin with the black squeeze frosting and then write a festive Happy Halloween (or other) message on the top of the cake.

Blood Fondue

1-cup heavy cream
1/2 stick unsalted butter
2 12-ounce packages white chocolate morsels
Red Food Coloring, Blue Food Coloring
Strawberries, pound cake squares, Rice Krispie treat squares, bananas, etc. for dipping
Fondue forks and a fondue pot.

How to prepare: in a large saucepan over medium heat, combine cream and butter. Bring mixture to a simmer, stirring constantly and then carefully remove pan from heat. Add the white chocolate morsels, stirring thoroughly until mixed. Continue to add 1 drop of red food coloring until a blood red color is achieved. If you need to darken the color, add 1-2 drops of blue food coloring. Cool slightly. Transfer to a fondue pot, chafing dish, or ceramic bowl. Serve with apples, bananas, strawberries, cookies, pretzels, and pound cake. Give each guest a fondue fork.

Cheesy Chicken Enchiladas

2 pounds skinless, diced or shredded boneless chicken breast meat
4 cups shredded cheddar cheese
1 1/2 cups sour cream
1/4 teaspoon chili powder (more or less to taste)
1 medium yellow sweet onion, diced
2 cloves of a shallot, minced
1 4-ounce can chopped green chilies, drained
1 package mild taco seasoning mix
10 green onions, minced
1-cup water
1.5-teaspoons butter
1.5-teaspoons lime juice
1/2-teaspoon onion powder
1/2- teaspoon garlic powder
5 enchilada-sized flour tortillas
1 10-ounce can enchilada sauce
1 6-ounce can sliced black olives
Salt and pepper to taste

How to prepare: in a large pot with water and 2 cans of chicken broth, add chicken and bring to a boil over high heat. Reduce to medium-low and simmer until chicken is done which is 15-20 minutes. Shred or dice the chicken and set aside.

Over medium heat, heat butter in a frying pan and sauté the onion and shallots for about 7-8 minutes until onions are golden brown. Add shredded or diced chicken, green chilies, green onions, taco seasoning and water. After simmering for 10 minutes, add the lime juice, onion powder, and garlic powder and continue to simmer for another 10 minutes. Salt and pepper to taste. In another pan, add the sour cream, cream of chicken soup, and chili powder in a saucepan. Simmer, stirring occasionally.

Mix 1 cup of the sauce with the chicken mixture. Fill the bottom layer of a 9x13 inch baking dish with the remaining sauce. Fill each tortilla with a portion of the chicken mixture. Before folding each tortilla, sprinkle a generous amount of cheddar cheese over the chicken filling. Fold tortillas with the filling inside and place seam-side down over the sauce at the bottom of the pan. Pour enchilada sauce evenly over the enchiladas and sprinkle the remaining cheddar cheese on top of the enchilada sauce. Sprinkle the rest of the chopped green onions and then place the sliced olives on top in a decorative manner. Bake about 25 minutes at 350°F until cheese is melted.

Scary Sopapilla Cheesecake...to Die for

1 16-ounce package of softened cream cheese
2 cups granulated sugar
1-teaspoon ground cinnamon
1-teaspoon vanilla extract
2 8-ounce cans refrigerated crescent rolls
1/2 cup softened butter
1/4 cup honey

How to prepare: grease a 9x13 inch baking dish with cooking spray or with butter and dusted with flour to prevent sticking. Combine the cream cheese with the vanilla extract and 1 cup of the sugar and mix thoroughly.

Unroll each can of crescent roll dough and knead together as one large piece of dough. Roll into 9x13 inch circles with a rolling pin. Press one piece into the bottom of the greased baking dish. Spread the cream cheese mixture onto the dough and cover with the second piece of rolled out crescent dough.

Stir together 1 cup of sugar, cinnamon, and butter. Spread this mixture over the top of the second layer of dough. Bake in the preheated oven at 350°F until the crescent dough has puffed and turned golden brown and this will take approximately 30 minutes. Remove from the oven and drizzle with honey. Cool completely in the pan before slicing.

Party Game Central

Chapter 19

Party Games- General Advice

Any of the following party games can be altered to fit your specific party theme. However, there are more theme-specific games in the Halloween, Slumber Party and Bridal-related chapters. The games below, unbelievably, can be played by all age groups so for this reason, they are not broken down by age groups.

If you think a group of sixty-somethings won't enjoy making necklaces out of weird items or smashing each other's crackers on their hips – you are wrong! Now, there are exceptions to that as there would be with *any* age group, but you know your group best!

Remember the Peter Pans from the adult party categories? Well, most of these more childish party games are ideal for that group of adults! Childish is definitely not a derogatory word! Childish should translate to *fun* as that is what kids are about! If you are no longer able to harness your inner child, which is unfortunate for you as you will never be able to experience true fun like you once did as a child. It's all right to be a child for a day – even if you are eighty!

There are more than 75 games to choose from in this chapter and with applying various themes to the games; you have endless possibilities!

Safety first! Always ensure there is an adequate and safe location for your game. Don't choose a field with hidden holes and uneven terrain to sprain ankles or a crowded living area where someone will lacerate an arm on an armoire during a relay race. An injury is a party killer, just remember that!

First, think of your group and imagine them in the challenge. You are probably thinking more conservatively than your group is but maybe grab a consultant to help you select the ideal games for your event. Tweak the games in any direction to make them more mature or even more childish (fun) as well as changing the theme as you need.

After you have your party games selected, make a master list that is sectioned by party game. Pay close attention to the game gear that is needed for each event. Gather these items and keep them together and in order of which you want to host the games. Designate a main party prop area for your party game props. Stick name tags on piles of props to show which game they go with so those that are assisting you in hosting during the party will know where to go to grab what you need for the next game.

Be sure that your area is conducive for the games you have selected. Don't do the crazy cracker smasher challenge in a small hotel room as there will not be room, you're likely to break things and you will leave a huge mess that you'll likely be charged for by the hotel. Use massive common sense when selecting games according to your location.

If you have older guests or older guests mixed in with your group in the case of a family reunion or wedding/graduation related event, you might not want to do the athletic games as you will exclude potential participants. Once Aunt Martha is a bystander it may become more difficult to get her to participate in future games.

Remember your theme. Try to select the parties that can go with your theme the best or that you can alter to fit your theme. It will make the most sense to your guests if you stick with your theme throughout your party.

Chapter 20

Ice Breaking Games

Famous Couples Trivia:

Game goal: to guess the famous fictional, historical or celebrity couple from a few fun facts.

Game play: do an internet search for 'famous couples' and write down five fun facts about this famous fictional, historical or celebrity couple. Print out decorative cards with this information along with the answer below the five facts.

Hand guests a card with their famous couple. As the guests mingle about during your meet 'n greet, they are to quiz each other on their famous couple. The one who guesses the couple with the least amount of facts wins! Then, the guests are to go on to the next person and so on until everybody has had a chance to mingle and quiz every other guest. Each guest can decide the order to give the facts to their partner – it doesn't have to be in the order written on the card.

Game gear: cards with the five fun facts and the famous couple (the answer) stated below the facts.

Game time: ~ 10-15 minutes.

What am I?

Game goal: to figure out the picture, word or phrase on the card that is on your forehead.

Game play: make cards (small paper squares) of items within the theme of your event and affix them with tape or other adhesive that is safe for the skin to your guests. Make sure there are not any reflective surfaces in your party area before you begin.

The guests are to ask yes /no questions to the other guests in order to figure out what is on their head. They are only allowed to ask questions of one person until they say *no* to any given question. At that point, the person that was answering questions is allowed to ask the person that was asking questions first. The pairs will switch and find someone else for their next line of questions. This will continue until there is a winner and then the loser is the last one standing. You might not want to wait until there is one loser but call the last five people standing the losers. That way, you don't single one person out.

Try to get an even range of difficulty with the squares. Don't make someone's card be a *famous artist* while someone else has a *dog*.

Game gear: small paper squares with any random item on it (word, phrase, and picture) within the theme of your party, scotch tape.

Game time: ~ 15-20 minutes.

The Twinkie Tower Challenge:
Game goal: to build the best and sturdiest Twinkie tower.

Game play: divide the guests into teams of four-five. When the host says go, the guests are to grab Twinkies from the main table and plan their strategy to build the most awesome and sturdiest tower out of the Twinkies.

They can use as many Twinkies as they need but the tower cannot lean and cannot crumble down or they are disqualified. They can add windows and staircases, doors, etc. but must create everything with only Twinkies. The Twinkies can remain in the wrapper or they can take them out. Altering of the Twinkies is acceptable but nothing but Twinkies is legal in the structure.

This is a timed event and the host is the judge but it will probably be obvious who the winner will be, as one team always seems to be the Twinkie Architects of the group.

Game gear: tons of Twinkies for as many groups as you will have.

Game time: ~ 10-15 minutes.

Survivor Challenge:

Game goal: to be the group that comes up with the best survivorship strategy with only 10 items for 20 days.

Game play: set the scenario to the group as a whole. Explain that they've been shipwrecked on a desert island where the weather is tropical but it thunderstorms every other day. There are coconuts available on the island and the ocean is available to them to hunt for food. They have only ten items, as that is all they could grab from the boat before it sank to the bottom of the ocean. Divide your group into teams of 5-10 players. Give them 10 minutes to devise the best strategy for survival. They should come up with the 10 best items for survival. The host declares the winner as the team that comes up with the best list.

 Albeit there might be arguments for other things that come up, the priority should be water, as you cannot live for more than three days without it. You can live without food for a couple of weeks or more but without water, you are history. In addition, drinking contaminated water will only speed up the impending doom as they will get sick and therefore, dehydrated. Therefore, the primary focus should be to harness the water from the storm (not the salty seawater) and to sterilize it (gauze, fire, etc.). They could survive on coconuts for 20 days but their second priority would be food and third is shelter from the rain.

Game gear: paper and pen for each team. A large easel to write down the ten items for each team for group comparison. Be prepared for a big group debate!

Game time: ~ 20 minutes.

Riddler Challenge:

Game goal: to find your match in the room by first solving your riddle and then locating the person who has a riddle answer that logically fits with yours.

Game play: for every two players in your party, you will have to come up with a simple (or complex) riddle with a clearly defined answer. For every riddle you write, you'll need to write a corresponding riddle that has an answer that logically fits with the first riddle. For example, if the answer to riddle #1 is *rose* and the answer to riddle #2 is *thorn*, those two would be a match.

Hand each player a card and allow him or her a minute to view his or her riddle. When the host says go, the players are to mingle about and locate the player in the room that has their logical match. Some riddle answers might seem to go together but you should make a very strong match between the riddles you want to go together.

For example, if riddle #3 has the answer *dirt* – the person holding the riddle #1 card might believe they are a match with the word *dirt* because *roses* need *dirt* for support and nutrients, etc. but *thorn* is a better choice. Especially since someone will hold riddle #4 in the room that will have the answer as *mud.*

If a pair believes they are a match and a third person comes around and has a stronger match to one person in the pair, the weak match player is thereby unpaired and must go to find their match! The first team to match their riddles is the winners and the last team to match their riddles is the losers.

Game gear: riddle cards.

Game time: ~ 15 minutes.

Name that Lie:

Game goal: to quiz each other on fun facts about yourself and coax each other into choosing the lie.

Game play: hand your guests a sheet of paper and a pen and ask them to write two fun facts about themselves. When everybody has done this, allow him or her to mingle about and instruct him or her to quiz everybody in the room and to keep track of how many people chose the lie as the truth! The person who coaxed the most people to believe the lie wins!

Game gear: pen and paper.

Game time: ~ 15 minutes.

Marvelous Marketeers:
Game goal: to come up with the ideal marketing strategy for a common household item.

Game play: give your guests a common household product such as a model of vacuum cleaner. Give them the going price and any specs that are available for this product. The product can essentially be anything you choose – bubble gum, disposable cameras, etc.
Divide your guests into teams of five-six and allow them to reinvent the marketing strategy for this item. Then, they are to propose it to the group. The groups can raise or lower the cost of the product but cannot reduce the profit margin. The best and most convincing marketing strategy wins!

Game gear: pen and paper.

Game time: ~ 20-25 minutes.

Chapter 21

Ultimate Challenge Party Games

Spunky Scramble Challenge:

Game goal: to be the first team to unscramble all of the scrambled words on your game sheet!

Game play: divide your guests into pairs. Give each team a copy of a scramble challenge sheet. A scramble challenge sheet consists of multiple words that you have scrambled. It is preferred to choose words within the theme of your party such as for a '70s party, select *disco ball, groovy, lava lamp, right on,* etc. When the host says go, the teams are to unscramble the words/phrases. The first team that unscrambles all of the words/phrases on their sheet wins! They're to raise their hand and shout *complete!*

In the case of a tie, the best two out of three on a rock, paper, and scissor tournament will break the tie.

An alternative way to play is to set a timer for five or ten minutes and the one who comes up with the most correctly unscrambled words - wins!

Game gear: the scramble sheets and of course, don't forget to make an answer key. Hit the web and search for 'scramble word' or 'word scrambler' and there will be some sites that will scramble words for you.

Game time: ~10 minutes.

From 3 to 20 Challenge:

Game goal: to be the team that comes up with increasingly larger words within the given theme the fastest!

Game play: divide the group into pairs. Within the theme of your party, write down a theme for all to see. Set the timer for 5 minutes.

When the host says go, the teams are to write down words in increasing size (starting with a three-letter word) that fit the given theme. For example, if the host says *zoo* is the theme, the team will write down *ba*t (3 letters), *bear* (4 letters), *zebra* (5 letters), etc. until they reach 20 letters. They can break up the words into a phrase as long as they fit the amount of letters. For example, *brown bear* would be appropriate for nine letters. However, *green bear* wouldn't make sense and would not be counted. The teams do not have to go in order of increasing size as they fill in the blanks on their answer sheets but the team with the most correctly applied words or phrases wins! The host calls the time and takes up the answer sheets, scores them and declares a winner!

Game gear: a pen/pencil and a sheet of paper for each team labeled 3 to 20. A large piece of paper, whiteboard or chalkboard to write down a word/phrase for all the teams to view.

Game time: ~ 8 minutes.

Word Hunt Challenge:
Game goal: to make the most words out of a larger word.

Game play: write a large word on a wipe off board or piece of paper and set the timer for two minutes. Divide your guests into teams of two or three.

When the host says go, they are to make as many smaller words out of the large word. The team that comes up with the most words wins!

In the event of a tie – set the timer for 30 seconds and have them come up with more words. If they keep tying, a scissor, rock, paper tournament with the best two out of three will claim a winner!

Game gear: a wipe off board or piece of paper, marker, and pens and paper for each team. In addition, a timer or a watch with a second hand will do fine.

Game time: ~10 minutes.

How many are there?

Game goal: to guess how many coins, jellybeans, pasta noodles, etc. are in a jar.

Game play: in a clean jar, put a designated amount of items. Seal the jar with the lid, decorate the lid within your party theme, and tie with ribbons for a fun effect. As your guests arrive to the party, have each guest write on a ballot their best guess of how many items are in the jar.

At the end of the night, reveal the amount of (precounted) items in the jar and a prize (maybe the jar of candy) is optional for the winner!

Game gear: a clear jar with a decorated lid; candy corns or other items that are small enough for the challenge; a ballot for each guest with a pen

Game time: ~5 minutes.

Don't Forget the Lyrics – Karaoke Challenge:

Game goal: to be the last one standing!

Game play: divide your guests into pairs and one at a time, have each pair come up to the karaoke stage. Flip a coin to see who will sing the first verse. Without the lyrics showing to the duo, the guests take turns singing a verse of the song without missing a lyric. They are to sing the chorus together and missing part of the chorus doesn't count against either of them.

The first player to miss a lyric is out of the competition and the winner of each pair goes to the next round. If there are only three verses in a song and neither misses a lyric, they will do another song of the host's choice and the order in which they are singing will continue until someone misses a lyric.

Can't get someone out? Increase the difficulty of the song! The rounds continue until someone is the last standing! The host can choose the song for the pairs to sing (suggested) or allow them to choose the song if they can agree upon one.

Game gear: karaoke machine with songs with scrolling lyrics (or a lyric sheet) for the host-judge.

Game time: ~30 minutes.

Fun Football Hoop Challenge:

Game goal: The objective is to be the one to throw the most footballs through the hula-hoop!

Game play: line up the guests. One player (or the host) must hold a hula-hoop at designated lengths away from the player in the front of the line (i.e. 10, 15, 20 feet, etc.). Hand the player a football and s/he must throw the football inside of the hoop for five points for the closest hoop, 10 points for the second closest hoop and 15 points for the furthest hoop. Once the player has had three tries at the various hoop distances, the player will either go to the back of the line for another turn or sit as part of the audience until the next game. Continue until everyone gets a turn. The host can decide how many turns the players should have before totaling the points and declaring a star athlete. The winner is the one with the most points at the conclusion of the game.

In the event of a tie, a throw off will need to be played. The host holds the hoop further than before and each player should get one try. If both players make it and there is still a tie among the players, the host is to back up further and repeat the process until a winner is declared. If neither player makes it, the host is to come closer until someone makes it.

Game gear: a Nerf football and a hula-hoop. It is advisable to mark off areas of the yard/ floor to determine where the hoop holder should stand and where the player should not cross to keep the difficulty of the distances even between players.

Game time: ~ 15 minutes.

Condiment Creations:

Game goal: The game objective is to be the team who makes the best picture out of swirling mustard and mayo in a spoonful of ketchup.

Game play: divide your guests into pairs. Give them access to ketchup, mayo, mustard and any other brightly colored condiments you choose. Give each team a large spoon and a toothpick. Set the timer for five minutes.

When the host says go, each team is to fill their spoon with ketchup as a base and then very carefully, add the other condiments and with a toothpick, they are to drag the condiments to make a beautiful picture. The teams can start over as many times as needed but will only have five minutes to complete their masterpiece. When the time runs out, it is toothpick's down! The host will judge the best condiment creation.

Game gear: a spoon for each pair, toothpick for each pair, and various colored condiments (i.e. ketchup, mustard, mayo, etc.)

Game time: ~ 10 minutes.

How Do You Do? Hey, I Know You! Or Do I?

Game goal: to figure out whom the most people are by only a handshake.

Game play: blindfold one guest and the other guests are to stand in a straight line in any random order - facing the blindfolded person. After the blindfold is secure, everyone is to switch positions and remain completely silent. The host will guide the blindfolded person to the first person in line. They will shake hands - and only shake hands! The blindfolded person must give a guess who this person is that they just shook hands with. This repeats until the blindfolded guest has shook hands with and guessed about every guest in line.

The host tallies up the amount of correct guesses and puts it on a score sheet. Each guest takes a turn being the blindfolded person until everyone has had a chance. The highest score - wins! In the event of a tie (or multiple tie) - the host will choose a number and write it down on a piece of paper and each person will guess a number between 1-100. The closest without going over will win the tiebreaker and therefore, the game!

Game gear: blindfold.

Game time: ~ 20 minutes.

Fantastic Movie Challenge:

Game goal: To be the team that can answer the appropriate movie with the corresponding tag lines, movie synopses, and / or movie quotes.

Game play: divide your guests into teams of four (or whatever number you choose). Select movies from websites such as www.IMDB.com. On this particular site, there are quotes, tag lines, etc. to select from for all movies. It is ideal to select movies within the theme of your party. If you're having a Wild West party, choose old westerns and new westerns such as Tombstone, etc.

Give the teams 15 minutes (or more) to fill in the correct movie in the blank next to the tag line, quote or synopsis.

When the time is up and / or the guests are finished, collect the answer sheets and score them using your answer key.

Game gear: copies of your challenge sheets, answer key and pens for each team.

Game time: ~20 minutes.

Chapter 22

Food Related Challenges

Do You Taste What I Taste?

Game goal: to be the one who can correctly guess the 10 random food items – while blindfolded!

Game play: gather 10 random food items of your choice using the list below or of your own choosing. One at a time, bring in the competitors and blindfold them.

Using a small plastic sample spoon (or other utensil); ask the blindfolded guest to open their mouth and spoon in sample #1. For example, if you choose sugar as food item #1, you will give them a spoon full of sugar to taste. They are immediately to guess what food item it is. Record their guess on the sheet and then proceed to the next item. Allow them to drink water in between food items. Proceed until all ten items are tasted and guessed before moving on to the next player. Each player that has already guessed the 10 items may remain in the room with you and assist you with the remaining players.
The one who guesses the most items is the winner! In the event of a tie, a best two out of three rock, paper scissor tournament will decide the winner.

Game gear: random food items (chosen either from the list below or of the host's choice.) Small plastic sample spoons. A blindfold. The guess sheets (below).
Example holiday-spirited palette testers:
1. brown sugar
2. cinnamon
3. raw pumpkin
4. nutmeg
5. yellow onion
6. egg yolk (cooked)
7. garlic or shallots
8. cream cheese

9.   sage
10. Worcestershire sauce
11. eggnog
12. balsamic vinegar
13. celery
14. mayonnaise
15. pecans

Game time: ~ 20 minutes.

Master Chef Guacamole:

Game goal: to be the ultimate culinary genius by making the best-tasting and best-looking guacamole dip!

Game play: Each guest can either compete individually or put them into teams of two to four.

Place all of the possible ingredients on a table where each guest has access to enough of the ingredient for their recipe (see the suggested ingredient choices below but feel free to modify as you choose). Give each guest a mixing bowl, a wire whisk (or just a spoon), and a set number of avocados.

When the host says go, the guests are to create the best-tasting and best-looking guacamole dip by using the best combination of the ingredients below along with the best technique for preparing the guacamole!

Each team can only take one ingredient from the ingredient table at a time - no grabbing all of the ingredients to sabotage the other chefs! They must return the container holding the ingredient in a timely manner before getting another one from the ingredient table! The teams immediately return all ingredients after their use (if not used in its entirety) or the violating team gets a one-minute penalty where they cannot continue until serving a penalty.

The following are the suggested ingredients to place on the table. Please make an announcement that by no means does it suggest that putting all of these ingredients into guacamole dip will be the best tasting! They are to create the best combination of the ingredients that they select and use the best techniques to prepare it!

Suggested food ingredients:

Mayo - maybe 2-3 different types to choose from
Soy Sauce
Mustard - maybe 2-3 different types to choose from
Paprika
1000 Island Salad Dressing
Salt & Pepper
Worcestershire Sauce
Cooked bacon (diced for them or not)
Avocados (have plenty)
Shredded cheese - a few types to choose from
Relish - sweet and a sour
Onions (diced for them - different varieties)
Pickles (diced for them)
Tomatoes (diced for them - different varieties)
Lemons (cut into slices)
Limes (cut into slices)
Cilantro (fresh herbs, minced)
Garlic (minced)
Spinach leaves (minced)
Parsley (minced)

*Since cooking challenges with knives lend to finger injuries, it is suggested not to require your guests to chop, dice and mince their own ingredients. Give the guests a time limit (i.e. 8 minutes) to create their culinary delight. When the host calls time, s/he will taste each team's guacamole and judge on presentation and taste. The best tasting guacamole dip wins!

Game gear: the food ingredients listed above - any variation of them and if you think of any to add - feel free! Mixing bowl and a spoon or wire whisk for each guest.

Game time: is approximately 15 minutes.

The Crazy Candy Bar Caper:

Game goal: to guess the most melted confections correctly!

Game play: purchase five-eight different types of chocolate candy bars. Divide them equally among the teams, place each on a separate plate, and melt each candy bar in the microwave. Stir the melted candy bars thoroughly while breaking up any cookies, caramel, etc. Make the mixture as uniform as possible. Designate the candy bar with a number and remember to make an answer key for you to reference when you score the guests' answer sheets.

For each contestant, line the numbered plates in a row and have them sample the melted candy bar (have plenty of mini spoons/spatulas available for tasting). They are to write down their guess for each melted chocolate bar on their answer sheet. They only have one shot - they cannot resample! Alternatively, if you decide they can resample, make it the same rules for all. If you didn't allow the first guest to do it, nobody else can!

The guest that guesses the most melted candy bars wins! In the event of a tie- a guess off can take place - melt two candy bars together and see if any of the tied guests can guess it correctly. If it's still a tie - make it three melted candy bars together and so on...until you get a winner!

Game gear: five to eight types of candy bars, melted on small plates. Small sampling spoons, pens/pencils and the candy guess sheets (below).

Game time: ~ 5-10 minutes.

The Smelliest Challenge on Earth:
Game goal: to guess the most food items from smell alone!

Game play: collect boxes of all sizes and shapes and cover them with fun décor. If any of these boxes carried food items within them, allow them to air out for a while prior to using them in this challenge.

Collect various food items with a strong smell such as barbecue sauce, olives, lemons, etc. and place each food item into a designated box. Be sure to fill out your answer key prior to sealing each box. Place any items that are semi-liquid into a secure container within the box (i.e. small Tupperware) with the opening facing the top of the box. Cover the top of the box with black mesh fabric so the guests cannot see the food items they smell.

One by one, allow your guest to smell each box and put their best guess of what the food item is on their answer sheet.

The host will score the answer sheets and declare a winner. In the event of a tie, the best two out of three with a rock paper and scissor tournament will declare a final winner.

Game gear: ten cardboard boxes, ten food items, black mesh fabric to cover the box tops, answer key. Guest answer sheets and a pen.

Game time: ~ 5-10 minutes.

Name the Ingredients!
Game goal: to guess the most ingredients correctly from a dish!

Game play: this is an individual challenge. The host will prepare (or purchase) a dish of their choice. It's preferred to stay within the party theme for this dish.
    One by one, the guests are to taste the dish (give clean utensils for each taste) and write down every ingredient in the dish.
    The guest who guesses the most ingredients correctly – wins!

Game gear: a prepared dish – preferably one within the theme of the party with multiple ingredients. Game guess sheets, pens for each guest and an answer key. Answer key of the ingredients used in the dish. Utensils for tasting.

Game time: ~ 10 minutes.

Chapter 23

Relay Race Party Games

Balloon Belly Relay:

<u>Game goal</u>: to be first team to get your balloon across the finish line after all of your team has crossed it carrying a balloon as their belly.

<u>Game play</u>: Divide the guests into two teams. Give each team a balloon and start the game. Within each team, either the members take turns taping a balloon to their belly with scotch tape or they can slip it underneath their shirt/costume as long as it doesn't fall off during the race. You will need to have an equal number of 'tapers' and 'underneath shirts' on each team to keep it fair. **Make sure to have judges available for this game!

Create a start line and a finish line about 10 feet away. This is relay style and each team should line up in a single file line behind the Start Line. When you blow the whistle, the first team member grab a balloon and are to create their balloon bellies (no help is allowed from their team members unless you decide to allow them to get help) and 'crab walk' across the racing path with their bellies intact. If any team member's belly pops and /or falls off – they are to start over at the Start line (obviously with a new balloon if it pops). Once they cross the finish line, they can remove their balloon belly and race back to the start line and hand it off to their teammate who is next in line. This continues until the last team member crosses the finish line.

<u>Game gear:</u>   two balloons for each team but have extra balloons on hand in case one more pop during the challenge.

<u>Game time:</u> ~20 minutes.

Perfect Popcorn Transfer:

Game goal: to move every piece of your team's popcorn from start to finish using a wooden spoon.

Game play: you will need a container for each team with the same amount of popcorn inside of each container at the start line. The empty container is located at the finish line.

When the host says go, one member from each group is to scoop as much popcorn as possible into their spoon and transport it into the container at the finish line. If any popcorn is dropped during the transport, the team member has to bend down and pick it up, place it back on his/her spoon - before moving on towards the finish line. Once a team member has dropped of their popcorn load into the container at the finish line, they are to come back to the start line and hand off the wooden spoon to the next player in line. This will repeat throughout each team until every piece of popcorn is transported into the finish line container. The team that transports all of their popcorn first – wins!
If any popcorn is stepped on and crushed during the challenge, the crushed pieces must be picked up and transported into the finish line container!

Game gear: two containers for each team, a start line, a finish line (~ 5-10 feet away), a wooden spoon for each team, and an equal amount of popcorn for each team.

Game time: ~10 minutes.

Tourist Versus Natives Relay Race:

Game goal: be the team that can fully dress your tourist or Hawaiian native the fastest!   Great for luau parties!

Game play: divide your guests into two groups. Mark off lines approximately 15 feet (or more) away from each other. The teams flip a coin to determine who the tourist team is and who the Hawaiian native team is. Each team will select their model.

Gather the following items for the tourist team: Hawaiian shirt, Bermuda shorts, visible sun block for the nose, flip flops, floppy hat, beach ball, etc. Gather the following items for the native team: a grass skirt, a coconut top or other top, a lei, a flower for the hair, lei wristlets and anklets, a ukulele, etc. Put an equal amount of items on either side of the two lines.

When the host says go, the models from each team will crab walk to the other side of the opposing line. Once the model has all four limbs across the line, their team members can put on one item from their pile. Then, the model is to crab walk back across the opposing line that is 15 or more feet away. Once the model has all four limbs across the line, the team members waiting on that side of the line are to place one item on their team member. If needed, the team member can stand up, etc. to get the item on. If at any time, an item falls off a model during their crab walk to the other side – they must immediately crab walk backwards to the side they were just on and have their team members put the item(s) back on.

This continues until the model is fully dressed in their attire (i.e. native or tourist). Once a model has all of their items on – their team wins!

Game gear: items for the tourist and items for the native to wear during the relay.

Game time: ~20 minutes.

An example set up of the Tourist versus Native Game:

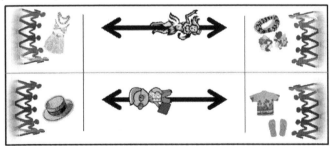

The Blarney Stone Pot O' Gold Toss:
Game goal: to land the most gold coins in the pot o' gold.

Game play: get any cardboard box, spray paint it gold, and decorate the bottom of the pot with green shamrocks cut out of construction paper. Allow at least 24 hours to dry before playing.   Purchase gold chocolate coins of various colors - or label each set of coins by taping small pictures of each guest on each coin.   (Also, purchase toy coins instead of chocolate coins).

Tape off a toss line approximately 10 feet away from the pot o' gold and allow each guest to toss either 5 or 10 coins into the pot o' gold.   The guest who lands the most coins - wins! There is a toss off for any guests that tie.   If they are making all of their coins into the pot - make it more challenging by moving back the toss line.   Change it up and play again by blindfolding your guests before they toss!

Game gear: a cardboard box, gold spray paint, green construction paper and scissors, gold coins (chocolate or toy), and a sheet of paper and pen to keep score.   An optional blindfold for a blindfolded challenge.

Game time is approximately 5-10 minutes.

Get the Party Started Relay Race:
Game goal: to work together and finish the relay the fastest!

Game play: split the guests into three teams of three.   A large area for a relay race is needed - preferably outside.   Place three random items from the theme of your party (i.e. a cowboy hat, a pirate eye patch, a birthday tiara, a plastic witch finger, etc.) at the end of each lane of the race.

Optional: outline the lanes for the relay race with crepe paper (streamers) weighted down by balloon weights so the guests will know where to run.   Tie helium-filled balloons to the balloon weights to help mark off the lanes.

The items of clothing can be anything that you have to put on within the theme of the party- i.e. hats, socks, pants, shoes, etc.   Try to keep the types of items even between teams - so don't give one team a bunch of hats while the other team gets all socks.   Line up the guests behind the starting lines and when you are ready, blow a whistle to start the race.

Upon the whistle blow, the three competitors in the front of the line from each team will race to the other end of the lane by pushing a balloon with their nose down the lane.   They are not allowed to use their hands to touch the balloon. If it goes completely off course – completely out of the lane – they must put it back at the start line and start over (the host is to judge whether it completely left the lane or not).

When they get to the end of the lane with the balloon, they must select one of the random items of clothing from the pile and put it on. The clothing has to be completely on before they can pick up the balloon and race back to the start/finish line. They are to transfer the item of clothing to the next team member in line.

The next team member must race to the other end of the line by pushing the balloon with their nose. When this player reaches the end of the lane, s/he must put on a second item of clothing on, pick up the balloon and run back to the third team member in line.

The second player must transfer *both* items of clothing to the third team member and so on until all players have received a turn. The first team to have their third member – wearing all three items of clothing – cross the finish line holding their balloon - wins! If the guests are having fun with this game, change it up and instead of running back down the lanes, try crab-walking, walking backwards, or even walking on their hands!

Game gear: Random items of clothing in the theme of the game, three balloons (and a couple of extra in case one pops), and crepe paper or tape to line off the racing lanes.

Game time: ~ 20 minutes.

Careful Cotton Carry Challenge:

Game goal: to transfer the most cotton balls from point A to point B while blindfolded!

Game play: place cotton balls all over the floor in about a 3' by 4' area or inside of a large bowl. Blindfold one guest, spin them around two times and hand them a large spoon or a small plastic shovel. The player is to scoop up as many cotton balls as they can with the spoon/shovel and then transfer them in to a bowl about five feet away. (Cotton balls are so light; the player will not be able to tell if they got any on their spoon/shovel.) The player can only use the ladle/shovel to get the cotton balls– s/he cannot touch the cotton balls with their hands or check to see if there are any present on the spoon/shovel. The player can touch the rim of the bowl with the hand not holding the spoon/shovel and then transfer the cotton balls (if any) with the other hand holding the spoon/shovel. Keeping the blindfold on, s/he can do this three times for three trips. The player is not allowed to check inside of the bowl at any time.

After three trips, s/he removes the blindfold and the host counts the cotton balls. Place the cotton balls back where they were and continue until all guests have had a turn. A prize or a certificate for the winner of the most transferred cotton balls can be awarded. If there is a tie, the player with the fastest time wins (you'll need to designate a person to keep time for each guest).

play this game in teams and add up the scores of each team member for a final score for each team.

Game gear: a few packages of cotton balls, a large spoon, ladle or small plastic shovel, and a large bowl.

Game time: ~20 minutes.

Jell-O'tastic Relay Race:

Game goal: to transport the most Jell-O cubes to an empty bowl while suffering various vertical challenges.

Game play: divide your guests into equal teams. It's no big deal to have an odd number team as the players rotate - the odd team will just have one extra player to rotate - no worries!

Fill a bowl with Jell-O cubes (make them with ice cube trays or prepare a sheet of Jell-O and cut into cubes) and place in front of each team. Place a plastic rounded toothpick by an empty bowl about 10 feet in front of each team. When the host says go, the first player on each team will run and grab the toothpick, come back to the Jell-O cube bowl, carefully stab a Jell-O cube and then transport it to the empty bowl. The players are not to touch the Jell-O cubes! If at any time, the Jell-O cube falls off the toothpick - or any piece of it falls off the toothpick -

the player must return to the bowl to get a new cube. *(Make sure you make plenty of cubes!)* After the player has transported a cube, s/he must rush back to their team, tag the next player in line, and hand them the toothpick (carefully)!

Here's where the difficulty comes into play: Each racer must get 'lower' than the team member in front of them did when they raced until someone has to lie down and scoot along the floor to the other side. Then, after the flat scooter completes their run, the next racer can start over by standing up.

For example: the first player walks upright, the second player can bend their knees slightly, the third player can walk on their knees, the next racer can sit down and scoot across the floor (or crawl) and then the next racer can lay down on the floor and scoot to the other side. Once each player gets to the other side to the bowl, they can stand up to put their cube into the bowl on a table - if it is on the floor - then there's no need to stand up until the Jell-O cube is inside of the bowl. If at any time the host (or other judge) notices that a team member is not transporting their Jell-O cube lower than the team member before, the player must go back to the starting point and start their turn over.

The host parent will decide the time limit and set the timer. Five to ten minutes are suggested time limits. Make sure you have enough Jell-O cubes for your time limit!

Game gear: plastic toothpicks, Jell-O cubes. A pair of kneepads for each team is suggested for the players who have to walk on their knees. Instead of kneepads, have long tube socks available and the players can tie these around their knees before their turn.

Game time: ~ 15 minutes.

Mummified Relay Extravaganza:
Game goal: to get all of your players across the finish line first!

Game play: divide your group into two or more teams. Have a roll of toilet paper for ½ of your guests and plenty of candy corn. Each team will need to split up into the following groups - the mummies and the mummifiers (two guests maximum).

Rope off (or just put pieces of tape at either end of the racing lanes) as many racing lanes as you have teams. Make the racing lanes as long as you wish. Designate one end as the start / finish and the other end as the mummification end. The mummifiers will wait at the mummification end of the racing lane with the toilet paper.

When the host says, one mummy from each team race to the other side of the racing lane to the mummifiers. The hard part is...each mummy must balance a piece of candy corn on their nose. If at any time the candy corn drops to the ground, the mummy must go back to the start and put a new candy corn on their nose. The mummies cannot use their hands in any way! Once a mummy gets to the mummification end of the racing lane, the mummifiers are to wrap an entire roll of toilet tissue around the mummy. They must wrap at least two times around each limb and the head - in addition to the body (torso). No toilet paper can be left behind. The mummy will race back to the start/finish line (no candy corn on the way back) and tag the next mummy in line, who must again, repeat the process by balancing a candy corn on their nose. This will repeat until all mummies have made it past the finish line. (Make sure to get many pics!)

Game gear: enough rolls of toilet tissue for each mummy (~8-10) and candy corn.

Game time: ~20 minutes.

Favorite Animal Relay Race:
Game goal: to get all of the animals on your team across the finish line first!

Game play: divide your group into two or more teams.
Prior to telling the team what the challenge is, have them write down on a team roster what their favorite animal is next to their name. Once everybody has filled in their favorites, announce that from this point on, until there is a winner, everybody must remain in the character of their animal they have chosen. Birds must flap their wings, snakes must slither on the ground, dogs

and other four-legged mammals must be on all fours, elephants must use one arm as a trunk and get on all threes, etc.

Rope off (or just put pieces of tape at either end of the racing lanes) as many racing lanes as you have teams. Make the racing lanes as long as you wish. Designate one end as the start / finish.

When the host says go, the first team member on the roster for each team must race to the finish line in the character of the animal that s/he chose. Once this player crosses the finish line, the next player on their team may race to the finish line and this will continue until the last member crosses the line. If, at any time, a member of either team steps out of his/her animal character, they must go back to the start line and start over. This includes those members waiting at the finish line for team members to cross the line!

It is suggested to have multiple judges for this contest! The winning team is the one who has all animal members across the finish line, first.

Game gear: a sense of imagination.

Game time: ~10 minutes.

Four-Legged Human Relay Challenge:

Game goal: to get of your four-legged human team members across the finish line first!

Game play: divide your group into two or more teams. Give each team a piece of fabric, bandanas tied together, or other item to tie two legs of two team members together. The teams will further divide into pairs. In the event of an odd number, one member of the last pair will also pair with the remaining player on the team.

Assemble half of the team on one side of the relay lane and the other half of the team on the opposing side.

Rope off (or just put pieces of tape at either end of the racing lanes) as many racing lanes as you have teams. Make the racing lanes as long as you wish. Designate one end as the start / finish.

When the host says go, the first two members will tie their legs together (one right leg, one left leg) and then race to the opposing end of the relay lane. After crossing the finish/start line, they will tag the next team members in line, remove their tie and hand it to the next pair. They will tie their legs together and race to the opposing start/finish line and this will continue until all members of their team have crossed a start/finish line.

The winning team is the one who has all four legged human members across the finish line, first.

Game gear: a tie long enough to tie two legs together – one for each team.

Game time: ~20 minutes.

Hula Hoopin' Relay Race:

Game goal: to get all of your hula hoopin' team members across the finish line first!

Game play: divide your group into two or more teams.

Rope off (or just put pieces of tape at either end of the racing lanes) as many racing lanes as you have teams. Make the racing lanes as long as you wish. Designate one end as the start / finish. Hand the first member in line a hula-hoop. They are to start hula hooping immediately and must continue hula hooping until they pass the finish line.

When the host says go, the team member must race across the relay lane, cross the finish line and come back to the start line to pass the hula-hoop to the next player in line. The entire time s/he must maintain the hula-hoop around their body without touching it. Even on their return to the start line to give the hula-hoop to the next player, they must keep the hula-hoop around them until the next player removes it!

If at any time a hula-hoop drops &/or a racer touches it with their hands, they must go back to the start line and start over. The first team that gets all of their hula-hoopin' members across the finish line – wins!

Game gear: hula-hoop for each team.

Game time: ~20 minutes.

Front to Back Relay Challenge:
Game goal: to get all of your players across the finish line first!

Game play: divide your group into two or more teams.
Instruct the teams to form a line at the start of the relay lane. Instruct every other team member to turn backwards.

Rope off (or just put pieces of tape at either end of the racing lanes) as many racing lanes as you have teams. Make the racing lanes as long as you wish. Designate one end as the start / finish.

When the host says go, the teams will race to the end of the line and back. The forward players must remain forward on the way down the relay lane and then must race backward on the return race. When they cross the start/finish line, they tag the next racer who will begin their race backwards on the way down the lane and then go forward on the return to the start/finish line. This will continue until all members have crossed the finish line! The first team to get everybody across – wins!

Game gear: patience.

Game time: ~20 minutes.

Treasure Hunt Relay Challenge:
Game goal: to get the most precious treasures across your finish line in three minutes!

Game play: divide your group into two or more teams.
Place a bowl full of rhinestones of all sizes and colors at one end of the relay-racing lane. Assign a point value for the various colors (i.e. clear is ten points, blue is five points, red is two points, yellow is one point, etc.).

Rope off (or just put pieces of tape at either end of the racing lanes) as many racing lanes as you have teams. Make the racing lanes as long as you wish. Designate one end as the start / finish.

Set the time for three minutes. When the host says go, one member of each team is to race to their bowl of jewels at the end of the relay lane. They are to select any five pieces they wish to return to their bowl at the start/finish line. If they come back to the start/finish line with more than 5 pieces, none of the pieces they have in their possession will count and the team member's turn is lost. (You'll need to post a judge at the start/finish line.) Play continues until the timer runs out. The judge will count the point value of the rhinestones in each bowl at the start/finish line. The team with the highest point value wins!

Game gear: two empty bowls for the start/finish line and two bowls full of various colors of rhinestones with assigned point values. Have a sign with their point values posted on a wall.

As an alternative for a pirate party, get treasure chests to house the jewels at the end of the lane and miniature ships at the start/finish lines for the teams to put their treasures into.

Game time: ~20 minutes.

Chapter 24

Arts & Crafts Party Games

The Fabulous Party Dress Challenge:

Game goal: to be the most fashionable and talented party dress designers at the party!

Game play: divide your guests into teams of three -four. Give at least six rolls of toilet paper to each team. Each team needs to select one party girl or guy (model) and the rest of the team is tailors.

The object is for the tailors to design and create the most fashionable party dress (or suit)...out of toilet paper only! Accessories can also be made...but only with toilet paper!

The timer is set for ten minutes and during the game play, the partier stands patiently during the fitting and the tailors frantically design and create the most stunning party dress while watching the timer closely.

When the bell rings – time is up! All models must immediately line up and one-by-one they are to model their dresses and suits in a trendy model walk for the rest of the group. The host can play music in the background to get the models moving! The host will judge or allow the guests to vote via secret ballot but they cannot vote for their own creation. If the secret ballot vote ends in a tie, the host will serve as the tiebreaker.

Game gear: toilet paper – six rolls for each team, a catwalk, and music for modeling.

Game time: ~15 minutes.

Frugal Fashionistas:

Game goal: to make the most fashionable runway outfit out of duct tape and newspaper!

Game play: split your group into at least three teams of three. Designate one team member as the runway model. Give each team one roll of duct tape (or other type of tape) and two -three newspapers. They are to design and create the most fashionable outfit for the runway show in the given time period (i.e. 10-15 minutes).

The outfit can contain anything fashionable (i.e. dress, shoes, jewelry, hat, purse, etc.). They cannot duct tape anything to the model's skin - the newspaper is the only thing that can touch the duct tape! (You don't want to deal with trying to remove duct tape off your guests!)

Find a good area to make your catwalk. Line it with streamers or tape of any kind and play a fun modeling song (i.e. Ru Paul's Supermodel) in the background to get the models moving! When the time is up, the runway models are to line up at the beginning of the runway, strut their stuff and sell that outfit to the judge(s)! Either the host can judge or the guests can vote via a secret ballot but they cannot vote for their own creation!

Game gear: duct tape, scissors, newspapers, a mapped out runway and a modeling song!

Game time: ~ 25 minutes.

One with Nature:

Game goal: to make the most awesome piece of jewelry out of things you collect on a nature hike.

Game play: this is an individual challenge. Take your guests on a nature hike through a predetermined route. Give each guest a basket / bag for collecting items during their hike such as leaves, rocks, etc.

Back at the party area, have a table ready with various craft items such as non-toxic glue, jewelry wire, wire cutters, non-toxic paint, string, etc.

Set a timer for 10 minutes and allow your guests to use their nature items to make the most fascinating piece of jewelry! The host will judge the winner after the items have had a time to dry.

Game gear: non-toxic glue, jewelry wire, wire cutters, non-toxic paint, string, etc. and nature related items collected during a nature hike

Game time: ~ 45 minutes.

Make Me A Necklace, Baby!
Game goal: to be the first to make the most beautiful necklace out of very, very strange items.

Game play: give each player a 24" length piece of yarn with two respective 'knots' on either side about three-four inches in to designate the beading length. The yarn on either side of the knots is used to tie the necklace and the knots should be tight & small enough not to prevent the items from being beaded onto the necklace. Place each 'item' into a bowl in a line - either on a table or on the floor. It is optimal if you can reach the bowls from either side. Space out the bowls as far apart as possible. When the host says go, the players are to start beading their necklaces with the items provided. The first one to make a complete beaded necklace and tie it securely on their necks is the winner. Additional Guidelines: no two items can be identical that touch each other and no piece of the yarn besides the yarn that is tied on the other side of the knot - can show. *An alternative way to play is to provide foil, glue, paint, construction paper, felt, and other craft items and instead of it being a timed challenge, allow your guests to have creative freedom and the most beautiful and creative necklace will win!

Game gear: Knitting yarn, any items with a hole in the middle (i.e. bolts, cheerios, olives, lifesavers, etc.)

Game time: ~ 10 minutes.

Foiltastic Jewelers:

Game goal: to be the first to make the most beautiful piece of jewelry out of foil!

Game play: give each player unlimited access to foil and jeweler's wire. Set the timer for 10 minutes and allow your guests to be as creative as possible designing the most awesome piece of jewelry out of aluminum foil and jeweler's wire (if needed).

Game gear: aluminum foil, jeweler's wire, wire cutters.

Game time: ~ 10 minutes.

Pasta Puppeteers:

Game goal: to create the best marionette out of uncooked pasta!

Game play: give each player unlimited access to uncooked pasta, quick drying non-toxic glue, non-toxic markers &/or paint, string and Popsicle sticks. Set the timer for 20 minutes and allow your guests to be as creative as possible designing the most awesome marionette doll out of uncooked pasta.
Have a puppet show after the dolls dry!

Game gear: uncooked pasta of all varieties, non-toxic markers, non-toxic paint and non-toxic quick drying craft glue. String and Popsicle sticks for controlling the marionette dolls.

Game time: ~ 20 minutes.

Secret Agent Disguise Challenge:

Game goal: to be the team that can best disguise your secret agent out of toilet tissue.

Game play: divide your guests into pairs. Give each team unlimited access to toilet tissue and clear tape. One member of the team is the designer and the other is the secret agent in desperate need of a disguise.

Set the timer for 10 minutes and allow your guests to be as creative as possible designing the best disguise out of toilet tissue. They are to disguise their secret agent with anything they can create such as a moustache, beard, glasses, wig, etc. The tape can only be used to assist in the creation of items out of toilet paper and to adhere these items to the secret agent. The tape cannot be used alone on the secret agent such as taping eyes wide open or taping nose flat, etc. Be careful with the tape on the model's skin, use common sense and don't apply tape where it will be harmful to the secret agent in any manner!

The team could just mummify their secret agent but that's not very creative! It's a challenge on being creative! The host will judge the best disguise!

Game gear: toilet tissue, clear tape.

Game time: ~ 15 minutes.

Chapter 25

Fun Party Games: Athletic (Non-Relay Race)

The Perfect Dance:

Game goal: The objective is to perform the best *perfect dance* out of the group!

Game play: have your guests sit in a circle. One at a time, each player will stand up and make up a 'four count' dance move of their choice. The next player in the circle will stand up, perform the previous player's dance move, and then add a 'four count' dance move of their choice. This will continue until everyone has had a chance to add a 'four count' dance move around the circle.

Then, go around the circle once more so each guest can practice the *Perfect Dance*. It is all right at this time for the guests to make mistakes and receive feedback from the group. Then, when everyone is ready, have the guests sit as an audience, play a groovy dance song and allow each guest to perform the *Perfect Dance* to music in front of the group.

An alternative way to play is to allow the guests to perform in groups of two or three. Some guests might not want to perform at all, and this is fine - don't try to force it as some people are shy and reserved.

The host is the judge or the guests can vote via a secret ballot for the winner - the winner is the one who performed the *Perfect Dance* the very best!

For lasting memories, have the group perform the dance together and get it on video!

Game gear: any dance song.

Game time: ~ 30 minutes.

The Bubble Walk Test:

Game goal: to get across the bubble wrap by popping the least amount of bubbles.

Game play: purchase about five feet of bubble wrap packing material for each guest. At packing supply companies, purchase a large roll for about 18-20$ that will be enough for most party sizes. The guests take turns walking the length of their bubble wrap strips. The first one to walk the length of the wrap without popping a bubble is the winner. If everyone does it without a pop – then change it up to walking on his or her knees, crab walks, front rolls etc.

Game gear: strips of bubble wrapping material for each guest.

Game time: ~ 10 minutes.

When the Cat's Away, the Mice will Play:

Game goal: to take out the mice before they find all of the cheese.

Game play: divide your guests into two teams – cats and mice. Give the mice colored bandanas to hang out of their back pocket or the back of their knee-high socks. These are what the cats will grab to take them out of the game. There must be at least five inches of bandana exposed (i.e. hanging) to be fair to the cats.

Keep the cats in one location and the mice in the opposite corner of whatever boundaries you have set to play the game. If they can see you, ask them to face the wall while you hide five pieces of cheese (the *cheese* can be a picture cut out, stuffed toy cheese, real piece/packages of cheese, etc.) throughout your home, yard or neighborhood or other location for the game. *(Hide ½ of the amount of cheese as you have mice. So if you have ten mice, hide five pieces of cheese and so on.)* If the two groups cannot see you and you have them separated into two opposite rooms, hide the cheese in midway points between the two groups. Tell your guests the boundaries for the hunt.

When you are ready, shout *get the cheese, mice* and the mice and cats are released from their respective locations.

The cats' objective is to locate the mice and take their bandana to take them out of the game. When a mouse loses their bandana, they immediately must stop foraging for cheese and take a seat against the wall in the room until the game is over. They are not allowed to continue to play by restraining the cats! If the mice collect all five pieces of cheese, the game is over and the mice win. If the cats get all of the mice out of the game before all of the pieces of cheese are collected, the cats win.

Game gear: bandanas (or other strips of fabric) for the mice, five (or more/less) pieces of cheese. The cheese can be anything you wish to hide and call cheese. Make the cheese out of felt, print out photos of cheese, use real cheese, etc.

Game time: ~ 15 minutes.

The Perfect Cheer:

Game goal: each guest contributes one line with a corresponding cheer movement to create the perfect cheer. Be the last one standing to perform the perfect cheer!

Game play: instruct your guests to sit in a circle. One at a time, each player will stand up and make up a line of a cheer about your party theme (i.e. Alice in Wonderland, Witches, Pirates) or stick with a traditional cheer. Along with the line, they are to choreograph a corresponding cheer move of their choice (i.e. 2,4,6,8 who do we appreciate)!

The next player in the circle will stand up, perform the previous player's cheer, and then add their own cheer line and corresponding cheer move of their choice. This will continue until everyone has had a chance to add a piece of the cheer around the circle.

Then, go back around the circle so each guest can practice the *Perfect Cheer*. It is all right at this time for the guests to make mistakes and get feedback from the group. Then, when everyone is ready, have the guests sit as an audience, and in any size group, they are to perform the *Perfect Cheer*. Basic guideline is the younger the group, the more you have in each performing group. For example, put four-five cheerleaders in a group of 6 year olds, pairs or trios for 8-10 year olds and then 16-year-old competitive cheerleaders should go it solo. The ages in between (i.e. 7 years old, 13 years old, etc.) – you make the call as you'll know your group the best. Not only will they need help remembering the cheer they just learned when they are younger, they are more apt to be insecure and shy performers. You are having a party and you want everybody to have fun and not be stressed and sad!

The host is the judge or the guests can vote via a secret ballot for the winner - the winner is the one who performed the *Perfect Cheer* the very best! For lasting memories, have the group perform the cheer together and get it on video!

Game gear: spunky attitudes!

Game time: ~ 30 minutes.

The Cheertastic Dance Contest:

Game goal: The objective is to be the most cheertastic dancers at the party!

Game play: divide your guests into pairs. Give the teams ten minutes (or more) to create a unique 30-second cheertastic dance routine to be performed to the song Holla Back Girl by Gwen Stefani or Mickey by Toni Basil. Any song that has a cheer theme is great. Each team should show their unique talents as cheer dancers! No need to be a good or technically sound dancer - just be unique! Play the song repeatedly in the background so the teams have ample time to practice with the music.

When the time is up and / or the guests are finished creating their routines, one at a time, the groups are to perform their routines for the other guests. The host will judge or the guests will vote via a ballot for the best cheertastic dance routine. In the case of a tie, the host will be the tiebreaker. *Note - there are no cheer stunts allowed in the routine and this dance routine must be unique and created by the teams. No dance moves (8's) from a past cheer or dance routine can be used.*

Game gear: any type of music playing source and a cheertastic themed song (playing any dance song is acceptable).

Playing time: ~ 30 minutes.

Stuntacular Challenge:

Game goal: to create the best cheer stunt under non-ideal conditions. *This game is only recommended for cheerleaders that are trained to perform stunts.*

Game play: the party guests should be teams of four (five or six people can be part of a group if there is an odd number). The objective is to create the most unique cheer stunt under non-ideal conditions in the allotted time of 15 minutes. No basket tosses or dangerous stunts are allowed and the host should elect safety monitors for each team and provide a safe, adequate area for this challenge.

Once the teams are selected, they are to choose which team member will have the following challenge during the stunt:

Cheerleader #1: must stay on his/her knees
Cheerleader #2: cannot use her right arm.
Cheerleader #3: is blindfolded.
Cheerleader #4: cannot use her left arm.
Cheerleader #5-6: cannot face any of the other cheerleaders during the stunt - s/he has to stand either to the side or with his /her back to the team.

The teams will perform their stunts and the host will judge or the party guests can vote via a secret ballot with the host / host parent being the tiebreaker.

Game gear: spunky attitudes, safety mats or a bouncy gym floor!

Playing time: ~ 20 minutes.

So You Think You Can Dance Contest:

Game goal: to be the most awesome dancers at the party!

Game play: pair the guests into groups of two to three. Create the types of dance strips, fold them and place into any container. Think of any types of dances for the dance strips such as Waltz, Fox Trot, Break Dance, '70s Disco, 7th Grade Couples Dance, etc. Each team is to draw from a hat or any other type of container – a dance strip.

Give the teams ten minutes (or more) to create a unique 30-second dance routine in their type of dance that they drew to be performed to any dance song of your choice. Play the song repeatedly in the background so the teams have ample time to practice with the music. If the team doesn't know the style of dance - they can re-draw, look it up on the internet (i.e. how to video on YouTube.com) or trade with someone who does…or just give it their best shot!

When the time is up and / or the guests are finished creating their routines, one at a time, the guests are to perform their routines for the other guests. The host will judge who came up with the best interpretation of the dance style and fit it best with the music. The guests can vote via a ballot for the best dance routine (and they cannot vote for themselves). In the case of a tie, the host is the tiebreaker.

Game gear: any type of music playing source and a dance song. The dance type strips are folded and placed into any container (i.e. hat, bowl, large sock, etc.) There is a So You Think you can Dance mp3 available for instant download on My Mystery Party in the Mystery Prop Emporium at http://www.mymysteryparty.com/mypapr.html.

Game time: ~30 minutes.

The Great Watermelon Toss:
Game goal: to toss the most beanbags on the watermelon!

Game play: locate the largest watermelon you can and place three to five feet away from the toss line. (Consider making a paper mache watermelon instead.)

Using small beanbags and / or hacky sacks, allow your guests to stand behind the toss line and have three attempts at a toss to the watermelon. The person who gets the most beanbags or hacky sacks to remain on top of the watermelon wins!

Game gear: beanbags and a watermelon and tape to mark the toss line.

Game time: ~5 minutes.

Monster Mayhem:
Game goal: not to be the monster in the middle!

Game play: the monster in the middle (the one who is it) calls out *Monster Mayhem for everybody who is:_____.*

The blank can be absolutely anything – wearing green, has a cat, has a sister, drives a white car, etc. Those matching the description are to immediately stand up and switch with another player who also fits the description. The monster in the middle must fight for one of the open seats and the last person standing without a seat is the monster in the middle.

It's just like musical chairs but without the music. If only one person stands during monster mayhem, they are automatically the monster in the middle. The person who had to be the monster in the middle the least amount of times after the end of game play is the winner! *During monster mayhem, a person cannot re-sit in his or her own chair.* If only one person stands during monster mayhem, they are automatically the monster in the middle.

Game gear: chairs for each player besides the monster in the middle.

Game time: ~15 minutes.

Ping Pong Madness:
Game goal: to be the team that obtains the most ping-pong balls with the highest point values.

Game play: divide your teams into groups of two -three players each. Write an arbitrary point value on as many ping-pong balls as you choose to play with and dump them in the middle of the pool.

When the host says go, one member from each team can enter the pool without splashing and retrieve a ping-pong ball. They come back to the side, exit the pool and place it in their team's bucket. When their entire body is out of the water, the next player on their team can enter the pool to retrieve the next ball and so on. Jumping or diving into the pool is illegal (it can get too dangerous) so the players must enter the pool without splashing. Anyone who splashes while entering the pool must exit the pool and reenter the pool before retrieving their next ping-pong ball.

First Game Variation: put a colored dot on each ball, the players can only collect the balls with their color dot on them, and the first team to collect all of their balls - wins!

Second Game Variation: allow all players to enter the pool on go and race to fetch as many balls as possible as quickly as possible.

Game gear: swimming pool, ping-pong balls and buckets for each team to collect their ping-pong balls in.

Game time: ~20 minutes.

The P.G.A. (Party Golf Association) Tournament:
Game goal: to be the team that can rack up the most points by a gentle putt of your golf ball to the bull's-eye!

Game play: divide the guests into groups of three – four. Cut out one color of construction paper (or thin felt) in about a three - inch (7.5 cm) diameter circle. With a different color, cut out a larger circle with a five-inch (12.5 cm) diameter and tape the smaller circle inside of the larger one, and repeat this process about four to five times until you've created a colorful bulls-eye. Write the applicable scores on the bulls-eye for each circle (i.e. 50, 40, 30, etc.). Tape this bulls-eye to the floor and mark a 5-foot line away from the bulls-eye on the floor. From this line is where the guests will putt their golf balls using the putter.

One at a time, using a putter, each guest gently putts a golf ball (or plastic Easter egg) towards the bulls-eye. The host records the score of where each ball (or egg) lands. <u>Where the actual ball touches</u> is the score that is recorded - it doesn't matter if the ball is hovering above a higher score - it ONLY matters where the ball encounters the paper of the target. Any ball that doesn't land on the target will be recorded as a try for zero points.

Each player on the team gets five tries and the top three scores are recorded. In the case of unequal teams, count an extra try for the applicable amount of guests on the smaller team to make it an even number of tries for all teams.

If the player requests a practice putt - this practice putt will not count towards the five tries but the score will not be recorded even if it lands on the bulls-eye.

<u>Game gear:</u> colored construction paper (or thin felt), scissors, tape, golf balls (or plastic Easter eggs) and a putter.

<u>Game time:</u> ~20 minutes.

Quick Thinker Balloon Contest:

<u>Game goal:</u> to be the team to keep your balloon afloat the longest by saying words within a theme in alphabetical order.

<u>Game play:</u> divide the groups into two teams. Give each team a balloon and start the game. *As an alternative, time each team and allow them to go separately to avoid chaos.*

Within each team, the members take turns hitting the balloon into the air – in a specified order - to avoid it touching the ground. The host is to pick a theme such as pirates or something related to the party theme. The team members designate a specific order in which they will come up with words in alphabetical order of this theme. For example, if you choose *animals* as your theme, player one will shout *Armadillo* and hit the balloon, player two will shout *Baboon* and hit the balloon;

player three will shout *Cat* and hit the balloon. When it is a team member's turn, they must say their word prior to hitting the balloon to keep it afloat. If at any time a team member goes out of order, fails to shout a word in the correct alphabetical order or shouts a word out of the designated theme, the game is over for that team and the host records what letter they were on when they got out &/or how many times through the alphabet they went. If you have two teams going simultaneously, the other team automatically wins – even if they haven't gotten as far in the alphabet (as long as they started at the same time). If you are doing separate trials, it is now time for the second team to go. The team that makes it through the most letters of the alphabet without making a mistake wins!

  If at any time a team's balloon hits a surface of any kind that is below the level of the team member, the team's trail is over. It is acceptable if the balloon hits a high part of a wall or ceiling but a table below the level of a player is not acceptable.

  ***Make sure to have many judges available for this game!*

Game gear: two differently colored balloons with a few balloon backups in case of an accidental popping.

Game time: ~ 15 minutes.

Balloon Popathon:

Game goal: to locate your opposing team's color of balloons and pop them all before your team's balloons are popped.

Game play: divide your guests into two teams. Have at least 10 balloons of two different colors and float them randomly throughout the room &/or game area that you choose (choose the entire house, etc.) Designate each team as a balloon color and this is the color that the team must protect.

  When the host says go, team members are to grab the opposing team's balloons and pop them. The team that has the last balloon intact wins!

Game gear: at least ten helium balloons for each team in two different colors.

Game time: ~10 minutes.

The Balloon Blow Challenge:

Game goal: to be the last team that keeps your balloon afloat by blowing on it.

Game play: divide the guests into two teams. Give each team a balloon and start the game. Within each team, the members take turns blowing their balloon into the air to avoid it touching the ground. No hands or any body part is allowed to touch the balloon or the team is disqualified and the other team automatically wins! Including any part of the face!

   The team must alternate the blowers and stay in the same order or they are disqualified. The first team to either not alternate blowers, use a body part or other object to hit the balloon, or to allow their balloon to touch the ground is the losing team. **Make sure to have many judges available for this game!*

Game gear: two differently colored balloons with a few balloon backups in case of an accidental popping.

Game time: ~ 10 minutes.

Capture the Balloon:

Game goal: to locate the opposing team's hidden balloon and pop it before your team's balloon is popped.

Game play: divide your guests into two (or more) teams. Give each team a balloon to hide in a designated game area (i.e. house, backyard, neighborhood, etc.) Allow the guests to scatter around the play area and when the host says go; the guests are to look for the opposing teams' hidden balloon(s). The last team with their balloon intact – wins!

Game gear: a balloon for each team.

Game time: ~20 minutes.

Let's Do Business with Balloons:

Game goal: to find the highest point total balloon!

Game play: with at least 20 balloons, insert slips of paper with various dollar amounts into the balloons prior to filling up with helium.

This is an individual challenge where two players can play against each other. Each guest is to select a balloon and hold on to it. They are not allowed to try to view the piece of paper inside so have them keep the balloons afloat above their head.

At this time, the host is to take two balloons out of play and put them aside.

With the remaining 16 balloons, each player is to take a turn selecting a balloon, pop it and open the slip of paper inside of them, revealing the point total. They can choose to stick with the new point total of the balloon they just popped or stick with their original choice, which is floating above their head. If they stick with their original choice, the point value they selected is out of play and play continues with the players alternating. Play continues until one player picks the high point total balloon or once all of the 16 balloons have been popped open. If a player remained with their original choice, they can pop this balloon and reveal the point total at the end of the challenge. The player with the highest point total balloon wins!

Game gear: 20 helium filled balloons with slips of paper containing various point totals on them.

Game time: ~20 minutes.

Chapter 26

Fun Party Games: Non-athletic

Excellent Charades:

Game goal: to earn the most points by guessing the charades correctly!

Game play: one player draws a charade topic from a hat and acts it out for the other players. The first one to guess correctly the charade topic gets a point. Play continues until all of the topics are guessed correctly.

The actor of the charade may not speak, point to an object, or acknowledge the other players until they give a correct guess. Decide if the actor is allowed to hold up the amount of words in the phrase with their fingers before starting. Also, decide if they can cup their ear to act out words that 'sound like' other words. Whatever you choose, make it known before the game begins.

This game may also be played in teams.

Example charade topics are as follows but you should choose charade topics within the theme of your party:

Fingernail polish	Chocolate Donut	Apple a Day
Sports Car	Wart Hog	Jelly Bellies
Light Microscope	English Teacher	First Cousin
Octopus	Doberman Pincher	Rock Salt
Yellow Submarine	Trumpet	Court Jester
Deputy	Superhero	Dog Food
Kitty Litter	Board Game	Hamburger

Game gear: paper strips, pen (or word processing program and printer), and a hat (or any container to hold the pieces of paper with the charade topics).

Game time: ~20 minutes.

Human Bingo:

Game goal: to be the first one to bingo by finding guests who can answer *yes* to the squares on your bingo sheet!

Game play: make bingo sheets with as many squares as you desire. A typical sheet will have either four by four or five by five format. Put a random event in each square such as 'owns a red bicycle, has seen all Harry Potter films', or 'has been to Las Vegas.'

When the host says go, the guests will start asking each other questions on their bingo cards. If anyone says yes to a question, the guest that said yes is to sign the square on the bingo card. If they say no to the question, the one asking the question must first answer a question for the player they just asked and then they may move on to ask someone else. The first player to get five across, down or diagonal – wins the first bingo.

The game can continue with the first to get two lines across, down or diagonal and then the first guest to blackout. If at any time it is discovered that nobody at the party can answer yes to a question – everyone gets credit for it immediately. In the event of a tie on the first bingo, the tiebreaker will be the first one to get another square signed.

As an alternative to this game, if this is performed for a company icebreaker, make it company-specific events in the bingo boxes or within your line of work, etc.

Game gear: bingo sheets and a pen/pencil for each guest.

Game time: ~ 5 -10 minutes.

Catch Me If You Can!

Game goal: to guess who the thief is before everyone in the group becomes a victim of the thief!

Game play: make strips that say innocent for each player in your game besides two – and the last two strip should read 'detective' and 'thief.' Fold the strips and put into a hat (or any type of container) and each player draws one strip and secretly reads their role in the game. Make sure to have the exact number of strips as players (only remove innocent strips as there must be a detective and a thief). A signal is chosen by the group (i.e. pointing finger, wink, stick out tongue, etc.) before the game commences. The detective goes to the middle of the circle where s/he must guess the identity of the thief before the thief steals everybody's prized possessions. The thief claims victims by secretly using the signal. If any player detects the signal coming from the thief s/he must frantically pretend she is missing something very important in an overly dramatic manner and cannot disclose whom the thief is. This player is to scoot back from the circle as they are out of the game.

The detective only has three guesses to guess the thief (more guesses can be given if the group agrees *before* the game commences). If the detective fails to guess in three guesses or in five minutes or if everyone besides the thief becomes a victim of the thief - whichever comes first - the thief wins the game and the game starts over by players drawing new roles out of the hat. This is repeated until nobody is willing to continue ☺ If you play long enough, give a prize to the best detective (best sleuther) and the best (most evasive) thief.

This game can be altered by changing the word thief to 'murderer' and then the guests that become victims must die in an overly dramatic manner when the murderer murders them.

Game gear: game strips of the same amount as there are players in the game and a hat or container to hold the strips.

Playing time: ~ 20 minutes.

Eyewitness Testimonies:
Game goal: to remember the most details about the crime you just witnessed.

Game play: the host explains that there has been a burglary (or other crime that you choose) reported in this area.

Choose a volunteer to be the 'burglar' and they are to go into an adjacent room. The burglar (or other criminal) is to dress up in an assortment of clothes – the sillier the better – with lots of accessories (i.e. sunglasses, a hat, a fake beard, a rolled up newspaper, a purse, etc.).

Then, announce to the players of the game that the suspect was last seen running away from the scene. Then, shout *there s/he is* and the volunteer burglar outside runs into the room and walks very quickly around and then leaves the room again. Then, explain that now they are all eyewitnesses, they will need to leave an account of what they saw as far as the suspect's description is concerned. The players then write down anything that they can remember about the suspect's appearance. The one with the most accurate list wins and s/he becomes the next burglar.

Game gear: an assortment of clothes and props for the burglars. Pens and paper for the eyewitnesses.

Game time: ~ 20 minutes.

Unmentionable Declarations:
Game goal: to be the team to answer the most secret words correctly without saying the prohibited descriptive words.

Game play: divide your guests into two teams. One team chooses a member to draw a secret word card. The secret word cards should include a secret word (or phrase) in bold, large font at the top and then below it, a list of forbidden or *unmentionable* descriptive words in smaller, un-bolded font. For example, if you select the secret word *juice*, then the unmentionable words below should be *drink, beverage, fruit, liquid, sweet.* Make at least five secret word cards for each team. It is preferred to select secret words or phrases within your party theme. For example, with a pirate party, make the secret word/ phrases *pieces of eight, spyglass, cutlass,* etc.

Set the timer for 30 seconds. The player is to describe the secret word or phrase at the top of the card without using any part of the secret word or phrase or the unmentionable words at the bottom of the card. The team member cannot say any form of the word(s) s/he is describing or any form of the prohibited words on the card.

One person from the opposing team is allowed to monitor the player that is describing the word to ensure that the rules are followed and s/he hasn't accidentally (or intentionally) said a forbidden word. A point is given when the guessing team members say the correct word - exactly how it written on the card - within the 30 seconds. Play alternates between teams until all cards are played.

Game gear: secret word cards placed in a pile face down. Any 30-second timer.

Game time: ~ 20 minutes.

No Mirror Prom Night:

Game goal: to be the team that works together to put on the best prom night makeup...without a mirror!

Game play: divide the guests into pairs. Each team is to have a dark–colored lipstick, three colors of eye shadow with applicators, eyeliner, blusher (rouge) with a blush brush, and lip liner and any other type of makeup you wish to use. It is not suggested to use mascara, as you do not want them to injure their eyes applying mascara without a mirror! Also, instruct them to close their eyes while applying the eye shadow as to not get eye shadow into their eyes.

Set the timer for two minutes and when the host says go, the team is to work together to put on one team member's (i.e. the prom date's) prom night makeup.

Instruct the pairs to face each other. There is to be no reflective surfaces in the room. One member is the instructor and the other is the prom date. The prom date is to clean their face prior to the game and not start with *any* makeup on their face. When the host says go, the instructor will coach the prom date how to apply the makeup to their own face. The instructor is not allowed to touch the prom date in any manner.

Allow each team two minutes to complete the makeup application (or do this simultaneously if you have enough sets of identical makeup). When every prom date is ready for the prom, (i.e. their makeup is applied), the host judges the best applied makeup! A prize is optional for the winning pair.
If this is a co-ed party, the boys are to be the ones to direct the application of the makeup.

Game gear: a set of makeup (or sets for each team) and a timer. Optional to have a set of makeup for each team to do the challenge simultaneously.

Game time: ~20 minutes.

Sightless Mona Lisa:
Game goal: to be the team that works together to create the best drawing of their object.

Game play: divide the group into pairs. Blindfold one member of each team and give them a pad and pencil. Give their teammate any random object (i.e. stapler, umbrella, etc.) after the blindfold is secured.

Set the timer for two minutes and when the host says go, the sighted member holding the object must direct the blindfolded team member how to draw the object without telling them what the object is or allowing them to touch the object in any way. All they are allowed to do is give directions on what to do with the pen/pencil (i.e. turn to the right, make a 'squiggly line', make a circle, etc.).
The host is to judge and select the best representation of a team's object. Optional to have prizes for the winners.

Game gear: a pen/pencil and a notepad/ sheet of paper for each team and random objects.

Game time: ~ 8 minutes.

Actors, Writers, Directors and Producers:
Game goal: to perform the most fabulous and hilarious skit given your scenario.

Game play: pass out one of the scenarios to teams made up of two or three guests. Feel free to write your own random scenarios by giving character names and a premise for the skit but don't give too much information or the guests' creativity will not shine.

Give them 10 minutes to come up with a one -two minute skit based upon the characters and vague premise given to them. If you assign a scenario to three guests, they can create the third character.

At the end of the 10 minutes, each team will perform their skit in front of the group. The host will judge the skits based upon who is the most creative and who executes the skit the best...and the best skit wins! Prizes are always optional.

Game gear: scenario sheets

Here are some example scenario sheets.

Character 1	Character 2	Scenario
Miss Mary Merryweather - a grouchy elderly lady who lives in a big shoe house	Alvi the Elf - a spunky shoemaker who runs a shoe repair shop	Miss Merryweather is very upset because Alvi created pointy toes on her best dress shoes and she only asked for the soles to be repaired.

Character 1	Character 2	Scenario
Patti Peterman - a very busy secretary who wants to get her job done	Gipper Gipman- a bored co-worker of Patti who doesn't want to do work	Patti Peterman is trying desperately to work and do a good job and Gipper Gipman wants to goof around and gossip about other people.

Character 1	Character 2	Scenario
Martha Mouse - a very clean mouse	Gertrude Mouse - a very messy mouse	Martha is angry that Gertrude keeps messing up the mouse hole that they share. Martha wants Gertrude to go and find another hole in the wall because she is tired of living in Gertrude's awful mess.

Character 1	Character 2	Scenario
Dr. Sarah Strangeheart - a mad scientist	Bertha Poindexter - her lab assistant	Dr. Strangeheart just exploded a beaker full of unknown black goo that she accidentally created. Bertha is afraid...very afraid! Dr. Strangeheart acts like nothing in the world is wrong with what happened.

Game time: ~ 25 minutes.

Scary Bedtime Stories:

Game goal: to come up with the scariest story to scare your friends!

Game play: instruct your guests to sit in a circle in a darkened room or at night during a camping trip by the campfire. One by one, each person is to take the flashlight and put it underneath his or her chin for a scary effect. The guest draws a story starter (examples below) and has two minutes to tell the scariest story s/he can think of! Continue until everybody gets a turn!

Game gear: the story starters, a dark area and a flashlight!
*As an alternative, the player that draws the story starter will start the first sentence of the story and the person to their right will add on a sentence and so on until the story is complete.

Game time: ~20 minutes.

Here are some example story starters:

It was twilight and the vampire awoke…	The werewolf howled at the moon as the young boy hid behind a tree…	The door slowly creaked open…	The lightening bolted down on the roof of the old farmhouse….
The four boys were lost deep in the forest. They heard a low growl…	The guard went to check on the strange moaning coming from the graveyard…	In a crowded movie theater, a skeleton appeared…	A bold knock at the door echoed throughout the house. It was 3 AM…
The witches cackled as they stirred the brew in the cauldron…	The witches cackled as they stirred the brew in the cauldron…	She walked into the hallway and swore she saw a ghostly apparition…	He woke up from an intense nightmare to hear…

French Expression Challenge:

Game goal: to come up with the most English Expressions that involves the word French.

Game play: divide your guests into pairs or groups of 3. Pass out a pencil and a French Expression Challenge sheet, which contains blanks for the guests to write their words on.

Set the timer (or look at a watch/clock) for 10 minutes and instruct the players to come up with as many expressions in the English language that include the word French. The team with the highest amount of valid expressions – wins!

Game gear: answer sheets and a pencil. Here are some examples of French Expressions. *You can find a more complete list on the internet, however.*

French Bean	French Harp	French Roof
French Boxing	French Heel	French Press
French Braid	French Hen	French Pleat
French Bread	French Saddle	French Kiss
French Bulldog	French Horn	French Seam
French Chop	French Knot	French Manicure
French Cricket	French Toast	French Cleaners
French Cuff	French Twist	French Onion Dip
French Curve	French Vanilla	French Roll
French Cut	French Pastry	French Onion Soup
French Dip	French Fry	French Dressing
French Door	French Drain	French Mustard

Game time: ~ 10 minutes.

Karaoke Reinvention:

Game goal: to be the one to come up with the most original 30-second performance of a chosen song.

Game play: choose any 30-second segment of a popular song. The guests who will compete are to reinvent the song in any manner that they choose (i.e. change up the lyrics, sing in a different accent, etc.) and perform this 30-second masterpiece for the rest of the group. The one who reinvents the song the best wins!

Game gear: a chosen karaoke song and a stage / performance area.

Game time: ~15 -20 minutes.

Balloon Truth or Dare:

Game goal: to pick the easiest dare balloon and accomplish the task without the blink of an eye!

Game play: write funny dares on small, folded slips of paper and slip into balloons before filling with helium. Use colored balloons within the theme of your party. Tie a long ribbon onto each balloon and allow the balloon to float to the ceiling. The ribbons should be long enough for your guests to reach.

One by one, as the guests pick a balloon, they are to sit on it and pop it, get the dare slip and then fulfill the dare. If they refuse to do the dare, they have to tell a truth that nobody knows about them. *(This is a great way for a group to get to know one another!)*

Game gear: Balloons, ribbons, dare cards and the corresponding items to go along with the dares (i.e. if the dare says to eat a jalapeno covered in whipped cream – make sure to have jalapenos available.)

Game time: ~20 minutes.

Chapter 27

Swimming Pool Games

Shove My Darling Duck Game:

Game goal: to be the first team to get their rubber ducky to the other end of the pool.

Game play: divide your guests into teams of three - four and have them start at one end of the pool, handing each team a rubber duck.

When the host says go, one member of each team must use their nose to push the duck to the other end of the pool. They can also blow the duck forward. However, they **_cannot_** use their lips or teeth to move the duck in any manner and cannot touch the duck with their hands or feet. The other team members will protect the duck advancer from the other team. Game defense: the opposing team is allowed to prevent the advancement of the opposing team's duck by splashing water either in the team's faces or toward their ducks. However, they can't touch any member of the opposing team or the other players' ducks in any way or they must go back to the starting end of the pool. In addition, they cannot stand in front of the duck – they can only attack from the side. They can **_only_** defend with water and words if they wish to taunt! ☺ The offensive players can splash back at the defending team but cannot, by doing so, advance their duck. In other words, if they are splashing to the side at the defenders, this is acceptable but they can't splash in the same direction as the duck is traveling. The first team to get their duck to touch the other end of the pool is the winning team.

Game gear: swimming pool, a rubber duck for each team of three - four players and an unbiased judge who can determine any game infractions, as there will likely be many made.

Game time: ~ 20 minutes.

Treacherous Sharks and Swashbucklin' Pirates:

Game goal: be the pirate crew to pillage all of the treasure before the sharks eat them...or be the shark team that eats all of the pirates before they can capture all of the treasures!

Game play: divide your guests into three groups. Designate one group as the sharks and the other two groups as pirates. The pirate groups must enter the pool and commandeer their ships (one of the pool mats/rafts) and all members climb aboard. Split up the treasure evenly among the two pirate crews. Once the pirate crews are settled and sailing abroad with their treasure, allow the sharks to enter the pool.

The pirate ships sail in the open pool sea with the focus of stealing the enemy ships' treasures. During the pirate duels, the sharks in the water try to capture the pirates by pulling them into the pool and off their ship (i.e. boats, rafts, noodles or mats). Once a pirate is off their ship completely, they become a shark and must release the floating treasures into the pool for the remaining pirates to retrieve. Once a shark releases the treasure - it is fair game for any pirate to claim.

Sharks cannot hold on to treasures - their fins simply don't have opposable thumbs!

A *pirate crew* can win the game by being the first pirate crew to claim all of the treasure before all of its crew becomes sharks. As long as one pirate is left when all of the treasures are stolen from the enemy ship, this pirate wins. The *sharks* team can win if they make all of the pirates in the pool a shark before either of the pirate crews steal the treasures. *Once a pirate is made into a shark, they become a member of the shark team and do not get to claim victory with their original team. This will prevent shark sabotage!*

Game gear: swimming pool, water mats/ rafts/noodles/pool boats for each of the pirate crews, pirate treasures (i.e. floating pool toys, etc.)

Game time: ~ 20 minutes.

Super Saturated Sweatshirt Race:

Game goal: to be the first team to race to opposing sides of the pool while wearing a super saturated sweatshirt!

Game play: divide your group into two teams and give them each an XL or XXL sweatshirt. For each team, half of the team will go to the opposite ends of the pool.

When the host says go, the first person of each team puts on the sweatshirt (over their swimming suit) and swims to the other side in any manner they so choose to their teammates. They are to remove the sweatshirt and put it on the next person on their team. This continues until each player on a team is on a *different* side than they started on and the first team who gets their whole team on the opposite side they started from wins.

Game gear: an XL or XXL sweatshirt for each team.

Game time: ~ 20 minutes.

Chapter 28

Ultra-Silly Party Games
Fun with Funyuns:

Game goal: is to get as many Funyun snack chips to stick on your teammate's whipped cream covered head!

Game play: separate your guests into two teams. With masking tape, tape two X's on the floor a designated length (i.e. five feet) from two corresponding 'do not cross' lines on the floor (i.e. for two teams). Have each team designate one member as the Funyun Head. The Funyun Head will put on a shower cap and cover their head with thick (chilled) whipped cream. The Funyun Heads will stand on the designated X and their respective team members stand behind the corresponding 'do not cross' line. When the host says go, the team members toss Funyun snack chips (or other chips that you choose) onto the Funyun Head team member's whipped cream covered head. The team that gets the most Funyun snack chips to stick *and stay* on their Funyun Head's head…wins! The host calls 'time' after three minutes and everyone is to freeze until the chips are counted – especially the Funyun Head. Any Funyun that drops off the Funyun Head's head that was sticking to their head when time was called - *should be counted.*

When the game is over, the losing team must eat the remaining Funyuns off the winning Funyun head's head because 'waste not, want not!' Yummy!

Game gear: Masking tape, Funyun snack chips (or other chips of your choosing), whipped cream (thick, chilled), any timer, two plastic shower caps and a big cleanable area!

Game time: ~ 20 minutes.

Monkey Feet Fandango:

Game goal: to be the team who can pass the banana to the end of the line and peel it the fastest...with their *feet!*

Game play: divide your guests into two -three teams. Each team is to sit in a straight line - parallel to each other with each member sitting on the floor - facing front - behind each team member. When the host says go, the first person in line will grab a banana with their feet and pass it to the person behind them - to their feet. Once the player's foot touches the banana, they must make monkey noises until the banana is passed to the next player. It is suggested to do a 'back roll' to pass the banana but any method that you wish to pass is fine as long as it is *feet to feet*. Hands are not allowed during this challenge! Once the banana gets to the last person in line, the last person is to peel the banana with their feet only – again, no hands are allowed. The first to peel the banana completely wins! Other team members can help peel as long as they only use their feet! Watch out because too many monkeys can spoil the banana!

Optional: once the banana is peeled, it is to be removed from the peel completely and passed back up the line to the first person in line. If the banana is in pieces, all pieces must reach the first person in line with the exception of 'residue' on the floor – go ahead and leave it be.

Once the first person receives the peeled banana (or all banana pieces)...that team wins! Place a tarp on the floor or do this game outside, as it would make a mess going back up the line!

Game gear: enough bananas for as many teams as you will have and a tarp (optional). A camera for goodness sake, this will be hilarious!

Game time: ~ 20 minutes.

Who Can Cook the Beef Stew?

Game goal: to be the one to get all of the beef stew ingredients in your pot.

Game play: with any word processing program, select five (or more, depending upon how many players are in the game) different items to put in your beef stew and print off pictures of these in small ~ 2" squares (i.e. beef, gravy, carrots, potatoes, etc). You will need one picture per guest of each ingredient. Each player will have a separate ingredient on his or her back. If you had ten players in the game, you would put ten beef cards on Player A's back, ten carrot cards on Player B's back and so on until every guest has a different ingredient on their back. For an alternative challenge, assign the same ingredient to two (or more) players.

Make a recipe card for your beef stew and post it on the wall in plain view of all of the contestants. Give each player a small plastic pot or a simple picture of a pot and scatter around the room but be sure that each guest knows where their pot is located. It's probably best to put their names on them to prevent any disputes. Tape five (or more depending upon how many players you have in the game) copies of the same ingredient on each player's back. Each player represents an ingredient. Try to have equal amounts of the ingredients available in the game play. Each player should have a full set of ingredients per the recipe card.

When the host says go, the players view the recipe card and collect the ingredients from each other's backs. The first to collect all five ingredients and get the ingredients to their pot first makes the beef stew and wins! The players are to *defend* their backs, but at the same time, they are trying to collect the ingredients – get ready for some chaotic fun!

Game gear: ingredient squares, plastic pots for each guest (real plastic or pictures) and the recipe card for the beef stew.

Game time~ 10 minutes.

Rambunctious Rap Off:

Game goal: to be the most awesome rapping duo at the party!

Game play: divide the guests into pairs. Give the teams ten minutes (or more) to create a unique 30-second rap routine to be performed to the group. Choose a theme for them to write their lyrics to such as 'being an elf' or 'about their job' or simply instruct them to be creative. Play any rap beats repeatedly in the background so the teams have ample time to practice with the music. There are instrumental rap beat tracks (rapmania) on My Mystery Party in the mystery props section (http://www.mymysteryparty.com/mypapr.html). As a fun and potentially hilarious alternative, don't allow any time for your guests to write lyrics and ask them to come to the microphone (microphone is optional)/ stand in front of the group and show how they can *lyrically flow.*

When the time is up and / or the guests are finished creating their rap routines, one at a time, the guest duos are to perform their rap routines for the other guests. The host will judge or the guests will vote via a ballot for the best rap routine. The guests are not allowed to vote for their duo. In the case of a tie, the host will be the tiebreaker.

Game gear: any type of rap beats and a music-playing source. There are rap beats available for instant download at the My Mystery Party Prop Emporium at http://www.mymysteryparty.com/mypapr.html.

Game time: ~ 30 minutes.

Crazy Cracker Smasher:

Game goal: to be the last one with an intact cracker!

Game play: cut 10" pieces of dental floss, fishing line, yarn, or equivalent type of thread. Thread the piece of floss (or material of your choice) through one -two holes of two saltine crackers. Tie one of these saltine necklaces to each guest - through a belt loop preferably. If the guest doesn't have a belt loop, grab a piece of their shirt and tie it around the bundled up shirt material. Get a newspaper (or two) and roll up equal amounts of paper for each guest. Play this game outdoors as it makes a big mess!

When the host says go, each guest is to swat at each other's crackers and knock them off their floss until someone is standing with the last intact cracker. The last one with an intact cracker wins! In the case of a tie - a re-match between the guests that tied should take place. Prizes are optional.

Game gear: dental floss (or equivalent), saltine crackers (or other food item that is breakable and can be threaded onto a string), newspapers.

Game time: ~ 5 -10 minutes.

Let's Do Business:
Game goal: to be the member of the audience who makes out with the big prize!

Game play: assemble the players in an audience and the party host is the game show host. Before the party, prepare some fun boxes with assorted booby prizes such as cooked spaghetti (call it zombie brains) and then others with great prizes such as a gift certificate to a store or maybe a simple delicious candy bar.
    Randomly select guests from the audience and offer them a prize of a candy bar (or other small token prize that's good enough to want). Then, offer them to trade with what is inside of a random mystery box, and so on...until you've given away all of the prizes. The guests will enjoy watching the stress of it all!

Game gear: gag prizes, good prizes, small pieces of candy for the starter prizes (that are good and *not* available as party food) and random containers / boxes to hide the gag and good prizes inside of.

Game time: ~20 minutes.

Red, Red Wine Musical Chairs:
Game goal: to be the last one with a chair!

Game play: while playing karaoke, assign someone to sing the song Red, Red, Wine by UB40/Bob Marley (or simply play the song). Put five chairs in a circle and get six volunteers to play the game (*the rest will enjoy watching the hilarity*).

When the song begins, the players are to dance around the outside circle of the chairs (just like musical chairs but they have to dance). When the singer sings a lyric involving a body part of any kind (i.e. heart, hand, etc.), the players are to grab a chair immediately. The one left standing is out. The host must remove one chair and the game quickly proceeds until there is one player left!

Game gear: karaoke machine (optional), the karaoke song Red, Red Wine – either the karaoke version or an mp3, and five chairs with enough room to walk around the chairs in a circle.

Game time: ~8 minutes.

Pint the Wart on the Celebrity's Nose:

Game goal: to get your wart closest to the tip of the celebrity's nose.

Game play: download a picture of your favorite celebrity's face from the web and print the picture. Hang this picture on a wall at eye's level. Give each player a pea sized portion of play dough (green preferred).

One by one, blindfold on the player, spin them around a few times and then gently direct them towards the celebrity's face. With one hand, they are to put the wart on his/her face. They cannot feel around the paper and when the play dough hits the paper, that is where it must stay! Whoever gets closest to the tip of the nose wins! *(put a small X on the tip of the nose with a sharpie marker to designate where the winning wart should be closest to – to prevent any variable interpretations of where the tip of the nose might be located.)*

Game gear: a printed celebrity's face-either a poster or downloaded picture from the web, sharpie marker, blindfold, green play dough and have a ruler to determine the winner. Also, if you want to remove the play dough after each player, get variable colored pens and put a small dot where each player lands their wart before the next player is to go. Remember which color goes with what player.

Game time: ~20 minutes.

Poetic Justice:
Game goal: to be the best poet at the party!

Game play: this is an individual challenge. Whatever your party theme is, you are to instruct your guests to create the best poem about the theme of the party. Give your guests a set time limit to write their poems and a pen/paper.
When the time is up, each guest will recite his or her poem in front of the group. Play a low jazz beat in the background for ambiance. The host will judge the winner or the guests can vote via secret ballot. Get your video camera ready, as this will be awesome to watch later!

Game gear: a pen and paper for each guest, optional low jazz style beat as ambiance.

Game time: ~ 30 minutes.

Ping Pong Ball Droppers:
Game goal: to get as many ping pong balls in your team's bucket before the timer runs out!

Game play: divide your guests into as many groups as you wish. Give each team a bucket in the center of the room and a pile of ping-pong balls of a designated color (use markers on them to write a symbol, etc.) The buckets should touch and cluster together in the center of the room. Each bucket should be of the team's color or marked clearly (use tape and a marker to put the same symbol as the ping-pong ball). Each team should have a start line designated with tape an equal distance away from the buckets. Make sure the teams are spaced appropriately and their buckets in the center are facing them. For example, if you have two teams playing, place their start lines at opposing ends of the room. With four teams, use the four corners, etc.
     Set the timer for ~ three minutes (or whatever time you choose). When the host says go, every member of the team will bend down and pick up a ping-pong ball and place it between

their knees. They may use their hands to place it between their knees but they may not use their hands after they leave the start line.

Each person races to their center bucket with the ping-pong ball in between their knees and drops their ping-pong ball into the correct bucket. If they get a ball into another team's bucket, they receive 2 points for it whereas each ping-pong ball placed into the correct bucket is 1 point. If at any time they drop their ping-pong ball from between their knees, they must go back to the starting line and start over. The teams are not allowed to retrieve any ping-pong ball from any bucket. Once a ping-pong ball lands in a bucket, it is final. Anyone that spills a bucket's ping-pong balls will receive a five-point penalty for their team for each bucket knocked over.

The host notifies everyone when the timer goes off and everybody must freeze. No additional ping-pong balls may enter a bucket after the time is up. The team with the most points wins!

Game gear: ~20 ping pong balls for each team and a bucket for each team, any timer.

Game time: ~ 20 minutes.

Braiding Frenzy:
Game goal: to be the team that can put the most length of braids in your team's hair.

Game play: divide your guests into teams of four. Try to make it as even as possible with hair lengths of the team members. Provide each team with multiple mini hair rubber bands to secure their braids.

Set the timer for three minutes. When the host says go, the teams are to put as many braids in each other's hair as possible. The team can strategize to braid each other's hair or focus on one team member – it is their decision. The braids can be any length the teams' decide. When the time is up, the host will ask the guests to secure their last braid with the rubber band immediately.

With a ruler or measuring tape, the judge is to measure the length of the cumulative braids in the team's hair. The braid is measured from when the actual braid begins to the rubber band – given that the braid goes through to the rubber band. If the braid doesn't go through to the rubber band, the judge will have to make the determination when the braid ends and measure to that point. Measure in any units you wish (i.e. .inches), but record each teams' number. The winning team has the longest total length of braids!

Game gear: a ruler or measuring tape, timer, mini hair rubber bands.

Game time: ~ 10 minutes.

Sightless Stylists:

Game goal: to create the best up-do hairstyle while being blindfolded.

Game play: divide your guests into teams of 3. One guest is *going to the prom* and needs their hair done. The other two are the sightless stylists.

Blindfold the two stylist team members and then hand them a large plastic comb (do not give them sharp tools since they will be blindfolded) and various hair fasteners such as large clips, rubber bands, etc. Ask that the person getting their hair done wear a visor to protect their face from the blindfolded stylists. Also, have a few safety people watching to make sure the stylists are focused on their client's hair. No heated appliances are to be used in this challenge, that would be entirely too dangerous!

Set the timer for five minutes. When the host says go, the stylists are to work together to create the most innovative and lovely hairstyle for the prom!

When the time is up, the host is to shout *freeze* and the stylist are to put their hands in the air. The host will judge the best hairstyle!

Game gear: various hair fasteners such as rubber bands, large clips, large plastic combs. Blindfolds for 2/3 of the guests.

Game time: ~ 10 minutes.

Beard Builders:

Game goal: to create the longest beard out of whipped cream!

Game play: divide your guests into teams of two. Give each team access to as much chilled cool whip as they need. Set the timer for 90 seconds. When the host says go, they are to use whatever technique they can to build the longest beard on their teammate out of whipped cream.

When time is up, the host will measure the longest part of the beard from the face to where it hangs down. The beard has to be free hanging from the face – the teams cannot attach it to any substrate. If the player already has a hanging beard, this player cannot be the beard model. The team with the longest cool whip beard – wins!

Game gear: a timer, plenty of chilled cool whip, a measuring tape or ruler.

Game time: ~ 8 minutes.

Reindeer Shake Challenge:

Game goal: to be the best dancer doing the *Reindeer Shake* dance– great for a Christmas Party!

Game play: either purchase the Party of 2 Ultimate Merry Christmas Dance Party CD or download the song *Reindeer Shake* (iTunes, My Mystery Party Prop Emporium) and instruct your guests to spread out on the dance floor. The host will serve as the judge or elect a panel of judges. Start the song *Reindeer Shake* and the guests are to compete against each other as the best dancers. All guests must follow the instructions of the song and perform their version of the Reindeer Shake dance with technique, enthusiasm and excitement. One by one, the judge is to eliminate people by handing them a festive ornament (i.e. cut them out of construction paper). The last three dancers must do a 30 second dance to any other Christmas spirited song (i.e. *Year*

Round Christmas etc.) and the guests will vote for their favorite dancer on their ornament cut outs. The host will announce the winner!

Game gear: festive ornaments cut out of construction paper for all but three guests, pens for all but three guests, the song Reindeer *Shake* and any other Christmas spirited song.

Game time: ~ 15 minutes.

Chapter 29

Halloween Party Games

Any of the party games in this book are great for a Halloween party. Just change the name of the game to a spirited Halloween name! The following games are already in the spirit of Halloween!

Pumpkin Panic Dance Challenge:

Game goal: to be the best dancer doing the Pumpkin Panic!

Game play: either purchase the Party of 2 Halloween Dance Party CD or download the song *Pumpkin Panic* (iTunes, My Mystery Party Prop Emporium) and instruct your guests to spread out on the dance floor. The host will serve as the judge or elect a panel of judges. Start the song *Pumpkin Panic* and the guests are to compete against each other as the best dancers. All guests must follow the instructions of the song and perform their dance with technique, enthusiasm and excitement. One by one, the judge is to eliminate people by handing them a pumpkin (i.e. cut them out of construction paper). The last three dancers must do a 30-second dance to any other Halloween spirited song (i.e. *Black Cat Mambo,* etc.) and the guests will vote for their favorite dancer on their pumpkin cutouts. The host will announce the winner!

Game gear: orange pumpkins cut out of construction paper for all but three guests, pens for all but three guests, the song *Pumpkin Panic* and any other Halloween spirited song.

Game time: ~ 15 minutes.

The Creative Pumpkin Challenge:

Game goal: to make the most beautiful pumpkin!

Game play: put an assortment of craft items on a table for the guests to choose from. Purchase or cut out ovals of orange paper or felt ~ 10" by 14". When the guests arrive, allow them to decorate their own pumpkin using the materials. Allow the pumpkins to dry during the party and they can take their creations with them when they leave!

Game gear: Enough orange paper for up to ten (or as many guests as you will have) 10" by 14" ovals. Glue (i.e. Elmer's, fabric glue if you use felt, etc).   Markers of all colors, pieces of felt in all colors, aluminum foil, strips of ribbon, buttons, sequins, etc. and scissors.

Game time: ~ 20 minutes.

Eyeball Bounty Hunters:

Game goal: to be the one who finds the most ping-pong balls (aka: eyeballs) in a set amount of time.

Game play: cook plenty of spaghetti noodles and assemble them into large buckets for as many teams as you will have. Rinse the noodles thoroughly with cold water and allow cooling prior to placing into the bucket. Allow the noodles to remain a little wet, as you don't want them to dry and become sticky. Draw eyeballs on the ping-pong balls and bury as many balls in the noodle bucket as you can. As an alternative, assign a point value to the balls.

Set the timer for 30 seconds and when the host says go; each guest will hunt for ping-pong balls without spilling any noodles from the bucket! For each spilled noodle, they lose a corresponding ping-pong ball that they have collected. (This prevents guests from dumping the bucket and collecting them that way which is a huge mess!) The guest with the highest point total wins! In the event of a tie, have a 10 second timed faceoff of the eyeball hunting challenge between the guests that tied until you get a winner.

Game gear: ping-pong balls, markers, cooked spaghetti noodles, buckets for each team.
Game time: ~ 15 minutes.

Halloween 'Feel' Game – Can You Stand It?

Game goal: to guess what Halloween item is in the containers!

Game play: using any container such as a cardboard box, decorate the outside in a fun Halloween theme so you cannot see inside. Create a hole wide enough to get a hand inside to feel the item. If you are using containers that you cannot cut into, purchase some felt and make a slit for a hand to get through and secure the felt with a rubber band around the rim of the container or glue to the rim of the container.

Choose 10 of the following items (or more/less) and put each of them into an individual box. Allow the guests to one at a time put their hand in the container and *before* withdrawing their hand, they must make a guess as to what Halloween item is in the box. The objective is not to guess the real item, but rather what the item simulates. For example – the guest must say *fingers* or more specifically *dead man's fingers* when they stick their hand into the lil' smokie sausage box. Make sure to have plenty of baby wipes available for the guests to clean their hands.

soft flour tortilla strips (add a few drops of oil) – witch's skin
dried corn kernels– dead man's teeth
little smokie sausages – dead man's fingers
pretzel sticks - petrified rat tails
tongue shaped cured ham – dead man's tongue
fake spider webbing from any party store – spider webs
cooked large egg noodles– tape worms
peeled, hard-boiled eggs – baby hearts
cooked spaghetti noodles (add a few drops of oil) - worms OR zombie veins
candy corn - vampire bat / vampire fangs
cooked rice (add a few drops of oil) – maggots
cornflake cereal – scabs
steel wool pad (tease off pieces of it)– witch's hair
broken sunflower seeds or almond slices – witch's fingernails
peeled grapes – zombie eyeballs
cornhusk silk – dead man's hair

Game gear: containers for the food (empty cereal boxes, etc.) random food items, baby wipes.

Game time: ~ 10-15 minutes.

Who Can Brew The Witches Brew?

Game goal: to be the one to get all of the ingredients in your witch's cauldron.

Game play: with any word processing program, select five (or more, depending upon how many players are in the game) different items to put in your witches brew and print off pictures of these in small ~ 2" squares (i.e. fingernails, mouse tails, fingers, etc). You will need one picture per guest of each ingredient. Each player will have a separate ingredient on his or her back. If you had ten players in the game, you would put ten fingernail cards on Player A's back, ten-mouse tail cards on Player B's back and so on until every guest has a different ingredient on their back. For an alternative challenge, assign the same ingredient to two (or more) players.

Make a recipe card for your witch's brew and post it on the wall in plain view of all of the contestants. Give each player a small plastic cauldron or a simple picture of a cauldron and scatter around the room but be sure that each guest knows where their cauldron is located. It's probably best to put their names on them to prevent any disputes.

Tape five (or more depending upon how many players you have in the game) copies of the same ingredient on each player's back. Each player represents an ingredient. Try to have equal amounts of the ingredients available in the game play. Each player should have a full set of ingredients per the recipe card.

When the host says go, the players view the recipe card and collect the ingredients from each other's backs. The first to collect all five ingredients and get the ingredients to their cauldron first makes the witches brew and wins! The players are to *defend* their backs, but at the same time, they are trying to collect the ingredients – get ready for some chaotic fun!

Game gear: ingredient squares, witches cauldrons for each guest (real plastic or pictures) and the recipe card for the brew.

Game time~ 10 minutes.

Hilarious Halloween Dance Contest:

Game goal: to be the most radical fun Halloween dancers at the party!

Game play: divide the guests into pairs. Give the teams ten minutes (or more) to create a unique 30-second fun Halloween dance routine to be performed to the song *Count Rapula* or other fun Halloween song of your choice. Play the song repeatedly in the background so the teams have ample time to practice with the music.
When the time is up and / or the guests are finished creating their routines, one at a time, the guests are to perform their routines for the other guests. The host will judge or the guests will vote via a ballot for the best fun Halloween dance routine. In the case of a tie, the host will be the tiebreaker.

Game gear: any type of music playing source and a fun Halloween song. The *Party of 2 Monstrous Halloween Dance Party Mix* is available for download on iTunes and My Mystery Party's Prop Emporium and it contains fun ambiance, dance party songs, a rap beat for a rap challenge as well as a ten-minute thunderstorm ambiance track and ten-minute monster track for your Halloween Party or Trick or Treat time.

Game time: ~ 30 minutes.

Creepy Disguise Challenge:

Game goal: to make the most creative disguise out of one roll of toilet tissue!

Game play: divide the guests into groups of two to three players. Give the teams ten minutes (or more) to create the most unique disguise by using one roll of toilet tissue. Scotch tape is allowed and should be available to all teams, as they need it. The teams can mummify *(easy and predictable)* or make weird intricate things out of the tissue to disguise one of their group members.
When the time is up and / or the guests are finished creating their disguises, one at a time the disguised guests are to model their disguises. The host judges or the guests vote via

a ballot for the best and most creative disguise. In the case of a tie via ballot, the potential winners will engage in a best two out of three rock, paper scissor tournament.

Game gear: one roll of toilet tissue per two -three guests.

Game time: ~ 15 minutes.

Guess the Ghost:
Game goal: to guess the most ghosts!

Game play: you will need multiple white (or other color) sheets for this challenge. If you can, cut out circles for eyes and replace with black mesh so the guests can see out but the guesser cannot see in. Number the ghosts as you would runners in a marathon (i.e. with bold numbers on a paper sign). Ask that all of the ghosts put on the same white socks (unless the sheets go to the floor). As the host, make an answer key each time as to which ghost was what number!

All of the guests besides the guesser are to go into an adjacent room and put on their sheet, socks, and number on the front part of their ghostly essence (i.e. on their chest / abdomen region).

When the host says go, the ghosts are to stroll into the next room with the guesser and the guesser has one minute to write down *who is what number ghost.* The ghosts can pretend to float around the room and do not need to stand in a straight line unless the host decides to go with that method. It will add more challenge if they are floating around as ghosts but be sure they can see where they are going – you want to prevent any accidents at all costs! When one minute is up, the guesser is to turn in the answer sheet to the host.

Continue until all guests have had a chance at being the guesser. Be sure that you write down the ghosts according to their number each time, as you'll want to switch this combination up for each guesser. *You don't want Jason being #3 ghost each time, as the guessers (after the first one) will all know his number!* An easy way to keep track is to make a table with each ghosts' name on the left column with a column beside them for each round. Each round, fill in their ghost number by their name. If it is their turn as the guesser, write N/A for not applicable as they were not a ghost when they were a guesser. Here is an example table for keeping track of a game played by four players. This table at the end of the game once it is filled out will serve as your answer key and you will compare and score the guesser's sheets by viewing this table.

GUESSERS→	Scot	Jason	Whitney	Lora
GHOSTS:				
Scot	**N/A**	#3	#2	#1
Jason	#1	**N/A**	#3	#2
Whitney	#2	#2	**N/A**	#3
Lora	#3	#1	#1	**N/A**

The one(s) who guess the most ghosts correctly – wins! Instruct the guests that they can do anything possible underneath their sheet to throw the guesser off – they can stand on their tippy toes, squat while walking under the sheet, hold it out a bit with their arms to disguise their body shape, etc.

Game gear: white sheets and uniform colored socks for each guest. Pens, paper for the guessers and a host-scoring sheet as shown above.

Game time: ~ 15 minutes.

Horrific Rap Contest:

Game goal: to be the team that gives the most awesome rap duo performance!

Game play: divide the guests into groups of two or three. Give the teams 10 minutes (or more) to write the most awe-inspiring and hilarious rap lyrics about Halloween. Play a steady rap beat in the background so the groups can get inspired and can practice.

When the time is up, allow each team to perform their rap song in front of the group. Each member of the team must play a role in the duo (or trio). The host will choose the best upcoming rap artist duo at the party!

<u>Game gear:</u> a cool rap beat (instrumental) to play in the background and during the performances. The Party of 2 Monstrous Halloween Dance Party Mix CD has an instrumental rap song for you to do this challenge. The CD is available on iTunes and My Mystery Party Prop Emporium at http://www.mymysteryparty.com/mypapr.html. There are also multiple rap beat songs to choose from on the My Mystery Party site to download instantly upon purchase.

<u>Game time:</u> ~ 15 -20 minutes.

Fun Halloween Movie Challenge:

<u>Game goal</u>: to be the team that answers the most correct fun Halloween movies according to the synopses (or movie quotes, tag lines, etc.) given!

<u>Game play</u>: divide the guests into groups of two or three. Give the teams 10 minutes (or more) to fill in the correct movie next to the Halloween movie synopsis, quote or tagline.
When the time is up and / or the guests are finished, collect the answer sheets and score them using the host answer key.
The best place to get synopses, quotes and taglines for movies is www.imdb.com. Use *Halloween* as a keyword search to find movies or if you have a specific movie you are looking for, simply search for it in their search engine on their front page.

<u>Game gear:</u> Halloween Movie Challenge sheets and an answer key. Pens for each team.

<u>Game time:</u> ~ 15 minutes.

Example movies to use:
1. It's The Great Pumpkin, Charlie Brown
2. Wallace & Gromit: The Curse Of The Were-Rabbit
3. Casper
4. Hocus Pocus
5. The Nightmare Before Christmas
6. Corpse Bride
7. Sleepy Hollow
8. Twilight
9. The Little Vampire
10. Monsters, Inc.

Balloon Truth or Dare:

Game goal: to pick the easiest dare balloon and accomplish the task without blinking an eye!

Game play: write funny dares on small, folded slips of paper and slip into balloons before filling with helium. Have the guests check with the host if any props are needed for the dare to ensure that every dare can be done.

Use black and orange balloons for a fun Halloween effect. Tie a long ribbon (orange or black) onto each balloon and allow the balloon to float to the ceiling, making sure the ribbons are long enough for the guests to reach.

One by one, each guests chooses a balloon, sits on it to pop it and retrieves the dare slip. They are to perform the dare. If they refuse to do the dare, they have to tell a truth that nobody knows about them. *(This is a great way for a group to get to know one another!)*

Game gear: balloons, ribbons, dare cards and the corresponding items to go along with the dares (i.e. if the dare says to eat a jalapeno covered in whipped cream – make sure to have jalapenos and whipped cream available.)

Game time: ~ 20 minutes.

Pumpkin Ring Toss:

Game goal: to toss the most rings on the pumpkin stem!

Game play: locate a tall, oval pumpkin with a large stem. Increase the stem length with paper mache. Allow the paper mache to dry and then paint the stem to match the original – adding glitter for a festive effect!

Using embroidery hoops (or other type of hoops – maybe created with cardboard, pipe cleaners or rope secured with duct tape), allow your guests to stand behind the line and have three attempts at a toss around the pumpkin stem. Halloween candies can be the prizes for the winners.

Game gear: a large, oval pumpkin with a large stem, embroidery hoops (or others), Halloween candy for prizes.

Game time: ~ 5 minutes.

Return the Witch's Wart:

Game goal: to get your wart closest to the real witch's wart!

Game play: using any word processing software, print off a picture of a witch's face (at least an 8" by 10" picture). Give each player a pea sized portion of play dough (green preferred). Put the blindfold on the player, spin them around a few times and then gently direct them towards the witch's face. With one hand, they are to put the wart on her face. They cannot feel around the paper and when the play dough hits the paper (or wall), that is where it must stay! Whoever gets closest to the bull's-eye – wins!

Game gear: a printed witch face, blindfold, green play dough and possibly a ruler if it is close to determine the winner.

Game time: ~ 20 minutes.

The Perfect Pumpkin Carve Off:

Game goal: to carve the most awesome face into a pumpkin!

Game play: Give each guest a marker, a piece of paper, a pumpkin and a pumpkin carving knife. *Do not play this game if the guests have had cocktails as accidents can happen with a knife - alcohol combo! If your guests will be consuming cocktails - either play this game before the cocktails or skip it☺
    Set the timer for 15 minutes and instruct the guests to design and carve the best face into their pumpkin. Tell them to plan their design on the paper and then draw the outline on the pumpkin before they start carving. When everyone is done with their creations, line them up on the table for judging! The host should appoint the winner or everyone should vote via secret ballot with the host being a tiebreaker.

 Game gear: pumpkins, carving knives, paper and markers for each guest.

Game time: ~ 20 minutes.

Best Costume Challenge:

Game goal: to have the most fabulous costume and to strut your stuff on the Halloween fashion runway the best!

Game play: all guests wearing a costume can participate individually. Create a fun Halloween fashion runway – simply designate an area or line your runway with tied down orange and black balloons, crepe paper, etc. Play a fun Halloween song while each guest models his or her costume down the runway – showing off every detail and remaining in character. The host of the party is the judge by default or elects a panel of judges who are not in the challenge.

　　　　After all of the contestants have modeled their costumes, if there is a tie, the potential winners must engage in a tie-breaking dance off. Each contestant must remain in his or her character for the dance off. For example, a vampire needs to insert vampire moves in their dance and a werewolf must dance like a werewolf. The remaining guests can vote via a ballot for the winner.

Game gear: a designated runway and a fun Halloween song.

Game time: ~ 20 minutes.

Fun Halloween Charade Challenge:

Game goal: to earn a point by being the player that is first to guess the charade correctly! The winner is the player with the highest point total!

Game play: one player draws a charade topic from a hat and acts it out for the other players. The first one to guess correctly the charade topic gets a point. The next player will draw a topic from the hat and act it out until one of the other players guesses it correctly. This continues until all of the topics are guessed correctly. The actor of the charade may not speak, point to an object, or acknowledge the other players until they give a correct guess. ***This game may also be played in teams.*

Example Halloween charade topics are as follows:

Candy Corn	Jack O'lantern
Pumpkin Patch	Candy Bowl
Trick or Treat	Halloween Costume
Bobbing For Apples	Shadows
Vampire Bat	Black Cat
Carving a Pumpkin	Skeleton
Frankenstein	Monster Mash
Chocolate	Graveyard
Tombstone	Spider Web
Caramel Apple	Worms
Tarantula	Dragon
Flashlight	Pumpkin Panic
Haunted Hayride	Count Dracula
Haunted Mansion	Zombie

Game gear: paper, pen, and a hat (or any container to hold the pieces of paper with the charade topics).

Game time: ~ 25 minutes.

Haunted Word Scavenger Hunt:

Game goal: to make the most sentences out of the eggs you find during the Halloween Egg Scavenger Hunt!

Game play: Phase 1: using sentence makers (example shown below), hide the slips containing the words inside of orange and black plastic eggs and then hide the eggs in a designated area. *They also sell eyeball painted plastic eggs at some local party stores.* Tell your hunters the boundaries of the hunt before you say go. Each hunter is to place his or her Halloween treat bag/basket in a designated area prior to the hunt.

When the host says go, the hunters are to collect as many eggs as possible that they can make full sentences out of but once they find an egg – if they choose to keep it – they must take it to their treat bag/basket and deposit it before finding the next egg. They will not want to take any eggs that contain words inside that they can't use, as they'll be penalized for having them during the next phase of the game. They do have the option to view inside the egg to see what the word is and if they don't want it – they decide to not take it and place it back in the exact location in which they found it. They are not allowed to re-hide a rejected egg in another location. After the eggs have all been found (you'll know by counting the hunter's eggs) or if the hunters are finished hunting (i.e. there are eggs left, but they have words in them that the hunters can't use) – move to phase 2.

Phase 2: when you say go, the hunters can take out the slips of paper containing the words and arrange them into as many sentences as possible. There is one point given for every word used in a sentence. For any words that are leftover that the hunter does not use – there is a one-point deduction per word. The sentences must be grammatically correct.   For example, if Scott collects 20 eggs and makes three sentences with six words each – he will earn 18 points but be penalized for the remaining two eggs that he did not use so his final score will be 16 points.

Game gear: sentence maker word squares and plastic eggs.

Game time: ~ 35 minutes.

Example sentence maker word squares- print and cut out as many as you want to play with and slip each into a plastic egg and hide:

The	Orange	Black	Witch
The	Tiny	Cat	Is
Halloween	Night	Monster	There
I	Want	To	Win
You	Can	Not	Make
Me	And	I	Am
I	Enjoy	Trick	Or
Treat	To	Get	And
The	Zombies	Scampered	Across
The	Graveyard	Alien	From
Scary	And	Hairy	Always
Screaming	And	Biting	Will
Are	So	Eerie	Scream
This	Fun	Go	Danced
More	Ran	From	Vampire
Count	Dracula	It	Are

Of	And	A	Are
Eat	Frightening	Candy	And
The	Coffin	Cauldron	Smoke
The	Light	Today	Fangs

The Great Pumpkin Drop:

Game goal: to get as many mini pumpkins in your team's witch's cauldron before the timer runs out!

Game play: divide your guests into as many groups as you wish. Give each team a plastic witch's cauldron in the center of the room and a pile of mini pumpkins of a designated color (there are white, orange, yellow varieties available or paint them.) The cauldrons should touch and cluster together in the center of the room. Each cauldron should be marked clearly for each team (use tape and a marker or adhere a fun Halloween item to the front to designate the teams).

Each team should have a start line designated with tape an equal distance away from the cauldrons. Make sure the teams are spaced appropriately and their cauldrons in the center are facing them. For example, if you have two teams playing, place their start lines at opposing ends of the room. With four teams, use the four corners, etc.

As an alternative cool effect, if you are playing in a large room or outdoors, add an additional center cauldron that is not assigned to a team. Add some dry ice and a flashlight with a red piece of saran wrap on top to make an eerie red smoke on top of the cauldrons. Place a piece of mesh on top of this cauldron to prevent any pumpkins from going inside. If anyone's pumpkin lands on the mesh, this pumpkin is out of play.

Set the timer for ~three minutes (or whatever time you choose). When the host says go, every member of the team will bend down and pick up a pumpkin and place it between their knees. They may use their hands to place it between their knees but they may not use their hands after they leave the start line. Each person races to their center cauldron with the pumpkin in between their knees and drops their pumpkin into the correct cauldron. If they get a pumpkin into another team's cauldron, they receive 2 points for it whereas each pumpkin placed into the correct cauldron is 1 point.

If at any time they drop their pumpkin from between their knees, they must go back to the starting line and start over. The teams are not allowed to retrieve a pumpkin from the cauldron. Once a pumpkin lands in a cauldron, it is final. Anyone that spills a cauldron's pumpkins will receive a five-point penalty for their team for each cauldron knocked over. The host notifies everyone when the timer goes off and everybody must freeze. No additional pumpkins can enter a cauldron after the time is called. The team with the most points wins!

Game gear: ~20 mini pumpkins for each team and a large plastic witch's cauldron for each team, any timer.

Game time: ~ 20 minutes.

Chapter 30

Easter Party Games & Hunts

Hoppin' Easter Bunny Relay Eggstravaganza:

Game goal: to be the team to collect the most pieces of Easter candy in the given time period!

Game play: if the party includes guests in a large age range, separate the guests by age into two teams with the younger guests on one team and the older on another.

Each team will separately compete in a timed trial. Arrange three different stations - one with plastic eggs (un-attached eggs), another station at least 10 feet away with any candy of your choice that fits inside of the eggs. It's best if multiple pieces of candy can fit inside of the eggs. The third station is a wicker basket - set this at least 10 feet away from the candy station and from the start/finish line (see suggested diagram). The team members are to form a line at the start/finish line. The host sets a timer for three minutes.

When the host says go, the first team member will put on the bunny ear headband and hop to the *plastic egg station*. They will select the appropriate pieces of one plastic egg (i.e. big piece, smaller piece) and then hop to the candy station. They are to fill their egg with as much candy as can fit in the egg and close it without popping the egg open.

Then, they hop to the *basket station* and place their egg carefully into the basket. Any egg that pops open will not count towards the total candy amount!

The player hops to the start/finish line and hands off the bunny ears to the next in line. The bunny ears must be on their head *before* the player can even touch the plastic egg or they have to go back to the start line. (The host is to watch carefully - and the opposing team will obviously monitor this too!)

When the three minutes are up - the host will call time and the team must freeze where they are and no additional eggs can be placed into the basket. The host will count the pieces of candy inside the intact eggs inside of the basket. If the host picks up an egg during judging that immediately pops open and the candy falls out - the candy in this egg is not to be counted. The stations are re-set and the opposing team will repeat the process. The team who collects the most pieces of candy in the basket wins! *(The host can decide on whether to allow smashed or broken pieces of candy to count toward the total - but either way - make the announcement before the game starts.)*

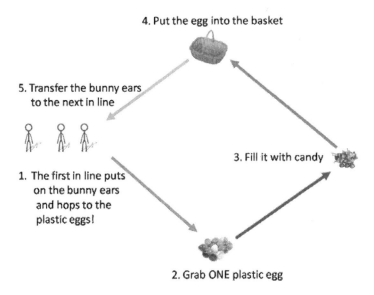

4. Put the egg into the basket

5. Transfer the bunny ears to the next in line

1. The first in line puts on the bunny ears and hops to the plastic eggs!

3. Fill it with candy

2. Grab ONE plastic egg

Even out the challenge for large age-ranged groups: any guest under 15 years of age must *hop on all four's* - just like a bunny. Guests that are 16-34 years old must hop backwards at all times. Guests over 35 years of age can hop forwards. Any guest over 55 doesn't have to hop at all!

Game gear: a bunny ear headband (available at your local party store or make one out of a headband and construction paper), plastic Easter eggs, Hershey's kisses or other candy that can fit inside of eggs - that you won't mind counting at the end. A wicker Easter basket and a timer / watch.

Game time: ~15 minutes.

Nose to the Grindstone: Eggtastic Rollin' Relay:

Game goal: to be the first team to transfer your plastic Easter eggs across the forest.

Game play: divide your guests into two teams and divide any number of plastic Easter eggs between the two teams. Mark off a starting point and a finish line that is about 5-10 feet away from the starting point. Create a forest between two points by placing any type of obstacles such as towels, buckets, etc. as the trees of the forest but be sure that the two forests are identical as to not give one team an advantage.

When the host says go, one member of each team transfers one egg from the starting point through the forest and across the finish line using only their nose. The moment the egg crosses the finish line, the next team member can begin to transfer their egg and this continues until all of the eggs have made it across the finish line. If you are transferring more eggs than there are team members, the first person who transferred is to get back in line and so on until every egg makes it across the finish line. The first team to get all of their eggs across successfully wins! *If any player touches an egg with their hand – they must go back to the starting point and start over.*

For an alternative challenge, take Easter basket shred and scatter it across the relay race lanes to make a textured *forest* terrain for the guests to push their eggs across.

Game gear: plastic eggs and random objects to create a forest in between a starting point and a finish line. Easter basket shred is an optional item.

Game time: ~ 10 minutes.

Project Easter Bonnet:

Game goal: to create the most fashionable Easter hat!

Game play: each guest receives a plain white baseball cap (or other type of hat). Purchase these at any local craft store.

On a main table, provide various materials such as plastic Easter eggs, feather boa (or individual feathers), sequins, buttons, ribbon, fabric, fabric paint, fabric markers, etc. Also, provide quick drying fabric glue or a hot glue gun (watch smaller kids around dangerous items).

Set a timer (or just pick a specified time) for 15-20 minutes and when the host says go, the players are to create the most fashionable Easter hat!

When everyone is done creating their hats, allow time for the hats to dry. In the meantime, line a fashion runway (with crepe paper, balloons or other material to designate where the runway is). When the hats have dried thoroughly, play fun supermodel music in the background, and allow each player to model their hat on the runway.

Either vote via a secret ballot and a player may not vote for themselves or the host will judge and pick the winner.

Game gear: white baseball caps, plastic Easter eggs and various craft items, fabric glue &/or hot glue gun.

Game time: ~ 25 minutes for the craft portion and the duration of your party for drying and runway modeling.

Knock Knock: What's In There?

Game goal: to be the one to guess the most hidden items inside of plastic Easter eggs correctly.

Game play: put various materials inside of 10 plastic Easter eggs such as feathers, coins, sand, flour, water, buttons, M&M candies, rocks, kidney beans, a pearl necklace, uncooked pasta, etc.

Ask all of the players to go into the next room and wait to be called upon. Escort each player one at a time into the challenge room. They are allowed to pick up each egg one at a time and pick it up, smell it, shake it – but cannot open it. If they accidentally open it – they will not receive credit for that egg. For each egg, they are to submit one guess as to what is hidden inside and you are to write their guesses on the score sheet (example shown below). The one who guesses the most correctly – wins!

Example score sheet:

Knock knock...what's in there? Score sheet					
	In the blank below the number, write what each player guesses is in the egg				
PLAYER name	1	2	3	4	5
Jason	flour √	sand X	water √	sugar X	beans X
Whitney	balloon X	sugar √	water √	curds X	pasta √
Correct answers	flour	sugar	water	wheat	uncooked pasta

In the example score sheet above, Jason got two correct and Whitney got three correct so Whitney wins!

Game gear: 10 plastic Easter eggs and various items to hide inside (i.e. feathers, coins, sand, sugar, water, buttons, rocks, beans, a necklace, uncooked pasta, etc.)

Game time: ~ 15 minutes.

Capture the Eggs - Scavenger Hunt Challenge:
Game goal: to be the team to hide your 10 colored Easter eggs the best!

Game play: divide your guests into two teams and allow them to draw for one color of egg (pink, blue, yellow, green, etc). *Example: one team will hide pink eggs and the other team will hide blue eggs.* Select two approximately equal-sized areas of your party area. The teams have five minutes to hide their 10 designated color eggs in the most difficult place they can within their designated area.

When the host says go, the teams are to hunt for the opposing teams eggs. The first team to find all 10 eggs - wins! *As an alternative, take turns in one room with team A hiding eggs and team B hunting for them and then switch. If you do it this way, you'll need to time each trial for each team and the best time wins.*

<u>Game gear:</u> two different colored eggs and a timer!

<u>Game time</u>: ~ 10 minutes.

Easter Egg Bowlathon:

<u>Game goal</u>: to score the highest point total in Easter egg bowling!

<u>Game play</u>: place a bowling pin in the middle of the room (i.e. white boiled egg with a black strip around it). Each player is given five plastic Easter eggs. The player who can bowl a plastic Easter egg closest to the bowling pin without moving the bowling pin – wins!

<u>Game gear:</u>   at least five plastic Easter eggs per player and a boiled egg for the bowling pin.

<u>Game time</u>: ~ 10 minutes.

Wordy Easter Egg Scavenger Hunt:

<u>Game goal</u>: to make the most sentences out of the eggs you find during the Easter Egg Scavenger Hunt!

<u>Game play</u>: <u>Phase 1:</u> Using sentence makers (example shown below), hide the slips containing the words inside of plastic Easter eggs and then hide the Easter eggs in a designated area. Tell your hunters the boundaries of the hunt before you say go. Each hunter is to place his or her basket in a designated area prior to the hunt.

When the host says go, the hunters are to collect as many eggs as possible that they can make full sentences out of but once they find an egg – if they choose to keep it – they must take it to their basket and deposit it before finding the next egg. They will not want to take any eggs that contain words inside that they can't use, as they'll be penalized for having them during the next phase of the game. They do have the option to view inside the egg to see what the word is and if they don't want it – they decide to not take it and place it back in the exact location in which they found it. They are not allowed to re-hide a rejected egg in another location. After the eggs have all been found (you'll know by counting the hunter's eggs) or if the hunters are finished hunting (i.e. there are eggs left, but they have words in them that the hunters can't use) – move to phase two.

Phase 2: When you say go, the hunters can take out the slips of paper containing the words and arrange them into as many sentences as possible. There is one point given for every word used in a sentence. For any words that are leftover that the hunter does not use – there is a one-point deduction per word. The sentences must be grammatically correct. For example, if Scott collects 20 eggs and makes three sentences with six words each – he will earn 18 points but be penalized for the remaining two eggs that he did not use so his final score will be 16 points.

Game gear: sentence maker word squares and plastic Easter eggs.

Game time: ~ 35 minutes.

Example sentence maker word squares- print and cut out as many as you want to play with and slip each into a plastic Easter egg and hide:

The	Pink	Bunny	Is
The	Tiny	Chicken	Is
Easter	Egg	Scavenger	Hunts
I	Want	To	Win
You	Can	Not	Make
Me	And	I	Am
I	Enjoy	Hunting	For
Like	To	Get	And
The	Rabbits	Hopped	Across
The	Chicks	Hatched	From
Cuddly	And	Cute	Always
Chirping	And	Pecking	Will
Are	So	Fun	Exciting
This	Fun	Challenge	Happy
More	Sentences	Than	From
Sure	Of	It	Are
Eggs	And	A	Are

Eat	Yummy	Candy	And
The	Front	Lawn	Chocolate
The	Egg	Today	Eat

Springy Time Charade Challenge:

Game goal: To earn a point by being the player that is first to guess the charade correctly! The winner is the player with the highest point total!

Game play: One player draws a charade topic from a hat and acts it out for the other players. The first one to guess the charade topic correctly gets a point. The next player will draw a topic from the hat and act it out until one of the other players guesses it correctly and this will repeat until all of the topics are guessed correctly. The actor of the charade may not speak, point to an object, or acknowledge the other players until they give a correct guess. Either type or write the charade topics on equally sized pieces of paper fold them and put them inside of a hat or other container.

The charade topics are as follows:

Flower Garden	Umbrella
Fuzzy Yellow Chick	Easter Basket
Bunny Hop	Cadbury Eggs
Easter Egg	Baked Ham
Coloring Easter Eggs	Family
Water The Flowers	Green Grass
Planting A Flower	Easter Dress
Sunshine	Jelly Beans
Peter Cottontail	A Chick Hatching
Chicken Laying An Egg	Easter Lamb
Easter Bunny	Blooming Flower
Easter Egg Hunt	April Showers
Prize Egg	Scavenger Hunt
Chocolate Bunny	Happy Easter!
May Flowers	Stuffed Animal Toy

Game gear: Paper, pen (or word processing program and printer), and a hat (or any container to hold the pieces of paper with the charade topics).

Game time: ~ 30 minutes.

Eggstraordinary Memory Challenge:

Game goal: to match the most pictures hidden inside of plastic Easter eggs by using your eggstraordinary skills of memory!

Game play: At least two players must play the game. Cut out as many memory squares (i.e. pictures of Easter items) as you wish to play with and slip each picture into a plastic Easter egg. Make sure that a matching picture is used with each picture.

In a designated area set by you (i.e. a five' by five' area in the living area of the home, etc.), place as many eggs as you wish to play with (up to 48 eggs) either in a grid design (see the example) or placed in designated locations (i.e. on the couch, under the chair, etc.). For an added challenge, use an entire room and hide the eggs throughout the room.

Taking turns, each player is to locate an egg, pick it up and view the picture inside. They must place the egg back in the exact location it was found in and they must try to find the egg that contains its matching picture. They find another egg, pick it up and view the picture inside. If it is a match, they can go back to the first egg, retrieve it, and put it in their basket. With each successful match, the players continue until they do not find a successful match. In the event that the second egg is not a match, the player is to close the egg with the picture inside and put it back in the exact location it was found and then return to the first egg and close the egg with the picture inside and return it to the exact location it was found.

Every time a player opens an egg and views a picture, the other players in the game have the right to see the picture in the egg. Players will rotate until all of the matches are made and then the player with the most eggs in their basket – wins!

Game gear: cut out memory squares below and plastic Easter eggs.

Game time: ~ 25 minutes.

Below is an example grid design within a five' by five' area.

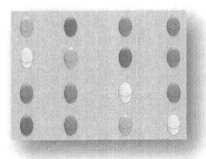

The Smashing Egg Toss Challenge:

Game goal: to be the pair who is crowned the most successful egg tossers in the land!

Game play: divide the players into teams of two. Divide the pairs into two lines that are about two feet apart with each pair facing each other. Give each team either an empty plastic Easter egg, a plastic Easter egg filled with various things (i.e. jellybeans, coins, water, etc.) or use real dyed Easter eggs or even a raw egg if you don't mind the mess!

When the host says go, the team member holding the egg is to toss the egg to their teammate. Any team member that misses the toss, drops the egg after catching it or breaks their egg is out of the game. This includes breaking apart the plastic eggs. The teams that successfully caught their eggs remain in the game and are to step backward away from each other in one-foot increments. Whenever you feel like it, ask that the tosser turn around backwards and toss the egg to their teammate or ask one or both team members to get on their knees during the toss, etc. As long as you are doing the same for all teams – it is fair. The last successful tossers are the best in the land!

Game gear: any kind of egg (i.e. plastic, real raw egg, dyed Easter egg) for each team of two players.

Game time: ~ 25 minutes.

Top Chef - Easter Style

<u>Game goal</u>: to be the ultimate culinary genius by making the best tasting and best-looking deviled egg! *(Great way to use those dyed Easter eggs for a tasty...or maybe not so tasty treat!)*

<u>Each guest can either</u> compete individually or put them into teams of two, three or four. Place all of the possible ingredients on a table where each guest has access to enough of the ingredient for their recipe (see the suggested ingredient choices below).

Give each guest a mixing bowl, a wire whisk (or just a spoon), and five hard-boiled eggs (cooled and sliced long-ways). When the host says go, the guests are to create the best tasting and best looking deviled egg by mixing their yolks with the best tasting combination of the ingredients below! Each team can only take one ingredient from the ingredient table at a time - no grabbing all of the ingredients to sabotage the other chefs! They must return the ingredient in a timely manner before getting another one from the ingredient table! After an ingredient is used, it must be immediately returned to the table or the team gets a one -minute penalty where they cannot continue until the penalty is served.

The following are the suggested ingredients to place on the table. Please make an announcement that by no means does it suggest that putting all of these ingredients into a deviled egg will make the best tasting egg! They are to create the *best combination* of the ingredients that they select!

Possible food ingredients:
> *Mayo - maybe 2-3 different types to choose from*
> *Soy Sauce*
> *Mustard - maybe 2-3 different types to choose from*
> *Paprika*
> *1000 Island Salad Dressing*
> *Salt, Pepper*
> *Worcestershire Sauce*
> *Cooked bacon (diced for them)*
> *BBQ Sauce*
> *Shredded cheese - a few types to choose from*
> *Relish - sweet and a sour*

Onions (diced for them)
Pickles (diced for them)

You don't want your guests to have to use knives or scissors on a timed challenge as you are simply asking for an injury. That is why you dice and slice everything for them in advance.

Cut the corner out of plastic sandwich bags and place on the ingredients table. The guests can put the egg yolk mixture in here and squeeze it out of the hole and into the egg white shell for the presentation points! Either tell them what to do with the bag or just offer it for them on the ingredient table and those who figure it out will have an advantage during the presentation part of the challenge! Give the guests a time limit (i.e. 8 -10 minutes) to create their culinary delight. When the host calls time, s/he will taste each team's egg and judge on presentation and taste. The best tasting and best-looking egg wins!

Game gear: the food ingredients listed above, plastic bags, and a mixing bowl and a spoon or wire whisk for each guest.

Game time: ~ 15 minutes.

Eggciting Mismatch Race:

Game goal: to be the first to repair your mismatched plastic Easter eggs!

Game play: Choose any number of plastic Easter eggs and snap different colored halves together (i.e. pink top, blue bottom, etc.). As many players as you wish can play at once. When the host says go, each competitor is to put their eggs back in the right uniform color combinations. The first one to have uniform, securely fastened eggs is the winner! A prize can be awarded for first, second and third place if a lot of players are competing.

Game gear: at least 10 plastic Easter eggs per player.

Game time: ~ 25 minutes.

What Spring Thing Am I?

Game goal: to be the first one to guess correctly the thing on your forehead and / or not to be the last one to figure out what thing you are wearing on your forehead!

Game play: select multiple spring clip art icons for each player and print them in ~ 2" sizes. Affix tape to the back of each item (cut out in a square) and affix a random thing sheet onto their forehead. Do not show the guests the thing that is being affixed to their forehead and make sure that there are not any mirrors or highly reflective surfaces in the party room during this game. When all of the guests have a sheet attached to their forehead, the game begins. The guests are allowed to ask each person one and only one yes or no question (i.e. Am I a person? or Am I blue in color)? No lying is allowed – that would be cheating - so all guests must answer the questions truthfully.

The object is to figure out what thing is on the sheet affixed to their forehead. If a player has asked every guest at the party a yes/no question and still cannot guess the thing on their forehead, s/he may start the cycle over with the first person that they asked a yes/no question and continue until the player can correctly guess the thing. There is one winner and one loser in this game. The winner is the first to guess correctly the thing and the loser is the last standing without a correct guess of the thing on their forehead. You might want to call time when there are more than one person standing at the end of the game as to not single one person out as the loser but rather multiple people as the losers. To be extra nice, just declare a winner and not a loser(s) however, many of the guests won't be able to guess their item and you're taking away a lot of the game play!

Game gear: Spring Thing squares, tape to adhere the squares to the guests' foreheads.

Game time: ~ 5-10 minutes.

Index

95768880R00193

Made in the USA
Columbia, SC
22 May 2018